Collaborative Happiness

Life Course, Culture and Aging: Global Transformations
General Editor: Jay Sokolovsky, University of South Florida St. Petersburg

Published by Berghahn Books under the auspices of the Association for Anthropology and Gerontology (AAGE) and the American Anthropological Association Interest Group on Aging and the Life Course.

The consequences of aging will influence most areas of contemporary life around the globe, from the makeup of households and communities and systems of care to attitudes toward health, disability, and life's end. Engaging a cross-cultural framework, this series publishes monographs and collected works that examine these widespread transformations with a perspective on the entire life course and a particular focus on mid/late adulthood.

Volume 8
COLLABORATIVE HAPPINESS
Building the Good Life in Urban Cohousing Communities
Catherine Kingfisher

Volume 7
PREVENTING DEMENTIA?
Critical Perspectives on a New Paradigm of Preparing for Old Age
Edited by Annette Leibing and Silke Schicktanz

Volume 6
BEYOND FILIAL PIETY
Rethinking Aging and Caregiving in Contemporary East Asian Societies
Edited by Jeanne Shea, Katrina Moore, and Hong Zhang

Volume 5
THE GLOBAL AGE-FRIENDLY COMMUNITY MOVEMENT
A Critical Appraisal
Edited by Philip B. Stafford

Volume 4
CARE ACROSS DISTANCE
Ethnographic Explorations of Aging and Migration
Edited by Azra Hromadžić and Monika Palmberger

Volume 3
AGING AND THE DIGITAL LIFE COURSE
Edited by David Prendergast and Chiara Garattini

Volume 2
UNFORGOTTEN
Love and the Culture of Dementia Care in India
Bianca Brijnath

Volume 1
TRANSITIONS AND TRANSFORMATIONS
Cultural Perspectives on Aging and the Life Course
Edited by Caitrin Lynch and Jason Danely

COLLABORATIVE HAPPINESS

Building the Good Life in Urban Cohousing Communities

Catherine Kingfisher

berghahn
NEW YORK · OXFORD
www.berghahnbooks.com

First published in 2022 by
Berghahn Books
www.berghahnbooks.com

© 2022, 2024 Catherine Kingfisher
First paperback edition published in 2024

All rights reserved. Except for the quotation of short passages for the purposes of criticism and review, no part of this book may be reproduced in any form or by any means, electronic or mechanical, including photocopying, recording, or any information storage and retrieval system now known or to be invented, without written permission of the publisher.

Library of Congress Cataloging-in-Publication Data

Names: Kingfisher, Catherine, author.
Title: Collaborative Happiness: Building the Good Life in Urban Cohousing Communities / Catherine Kingfisher.
Description: New York: Berghahn Books, 2022. | Series: Life Course, Culture and Aging: Global Transformations; volume 8 | Includes bibliographical references and index.
Identifiers: LCCN 2021037219 (print) | LCCN 2021037220 (ebook) | ISBN 9781800732391 (hardback) | ISBN 9781800732407 (ebook)
Subjects: LCSH: Housing, Cooperative—Social aspects. | Housing, Cooperative—Psychological aspects. | Lifestyles. | Well-being. | Happiness.
Classification: LCC HD7287.7 .K56 2022 (print) | LCC HD7287.7 (ebook) | DDC 334/.1—dc23
LC record available at https://lccn.loc.gov/2021037219
LC ebook record available at https://lccn.loc.gov/2021037220

British Library Cataloguing in Publication Data

A catalogue record for this book is available from the British Library

ISBN 978-1-80073-239-1 hardback
ISBN 978-1-80539-316-0 paperback
ISBN 978-1-80539-429-7 epub
ISBN 978-1-80073-240-7 web pdf

https://doi.org/10.3167/9781800732391

For my sisters Marguerite and Bernadette Pélissier, two of my favorite collaborators in life; and my son, Levi Kingfisher, who, among other things, made fabulous common meals at both Quayside Village and Kankanmori.

CONTENTS

List of Illustrations	viii
Acknowledgments	ix
Notes on Text	xii
Introduction. How Urban Cohousing Communities Can Expand How We Think about Well-Being	1
1. Kankanmori and Quayside Village: An Overview	35
2. Quayside Village	71
3 Kankanmori	108
4. The Exchanges	145
Conclusion. Policies of Well-Being	185
Appendix. The Film Shorts	216
Bibliography	220
Index	234

ILLUSTRATIONS

Figures

1.1 Kankanmori floor plan, first floor. Reproduced with the permission of NPO Collective Housing Corporation. 39

1.2 Quayside Village floor plan, first floor. Reproduced with the permission of the Quayside Village community. 54

4.1 Donya's view of high/low connection and socializing versus business at Kankanmori and Quayside Village. Reproduced with permission of Donya Metzger. 171

Tables

1.1 Adults at Kankanmori, by age and years in residence, 2017. Table created by Jamie Lewis (research assistant for the project). 43

1.2 Children at Kankanmori, by age and years in residence, 2017. Table created by Jamie Lewis (research assistant for the project). 44

1.3 Adults at Quayside Village, by age and years in residence, 2017. Table created by Jamie Lewis (research assistant for the project). 57

1.4 Children at Quayside Village, by age and years in residence, 2017. Table created by Jamie Lewis (research assistant for the project). 58

2.1 Color-coded meeting discussion and decision-making cards. Table courtesy of Kathy McGrenera. 80

3.1 Kankanmori committees and subgroups. Table courtesy of Kankanmori Collective House, Inc. 113

ACKNOWLEDGMENTS

I REMAIN TOUCHED BY THE overwhelming generosity and collaborative enthusiasm of Kankanmori and Quayside Village residents. For over six years, they patiently allowed me into their communities—their *homes*—and many eagerly participated in the research process, contributing ideas on topics to explore, joining in both formal discussion groups and endless informal conversations, patiently answering my endless questions, and including me in their rich social lives. Residents' involvement in this project exemplifies the spirit and practice of living in cohousing, marked as they are by both kindness and care.

While everyone gave freely of their time and handled my intrusions with great grace, a number of people in each community went above and beyond. At Kankanmori, Emiko Ura and Yoshie Sakamoto served as my main hosts. They facilitated my entry into the community and the launching of the project, coordinated various aspects of the work, offered invaluable feedback and direction, and helped me with the logistics of renting an apartment at Kankanmori. But this was not all: Yoshie baked me homemade rice buns and took me to the doctor, and Emiko routinely bought me special gluten-free treats, since I often had difficulty reading ingredients labels, and even took a weekend trip with me to Hakone, so we could visit the *onsen* (Japanese baths) and museums there. Both also organized many outings to restaurants and karaoke with others at Kankanmori, including especially with Katsuji Yutaka and Keiichi Fujiwara. I cannot thank them enough for their friendship, generosity, and the seriousness with which they took the research. Other members of the Kankanmori study group for this project—Yu Wada-Dimmer, Christian Dimmer, and Reiko Shiraki—were also invaluable collaborators. I am particularly grateful to Yu and Chris, who traveled with their families to visit Quayside Village. The intellectual contributions they made to the project are priceless. Keiichi Fujiwara and Yui Watanabe, along with Natsuko Nakatogawa and Yoshie Sakamoto, generously provided the personal narratives that are included in chapter 1. Natsuko Nakatogawa, a musician by training, also produced the music and narration for the Japanese clips in the film shorts. And Junko and Hideki Kawahara, Mayumi Otsuki, Yumiko Yanagisawa, Etsuko Adachi, Shoko Hosoi, and Katsuji Yutaka all went out of their way to make me feel at home at Kankanmori.

At Quayside Village, Stacy Pigg, fellow anthropologist, facilitated my initial entry into the community and provided early guidance on how to best unfold the project. Over the years, a number of residents—including Stacy, Carollyne Conlinn, Vera and Patrick Berard, and Natassja By—let me stay in their apartments when they were out of town. Mostly, however, I stayed with Kathy McGrenera and her daughter Elise, who tolerated my intrusions into their space on more occasions than I can count, and with whom I enjoyed endless hours of good conversation. Kathy, the hub of life at Quayside Village, provided more support and advice than I could ever have hoped for. Carol McQuarrie, grand matriarch of Quayside Village, tutored me in the history and, above all, the spirit of the place. Marylee Stephenson lent her sociological guidance to the project. Kathy and Elise, along with Peter Burch and Yuki Toyoda, contributed the personal narratives that are included in chapter 1. Connie Blundy, Donya Metzger, and Juhli Weiss, the three Quaysiders who visited Kankanmori, were invaluable co-researchers. They are, each of them, supremely competent observers and analysts—as are Yu and Chris from Kankanmori— and I am enterally grateful for their contributions and insights. Yuki Toyoda also visited Kankanmori, and added to the interpretations provided by Connie, Donya, and Juhli.

This book also benefits from the generosity and insights of a number of other collaborators. Gordon Mathews, John Clarke, Su Il Kim, Shin-Ichiro Ishida, Hulya Demirdirek, Yukiko Uchida, Vinnai Norasakkunkit, Yuji Ogihara, Doreen Indra, Norman Buchignani, Barbara Rylko-Bauer, Nanami Suzuki, Gillian Ranson, Masami Iwakasi-Goodman, Dan Goodman, Paul Vasey, Mary Kavanagh, Claudia Malacrida, Artit (Ryo) Markshom, and Jeremie Bouchard enriched my thinking and writing in so many ways, ranging from feedback on drafts, to brainstorming conversations, to opportunities to publicly present preliminary thoughts for discussion in group settings. I cannot thank them enough.

I'm also grateful to Mari Minamiyama for the interpretive work she did at Kankanmori when Connie, Donya, and Juhli were visiting, to Yu Wada for translating English passages from interviews into Japanese, and to Matt Treyvaud and Tomoko Greenshields for translating Japanese passages into English. All four dramatically increased the precision of the cross-cultural communication required for this project.

At the University of Lethbridge, I am particularly indebted to Don Gill, the artistic consultant for the project. He held workshops at both Quayside Village and Kankanmori on how to use the GoPro cameras, spent endless hours going through film clips, presented rough cuts to community members, advised on everything from sequencing to the font size for subtitles, and even contributed some footage. I also thank Jamie Lewis, Jake Vinje, and Chelsea Wittig for their superb research assistance, including putting together film clips and adding subtitles, transcribing audio and video tapes, collating data, searching various literatures, and formatting the manuscript. They were, each of them, stellar.

At Berghahn Books, I thank Marion Berghahn and Tom Bonnington for their encouragement and attention to detail, the anonymous reviewers for their insightful and very helpful feedback on both the prospectus and final manuscript, and Elizabeth Martinez for her excellent production work.

Support for this research was generously provided by the Social Science and Humanities Research Council of Canada, the University of Lethbridge Research Fund and Community of Research Excellence Development Opportunity, and a University of Lethbridge University Scholar Research Chair. I thank Mary Butterfield and Hector MacIntyre for their guidance on funding applications, and Jenny Oseen for her talented—and patient—organization.

NOTES ON TEXT

FOUR FILM SHORTS, SHOT MOSTLY by residents of Kankanmori and Quayside Village, accompany the text in chapters 1–4. References to particular clips are indicated with a ◗ icon. The URL for the clip is as follows:

https://drive.google.com/drive/folders/1WnPcxyyrL86VI5ifHc_cET12X AWdo4mj?usp=sharing

An outline of individual scenes is included in the appendix.

INTRODUCTION
How Urban Cohousing Communities Can Expand How We Think about Well-Being

> Human well-being, including happiness, is so intrinsically social that it is wrong to try to conceive happiness or freedom or sense of self-worth or any other aspect of well-being in terms of pure, disconnected autonomy.
> —Neil Thin, *Social Happiness: Theory into Policy and Practice*

ALL IS NOT WELL WITH well-being. Our lives, marked by decreasing social connectivity, are marred by patterns of isolation among the elderly, withdrawal and alienation among youth, increasing rates of interpersonal violence, and struggles with loneliness, anxiety, and depression. "Modern society," Robert Wright noted in an article in *Time* back in 2001, "is dangerously asocial."[1] This feature of contemporary life traverses a range of social systems, affecting societies as disparate as those of Canada and Japan.[2] According to Canada's 2016 census, for example, the number of one-person households now surpasses all other types of living situations, adding up to almost 30 percent—more than couples with or without children, single-parent households, or intergenerational households.[3] On the other side of the globe, in 2017, 18.4 million Japanese lived alone. This comprises only 14.5 percent of the population—much less than the 30 percent of Canadians who live alone—yet it is double the number of thirty years ago.[4] And while living alone or in smaller households does not automatically translate into isolation,[5] increases in solo living in particular and collapsing household size and reduced intergenerationalism in general have nevertheless been correlated with escalating rates of loneliness, leading to what some consider a public health crisis.[6] In 2017, for instance, a record forty-five thousand Japanese died alone, sometimes unnoticed for days or even weeks[7]—and sometimes even while part of a shared household.[8] There is even now a term for this: *kodokushi*, or "lonely death." It comes as no surprise, then, that the Japanese government's 2010 and 2012 National Survey of Lifestyle Preferences indicated that loneliness is *the* key determinant of well-being in Japan—not gender, age, income, educational level, or occupation but loneliness.[9] And in both countries, the percentage of people who report having relatives or friends to count on for support is on the decline.[10] Clearly, we are experiencing a crisis of social sustainability.

This crisis has given rise to an obsession with happiness and well-being. Endless academic conferences and publications, policy discussions and initiatives, newspaper articles, TED talks, podcasts, and self-help books testify to the centrality of the topic in our collective imagination. Although the concern with happiness has deep historical roots in a number of philosophical and spiritual traditions, the emergence of this latest iteration can be dated to the mid-twentieth century, when we began to see declines in psychological indicators of well-being—a downward trajectory that continued through to the end of the century and into the twenty-first.[11] Around the same time, Bhutan introduced the Gross National Happiness Index to replace gross national product as a measure of prosperity and well-being, providing an institutional framework for a focus on happiness. Since then, and with the support of the Organisation for Economic Co-operation and Development (OECD) and United Nations, well-being has become increasingly prominent in the policy orientations of governments across the globe. Fundamental to these orientations and interventions is the work of scholars in happiness economics and positive psychology, two recently emergent disciplines that have influenced not only governments but also popular culture. The result is a burgeoning, multibillion-dollar "happiness industry,"[12] composed of various approaches to therapy, self-help, medication, diet and exercise regimes, and so on.

Conventional approaches to loneliness and isolation, on the one hand, and happiness and well-being, on the other—two sides of the same coin—have tended to locate both problems and solutions in individual selves. Thus, the focus is on *individuals*, who are depressed, or lonely, or wanting to be happier; and the remedy is ingesting antidepressants, attending therapy, cultivating positive emotions, practicing gratitude, and so on. These methods, however, while useful in some contexts, also have the potential to exacerbate the problem of asociality that Robert Wright identified in his *Time* article, and that others, such as Robert Putnam in *Bowling Alone*,[13] have also documented. The connecting thread here, weaving together interpersonal disconnection and desires for personal well-being with particular responses and practices, is hyperindividualism: an overvaluing of excessive, individualized forms of consumption, and an overemphasis on personal autonomy and self-sufficiency. Both articulate with capitalist economic formations, and both ignore the social contexts of loneliness and happiness alike. If, as I argue below, hyperindividualism is indeed a problem, then it becomes imperative that we not only identify the dangers of individualized (and individualizing) orientations to life but also move beyond criticism of such frameworks to imagine—and practice—other ways of doing things.

Recognizing the problems associated with hyperindividualism, a number of people across the world have come up with one approach to doing things differently: living together in urban cohousing communities. A type of intentional community typically composed of architecturally designed buildings that provide both private apartments and common, communal spaces, urban cohousing communities allow for residents to simultaneously share space and time with each other, pool their resources, *and* maintain their autonomy and independence. A rather modest and unpretentious model for overcoming the debilitating isolation of contemporary society, cohousing has the potential to make significant contributions to social sustainability. This model, which positions happiness, well-being, and the good life as fundamentally about *connection* and *collaboration*, is the focus of this book. In what follows, I highlight the value of cohousing in general terms and illustrate its potential contributions to happiness and the good life in detail by means of in-depth explorations of two communities located in very different societies: Kankanmori, in Tokyo, and Quayside Village, in North Vancouver.

Why Urban Cohousing?

There are good reasons for paying close attention to urban cohousing communities in these times. First, and most obviously, we live in an increasingly urbanized world. As of 2018, 55 percent of the world's population lived in urban centers, and this percentage is projected to increase to 68 percent by 2050.[14] Yet urban life is becoming increasingly difficult: "Working distance, flexible working conditions and above all rising individualism . . . have made it hard for communities to survive in an urban context since the 1980s."[15] In *Happy City*,[16] Charles Montgomery uses the term *dispersed city* to describe the all-too-normalized, ever-expanding diffusion of business, industry, and housing in urban areas that reflects our long-standing "ideology of separation"[17]—in particular, for my purposes here, the valorization of privacy and private property ownership. The result is a dissolution of both spatial and personal connectivity, a problem highlighted in the 2019 *Global Happiness and Well-Being Policy Report*.[18]

Cohousing has the potential to remedy some of these patterns. Insofar as it is characterized by dense, interconnected living spaces located in close proximity to transit, businesses, schools, medical facilities, and entertainment, urban cohousing can help to ease some of the logistical difficulties generated by the ideology of separation and the dispersal it generates.

There are also economic benefits to living in cohousing: pooling resources to buy in bulk, growing food on site, and sharing everything from kitchen mixers and vacuum cleaners to large equipment such as washers and dryers reduces the economic burdens on individual households, thereby increasing the feasibility of living in city centers. Drawing on the expertise of residents—someone has experience in finance, someone else in carpentry—can produce further economic efficiencies.

These practical features of cohousing work to produce the kinds of connections that can mitigate the psychological difficulties—in particular, the loneliness—associated with the spread and fragmentation captured by the term *dispersed city*.[19] According to the Harvard Study of Adult Development, which has followed over two thousand people over the course of some eighty-odd years, social connection is *the* key to well-being. In a TED Talk on "What Makes a Good Life," Robert Waldinger, the current director of the study, stated that "loneliness kills. It's as powerful as smoking or alcoholism."[20] Similarly, in the 2018 *Global Happiness Policy Report*, Ed Diener and Robert Biswas-Diener note that "social connectedness is known to benefit health in a major way that surpasses the benefits of other known public health factors such as exercise, avoiding obesity, and not smoking."[21] This should come as no surprise: it has been over fifty years since social epidemiologists documented, unequivocally, that social and community ties have a greater impact on physical and psychological well-being than socioeconomic status, obesity, smoking, exercise, or alcohol consumption.[22] Yet even earlier, sociologist Émile Durkheim demonstrated that patterns in suicide—something considered profoundly personal—were in fact *socially* produced.[23] The alternative to single dwellings provided by an arrangement of space that works to balance interdependence and independence, allowing residents to maintain privacy *within* a rich social environment—markedly different from the high-rise living that, in some cases, seems to increase rather than decrease isolation[24]—is thus worth exploring.

The social and economic benefits of living in cohousing are intertwined with its positive environmental impacts.[25] The Intergovernmental Panel on Climate Change and the World Meteorological Organization remind us, on an almost daily basis, that we are in the throes of an environmental crisis, marked by rising temperatures and sea levels, increasingly erratic and severe storms, forest fires and droughts, rapid and widespread species extinction, and dramatic growth in the numbers of environmental refugees.[26] Admittedly small-scale, it is indisputable that having several people share a washing machine instead of having one in each household, eating food grown on site, and circulating used goods among community members and donating or recycling what is not taken up all serve to reduce the consumption of material goods and of the resources required to produce and transport them. Fossil fuel consumption is also decreased by living in urban centers as opposed to suburbs, given the opportunities for walking, cycling, and using public transit that cities provide.

Despite these benefits, urban cohousing remains on the margins of mainstream studies of social and environmental sustainability, and it has yet to be taken up in any robust fashion in policy-related circles. It is, however, gaining recognition in the popular media, and it is also becoming increasingly attractive as a model among those who are plugged in to circuits for the travel of information on intentional community. The goal of this book, then, is not only to describe what urban cohousing looks like but also to feed the increasing awareness of cohousing as a viable option and to argue for placing it on the list of interventions that can improve both our daily lives and the condition of our planet.

How We Got Here: The Narrow Focus on the Self

That the individual has served as the site of both investigation and intervention in our theories and practices of well-being is understandable. As Sam Thompson notes in the *Oxford Handbook of Happiness*, those aspects of happiness that have to do with social systems have received less scholarly attention than those related to biology and personality, if for no other reason than that the latter are relatively easier to study.[27] This may, in turn, reflect the context within which mainstream orientations to both loneliness and happiness operate; namely, a cultural and political system in which "society" has been eclipsed by a focus on the individual. As Margaret Thatcher famously stated in response to critics of her programs of economic restructuring, "They are casting their problems at society. And, you know, there's no such thing as society. There are individual men and women and there are families. And no government can do anything except through people, and people must look after themselves first."[28]

The concepts and methods of social science, however objective and universal its proponents may claim them to be, are not in fact immune to the influence of the cultures from which they emerge and within which they are situated. Thus, community psychologist Collin van Uchelen has argued that individualistic assumptions have been incorporated into psychological concepts and theories to such an extent that they are now taken for granted as universal.[29] Central to these individualistic assumptions is the idea that persons are self-contained autonomous units, a belief that produces both a self-other binary and a myopic emphasis on internal control and independence as signature markers of mental health. In a sense, then, the "ideology of separation" that Montgomery describes has informed not only how we design our built environments but also how we conceptualize the nature of the self.[30] Individualistic orientations are so pervasive in our social science frameworks, van Uchelen argues, that reflecting on their influence may be "like asking those who know only one language to reveal the ways in which it constrains and shapes the nature of their experiences and their ability to communicate about them."[31]

This narrow focus on individual selves was, at least initially, central to positive psychology, a key player in the mainstream approaches to happiness that emerged in the late 1990s. Its founders, Martin Seligman and Mihaly Csikszentmihalyi, argued that psychology as a discipline had come to overemphasize what is wrong (mental illness, loneliness, distress) and underemphasize what is right (strengths, capacities, positive emotions).[32] In order to remedy this, they claimed, we need to focus on enhancing the positive instead of fighting the negative; and the key method for this is work on the self, by means of therapy, meditation, medication, and various other techniques for developing positive thoughts—all with the goal of producing a positive attitude, itself considered a form of happiness.[33]

As van Uchelen's insights indicate, however, this emphasis on interiority, on what goes on inside our heads, and on positive affect/satisfaction—key indicators of happiness and well-being in positive psychology's framework—are culturally unique rather than universal. Anthropologists agree: cross-cultural comparison reveals that the *individual* pursuit of happiness is not, in fact, universally valued.[34] On the contrary, in many societies an orientation toward others and toward the group overrides any emphasis on the individual per se. There are enough cross-cultural examples to indicate that it is precisely the contemporary Euro-American model of independent self-sufficiency that is unique—not the other way around.[35] Nor are emotional satisfaction and positive affect universally considered paramount: feelings of dependence, subservience, and dissatisfaction are in some places more highly valued than independence and "feeling good," insofar as they foster relationships with others and boost motivation.[36] The pursuit of personal emotional satisfaction is even considered dangerous in some cultural contexts, since it can turn people away from the community; and in certain instances it is simply inconceivable as something that people would be primarily oriented to.[37] Three examples will serve to illustrate these points. Among the Yapese in Micronesia, happiness, or contentment—*falfalaen'*—is viewed negatively, since people who exhibit *falfalaen'* tend to be focused only on their own success and comfort, to the neglect of attention to the well-being of others. Instead, *gaafgow*, or suffering for others, is what is most important.[38] In Sierra Leone, the Kuranko concept of *kendeye* refers to *social* well-being rather than to individual physical or psychological health.[39] And finally, perhaps most relevant to this book, in

East Asian societies, personal achievement, considered a key determinant of well-being in Euro-American contexts, is deemphasized relative to relationships with others and a self-other balance.[40] Thus while Western cultures place a premium on independence, there are many societies in which Western-style independence and individualism are frowned upon—or even feared—and in which interdependence and relationality are more highly valued.

The work of cultural psychologists, like that of anthropologists, has also served to transcend the biases of individualistic frameworks. In contrast to the tendency of Western psychology to assume the universality of its constructs, cultural psychologists draw attention to "the critical role of culture in explaining psychological functions and behaviors."[41] Hidehumi Hitokoto and Yukiko Uchida thus introduced the concept of *interdependent happiness*, which works to broaden our understandings of where happiness is located (perhaps in between persons as much as inside of them) and how it might be produced (perhaps socially as much as individually).[42]

The focus on individual selves is historically as well as culturally unique. Indeed, the taken-for-granted focus on inner life that marks positive psychology emerged in Euro-American cultural contexts in full form only around the time of the eighteenth-century European Enlightenment.[43] Given these shallow roots, any attempt to assert this orientation as a historical universal reflecting human nature is troubling. To collapse and simplify a long and complicated history: in general, in Western culture, beginning with the early Greeks, happiness has followed a trajectory from an experience gifted to humans by the gods, to something that humans have control over, to something all humans should have access to as a right, to, in the contemporary context, something that we are personally responsible for and even obliged to achieve.[44] Over the centuries, then, we have moved from constructs of happiness as happenstance—as something outside of human agency—to ideas of happiness and well-being as artifacts of human will, under our control. This is no small shift. It turns happiness into a consumer item, as commentators on the "happiness industry" make clear,[45] and also into a kind of burden, a social imperative. "Permanent monitoring is the new job of modern life and seems exhausting," writes Suzanne Moore in *The Guardian*: "Now we're in the era of clean feelings, with the rise of emotional hygiene. When you are not flossing your teeth, you should be flossing your mind, getting rid of pesky emotions such as anger or self-doubt. Write them down. Reorder them. Cleanse your brain."[46]

Finally, with this history in mind, scholars writing from the perspective of critical psychology have explored the linkages between mainstream approaches to happiness and neoliberal, or market-based, forms of governance that devolve responsibility for happiness and well-being—as well as for loneliness and a range of social problems, like poverty for instance—to the individual.[47] Indeed, there is a correlation between the type of person most valued in positive psychology and the type of person most valued by neoliberalism: that is, someone who is self-examining, self-governing, "active," autonomous, and self-sufficient.[48] Some happiness economists have even suggested that governments can use measures of subjective well-being to determine whom to target with programs designed to increase resilience, in order to allow for cuts to welfare programs; and in some contexts (most notably in the United States and United Kingdom), benefits for poor people have been reduced and the money rechanneled to programs like Cognitive Behavioral Therapy,[49] as if there are no structural problems, only problems of attitude. There is a relationship, then, between certain scholarly approaches to happiness and government programs of austerity and restructuring.

Despite their shallow history and cultural specificity, ideologies of individualism and of individual responsibility, asserted as universal, have been spreading globally.[50] If, however, policy-makers adopt these orientations uncritically, they will be focused on producing the conditions of possibility for the *individual* pursuit of particular *internal* states, thereby reproducing constructs of persons as autonomous, independent entities and strengthening frameworks that position both the genesis and manifestation of happiness as primarily—perhaps exclusively—subjective. In the process, the idea of "human welfare," an expansive concept that "can only be imagined, and put into practice, in the context of a very clear social whole," is in danger of being replaced by frameworks that focus more narrowly on individual selves,[51] limiting both the experience of and responsibility for well-being to the individual person. Such individualized approaches may serve to exacerbate the disconnection and loneliness that give rise to the need for happiness in the first place.

Expanding Our Focus

Given the criticisms of anthropologists and cultural and critical psychologists, mainstream happiness scholars themselves have started to underscore the foundational importance to well-being of social relationships and engagements with society. Although recognition of the social was not completely absent in positive psychology's early days, it was often eclipsed by an overarching emphasis on the individual self.[52] This began to shift when scholars such as Ed Diener, a key figure in positive psychology, pointed out that ever since Aristotle, those who study well-being have recognized the importance of family, friends, and other forms of social contact. Despite this long intellectual history, economists and psychologists have tended over the past century to concentrate on individual needs and aspirations. Well-being has often been treated as an individual outcome that is based on the pursuit and achievement of individual goals. Both survey and experimental data on well-being, however, show the importance of the social context. Some of the most important factors that influence well-being revolve around the social features of people's lives.[53]

Following this, in 2012 Seligman added social relationships to his list of the basic building blocks of happiness.[54] More recently, Shelly Gable and Christopher Bromberg placed "healthy social bonds" at the center of their work on well-being,[55] mirroring Diener and Robert Biswas-Diener's claim that "the 'secret' to happiness—such as there is one—may be high quality social relationships. Humans are social animals."[56]

Some governments have taken notice. Japan, which established a Commission on Measuring Well-Being in 2010, provides a case in point. Under the advice of cultural psychologist Yukiko Uchida, the commission included among its five key orientations the need to "examine wellbeing not only at the individual level but also at a collective level. In addition, we should focus on inequity within societies."[57] The commission was disbanded by the Abe administration in 2013, undermining the influence of its broader approach to well-being on policy initiatives—ironically, at the same time as Western-style individualism was gaining traction in Japanese society as a whole.[58] Nevertheless, in locating well-being in the interpersonal as well as the intrapersonal, and in highlighting issues of social structure and political economy, the commission's orientation serves as a corrective to hyper-individualized theories and interventions.

Acknowledgment of the central importance of social connection has also made its way into popular culture texts. Stefan Klein's *The Science of Happiness* provides an illustrative example. Writing for a general audience, Klein highlights the work of positive psychologists and neuroscientists, emphasizing the need to cultivate positive emotions and to control negative ones—the *modus operandi* of positive psychology. He places the individual self in social context, however, when he outlines what he calls the "magic triangle" of well-being: a civic sense, social equality, and control over one's life.[59] All three elements of this magic triangle underscore the embeddedness of individuals in social settings.

This has not been a wholesale change in tack, however: many mainstream approaches, and certainly popular culture models, continue to highlight the individual more than social relations. In these contexts, connection and relationship are often positioned as a means to an end, as self-centered and instrumentalist "investments" in one's own well-being (so, for example, you give money to a homeless person because it makes you feel good and not because they need it).[60] Nevertheless, these recent developments in positive psychology can be taken to herald the beginning of a potential confluence of mainstream approaches, on the one hand, and more culturally and historically attuned ideas about how to think about and enhance well-being, on the other.

This emerging convergence around the need to position well-being as simultaneously subjective *and* social has focused attention on the range of venues and practices that foster connection, such as churches, community centers, clubs, and volunteer and activist groups. At the same time, the need to rethink privatized versus shared space has garnered the interest of city planners, urban studies scholars, architects, policy analysts, and activists alike. In the 2018 *Global Happiness Policy Report*'s chapter on "Social Well-Being," for instance, Diener and Biswas-Diener highlight interventions in zoning regulations, the design of parks, and community activities that work to encourage and enhance social connection.[61] Similarly, in the 2019 report's chapter on "Happy Cities Agenda," Aisha Bin Bishr points to the role of urban design and placemaking in the building of a sense of connection and community, that is, of belonging.[62]

What happens in these spaces that are now seen as foundational to the good life? How are connections established and maintained? While religious organizations, clubs, community centers, or activist groups could all serve as fruitful entry points for examining these mesolevel processes in more detail, this book zeroes in on urban cohousing communities—self-organized and -governing environments in which people live out their daily lives in close proximity to a group of known others. Given its unique features, the model provided by urban cohousing provides a particularly useful addition to our "tool kit"[63] for projects of well-being. Such a tool kit is ideally composed of "positive alternatives, contextualized in a way that avoids moral judgment—non-prescriptive, non-definitive options that might inspire other ways of looking at issues."[64] Urban cohousing, as a possible approach to living that transcends hyperindividualism, is thus good to think with—not only in and of itself but also in terms of its capacity to generate new ways of conceptualizing space, the public and the private, human connectivity, and human impacts on and engagements with the environment.

Quayside Village and Kankanmori, and places like them, thus offer one positive alternative to how we have organized society and how we think about and practice the good life: namely, one that locates the solution to loneliness and the generation of happiness and well-being in sets of social relations as well as in individual minds, hearts, and bodies. Cohousing communities tell us that while the experience of happiness may be subjective,[65] this does not necessarily mean that the production of happiness is purely individual, or that happiness is an exclusive characteristic or property of the self.[66] Attending to how urban cohousing communities operate and to the lives of those who live in them can thus broaden our approach to well-being: to how we define it, how we think about how and where it is generated and by what means, and how we might engage with it in our daily practices, ranging from envisioning what a good life might look like to participating in social and political activities designed to produce it. This is not to deny that well-being does indeed reside in individuals. Nor is it to claim that macrolevel structures and policies are irrelevant. Far from it: both are clearly crucial. But the meso—that space of groups and communities that sits between the macro and the micro and plays a key role in articulating the two, with implications for both—is equally fundamental.

Gordon Mathews and Carolina Izquierdo provide perhaps the most comprehensive framework for exploring happiness and well-being that combines the macro, micro, and meso, recognizing the importance of each.[67] They outline four dimensions of well-being: (1) the physical dimension, or conceptualizations/experiences of the body; (2) the interpersonal dimension, or constructions/experiences of relations with others; (3) the existential dimension, or conceptualizations/experiences of meaning and value; and, finally, (4) the national institutional and global dimension, that is, the larger contexts of and influences on well-being. In underscoring that "these dimensions are perceived through a prism of culture,"[68] they point simultaneously to universals (these dimensions are present in all societies) and specifics (they do not look the same everywhere). In exploring Kankanmori and Quayside Village, I focus on all four dimensions, with particular attention to the individual and the interpersonal, as situated within the context of collective constructions of meaning and value.

Intentional Community: Urban Cohousing

> The study of community acknowledges the inherent need for connection that exists among human beings . . . and affords opportunities to understand how this need is culturally configured and reconfigured with other human requirements in the face of change.[69]

Urban cohousing communities are a type of "intentional community." The term refers to "groups of people who share a common vision of the good life and who live and act together in order to try to realize this."[70] As early as the sixteenth century, Thomas More, in his book *Utopia*, idealized communal living, envisioning groups of thirty households (syphograncies) sharing property, space, and meals.[71] Over the years, others (among the most well-known being Robert Owen, Charles Fourier, and Le Corbusier[72]) produced a range of designs for collective living, and more than a few, including adherents of religious/spiritual sects, experimented with putting some of these designs into practice.[73] Aside from mid-twentieth-century state-organized and Marxist-inspired utopian socialisms, many such undertakings remained on the fringes of society. In the second half of the twentieth century, however, intentional communities experienced a resurgence, moving inward from the margins of society and taking a variety of contemporary forms ranging across the political spectrum: communes, ecovillages, kibbutzim, religious sects, disability communities, and—my focus here—cohousing communities.[74] This resurgence is part and parcel of increasing interest in the commons, forms of "self-organized cooperation (or solidarity)" that focus on the collective sharing and management of various resources and operate outside of the orbit of the state or market.[75] Examples here include the commoning of water, land, and other natural resources; participatory politics; alternative currencies; community gardens; and knowledge and health commons, to name a few.[76] Contemporary intentional communities, then, far from being outliers at the edge of society, are firmly situated within the context of these diverse efforts that together signal a movement away from capitalist forms of privatization and individualization.

Typically organizing themselves both spatially and socially in ways that encourage interaction and interdependence, members of intentional communities define the good life in various ways, focusing, for example, on environmental sustainability, income sharing, community self-sufficiency, spiritual development, or some combination thereof. In all cases, intentional communities in one way or another challenge exclusive nuclear family formation and rigid practices of private property ownership. In its most recent update, the Foundation for Intentional Community, which hosts the largest international database of intentional communities,[77] lists 1,059 communities worldwide.[78] Significantly, 455 of these are categorized as "in formation," indicating that intentional community, as both idea and practice, is gaining in popularity in certain sectors of society. Speaking at the 2013 International Communal Studies Association conference, Yaacov Oved claimed that "the globalization of the communal movement" was becoming "an integral part of global civil society";[79] and in his keynote address at the same conference, Robert Gilman went so far as to argue that the global spread of intentional community is part of a shift as significant as that from gathering-and-hunting forms of social organization to the more sedentary social systems that accompanied the rise of agriculture.[80] The claim, in other words, is that intentional communities comprise a global social movement. Indeed, many such communities participate in web networks, conferences, and site exchanges designed to spread knowledge of "best practices";[81] and they are also becoming increasingly visible in mainstream media[82]—something that many communities cultivate in order to increase awareness of their social and environmental advantages.[83] Robert Schehr notes in this regard that "actors in contemporary ICs [intentional communities] view their alternative lifestyle choices as laboratories for what is possible within civil society, conscious of their role as actors in (re)creating meaning."[84] Clearly, increasing numbers of people are seeing intentional community as an idea whose time has come. Nevertheless, as already mentioned, intentional community remains relatively underrecognized, and therefore underutilized, as a potential model in policy circles. Thus, while there may be a global movement of intentional community, it is one that travels along different circuits than those for the travel of orthodox approaches to well-being and the sharing of official policy frameworks. One goal of this book, then, is to contribute to efforts to make one particular form of intentional community—urban cohousing—more visible and relevant to policy-makers and members of the public alike.

The approaches to cohousing I explore in the following chapters emerged in Denmark, Sweden, and the Netherlands in the 1960s and 1970s and soon spread to the rest of Europe, North America, and beyond, including to Australia, Aotearoa/New Zealand, Korea, and Japan, among others.[85] In their influential book, *Cohousing: A Contemporary Approach to Housing Ourselves*,[86] Kathryn McCamant and Charles Durrett outlined shifts in the social landscape to which cohousing provided a productive response:

> Contemporary postindustrial societies ... are undergoing a multitude of changes that affect our housing needs. The modern single-family detached home, which makes up 67 percent of the American housing stock, was designed for a nuclear family consisting of a breadwinning father, a home-making mother, and two to four children. Today, less than one-quarter of the United States population lives in such households. Rather, the family with two working parents predominates, while the single-parent household is the fastest-growing family type. Almost one-quarter of the population lives alone. ... At the same time, the surge in housing costs and the increasing mobility of the population combine to break down traditional communities and place more demands on individual households. These factors call for a thorough re-examination of household and community needs, and the way we house ourselves.[87]

Bertil Egerö echoed this view at Stockholm's 2010 International Collaborative Housing Conference:

> Today, the growing numbers of single parent households, and the even more common one-person households, underline a need for social support and access to social togetherness. The 'ageing' process (relatively fewer young and more old in the age pyramid) adds dimensions such as care and security, mutual support and easier access to services.[88]

Cohousing, then, represents a response to dissatisfaction with contemporary social arrangements—in particular, with the mismatch between ideals, or norms (heterosexual nuclear families living in detached homes), and reality (demographic and economic shifts, and the range of actually existing household types). As Lucy Sargisson documents in her comparison of cohousing communities in Sweden, Aotearoa/New Zealand, the United Kingdom, and the United States, concerns about social systems that create "bad communities and unhappy people"—that is, systems characterized by alienation and the "inefficient use of social resources and human potential"—led many to turn to the alternative provided by cohousing.[89]

Criticism of current social arrangements and utopian desires for something better—a hallmark of intentional community[90]—is reflected in the design of community-specific approaches to space, community maintenance, and social life. Such designs reflect members' ideas about the kind of community they would like to live in—in particular, about the spirit of interrelationships they hope to engender—as well as the practicalities of living collectively. These approaches to the built environment and to the organization of social interactions regarding, for instance, the sharing of food, decision-making, and the resolution of conflict involve "a circular process ... in which the group intentionally designs" spaces and procedures "that will shape their own behavior"[91]—that lay the foundation, in other words, for the emergence of a particular vision of "community," composed of particular kinds of individual selves.

While *urban* cohousing communities, like other types of intentional community, represent forms of utopic imagining and practice that articulate claims about what is wrong with society and desires for "something better," they nevertheless remain fundamentally engaged with the societies within which they are embedded.[92] This distinguishes them from those intentional communities that "attempt to create ... [a] better life within the confines of the larger society but in various ways separate from it."[93] It also distinguishes them from cohousing communities that are situated on the outskirts of urban areas, locations that may reflect financial as much as philosophical orientations and constraints but serve, however inadvertently, to reduce the range of possible ties with society at large.

In being situated in urban centers and integrated with rather than segregated from their surroundings, urban cohousing communities transcend inside/outside, with/against binaries. They may emerge in response to a sense of alienation from current social arrangements, but they do not cut themselves off from them; on the contrary, "they strive to connect with neighbors and contribute to local economic, cultural and political life. This is perhaps cohousing's most significant deviation from communitarian tradition and its basis is a matter of principle, being a different reading of the process of social change."[94] The hybrid nature of their built environments and forms of social organization—emphasizing neither the individual nor the community to the exclusion of the other but both simultaneously—also transcends individualist/collectivist binaries. There is no effort to eliminate private property or personal space, but rather to place equal emphasis on shared spaces and resources: common rooms, gardens, laundry rooms, kitchen equipment, and so on. Similarly, residents remain responsible for their own units and personal finances while at the same time sharing expenses related to common spaces and resources. The response, then, to the failures of hyperindividualism is not hypercollectivism but something in between. This in-betweenness, or both/and, reflects a framework for living that challenges the radical individualism of mainstream approaches to well-being and consumption without being exclusively collectivist in orientation. In incorporating elements of both individualism and collectivism, and in maintaining ongoing connections with society at large, urban cohousing communities work within existing social and economic systems to model feasible alternatives that move society in the direction of greater social and environmental sustainability.

(Co)Housing and Well-Being

In their analysis of a survey questionnaire distributed to over 250 intentional communities in North America, with responses received from over 1,000 people living in almost 180 communities, Bjørn Grinde et al. found that cohousing residents ranked high on measures of life satisfaction, meaning and purpose, and connectedness and relatedness.[95] They conclude that "on average the ICs [intentional communities] appear to offer a life less in discord with the nature of being human [the need for social connection] compared to mainstream society."[96] They also note that intentional communities' environmentalist orientations and practices—one of the factors respondents highlighted as central to their decision to live in intentional community—indicate that "ICs may serve as models for a way of life that combines happiness with sustainability."[97] In another review, Amy Lubik and Tom Kosatsky point to a series of case studies demonstrating that "when communal spaces are shared by close neighbours, a common sense of belonging, ownership, and the facilitation of regular interaction reduces social isolation."[98] The strong relationship between the built environment and physical and psychological health established in these studies leads Lubik and Kosatsky to position cohousing as a public health intervention.[99] Epidemiologist Lisa Berkman concurs: in a 2017 PBS NewsHour interview, she described how cohousing works as a prophylactic against loneliness and social isolation, which in turn has a positive impact on public health.[100]

In an expansive study of both primary and secondary sources in the United States and Europe, Jo Williams documents a wide range of social, economic, and health benefits associated with living in cohousing, including increased opportunities for socializing and sharing interests, greater capacity to influence one's surroundings, reduced costs resulting from the pooling of resources and sharing of expenses, and mutual care and support in the face of physical and mental health challenges—all of which lead to an increased sense of belonging, safety, and self-esteem.[101] Lucy Sargisson, who coupled face-to-face interviews with an analysis of statements posted on cohousing communities' websites, similarly found

> an increased sense of well-being, happiness or satisfaction with their quality of life, pleasure about their reduced impact on the environment, and celebration of an increased sense of community. This latter involves greater involvement in the lives of neighbours (with well-protected privacy), shared responsibility for decisions that affect the group, and increased autonomy.[102]

Elsewhere, Sargisson highlights cohousing's positive impact on residents' civic participation,[103] indicating that the advantages of living in cohousing may accrue to society as a whole, as cohousers' engagements in community are not directed exclusively inward but also radiate outward.

Significantly, many of these benefits—connectedness, relatedness, belonging, mutual care and support, security, agency, and self-esteem—are precisely the ideals that we attach to the concept of *home*.[104] Indeed, housing is now recognized as a key determinant not only of physical health but also of happiness. Aisha Bin Bishr writes in this regard that "a lack of affordable housing is a major detractor from happiness."[105] David Clapham expands on this theme to argue that housing policy needs to move beyond frameworks that position housing instrumentally as "units of accommodation"[106] toward approaches that take into consideration the intimate connections between housing, on the one hand, and meaning, identity, self-esteem, agency, and human relationship, on the other. In other words, while housing policy obviously must address issues of accessibility, affordability, and adequacy, it should also be oriented to the idea of *home*, or *dwelling*, in an expansive sense.

This expansive sense of home includes recognition of "home-as-process," as something that we *do*.[107] And it is here that, in these times, cohousing can provide a fruitful model for thinking differently. The ongoing work that goes into community building and maintenance in cohousing facilitates an appreciation of home as a verb, not just a noun. This means that the desires for intimacy, security, mutual care, belonging, and self-realization that we project onto the idea of home are not automatically given—indeed, home can be a site of oppression and domination as well as of refuge and security[108]—but have to be actively produced. Cohousing also prompts us to recognize the larger, and largely taken for granted, conditions under which we realize (or don't) our ideals, conditions currently marked by an ideology of separation and the practices that index this ideology: separate, often isolating as well as isolated living spaces, a pattern that reflects the historical emergence of distinct public/private spheres with supposedly distinct characteristics—dog-eat-dog competition in the public sphere versus the safe haven of the private.[109] This model, which includes not only the separation of the public from the private but also separation *among* private households, poses problems for both social and environmental sustainability. Cohousing, in contrast, crosses these public/private boundaries, offering a different entry point into constructions and practices of *homing*[110] and functioning as a node of connection between "home" and "society." As such, cohousing works to expand the parameters of our conversations about housing and well-being to include "different choices about what is equitable, politically possible, and socially responsible"[111] in the context of an overall desire to make our world better.

Quayside Village and Kankanmori

Most publications on cohousing focus on how to physically and socially build such communities, and/or provide overviews of a number of communities, often in different countries.[112] These are extremely useful: in presenting information on patterns of development and organization, including pitfalls as well as "best practices," these studies and guidebooks offer insight both into what cohousing communities share as a model of the good life and into the contributions they make to social and environmental sustainability. My goal in this book is to build on these efforts by complementing breadth with depth—by providing a full-length movie, as it were, to fill out the snapshots. I do this by focusing exclusively on Quayside Village and Kankanmori, exploring in detail the structure and feel of these two communities and the nuances of their residents' everyday lives and experiences.

Kankanmori and Quayside Village are the first cohousing communities in their respective cities, and both are well-established: in 2018 Kankanmori celebrated its fifteenth anniversary and Quayside Village its twentieth. As I describe in the chapters that follow, they are quintessential examples of urban cohousing: architecturally and socially designed to balance independence and interdependence, self-governing, cross-generational, and integrated with society at large. Both are also located in countries that are witnessing the negative impacts of extreme individualization at the same time as individualized approaches to well-being are gaining in popularity. This is occurring even in Japan, despite the fact that individual happiness has not been at the forefront of Japanese culture historically.[113] Mirroring the pattern in Canada, the contemporary "quest for happiness" in Japan is manifested in mounting numbers of popular publications on the topic, the increasing circulation of discourses of well-being in the press and in politics, and an escalating pattern in advertising of coupling happiness with consumption—all in keeping with the global circulation and popularity of aspects of the "western tradition."[114] And yet, despite this, Kankanmori and Quayside Village, which emphasize *living together*, embody alternatives that both reject the current hyperindividualized order and offer a potential "yes"—that is, a direction in which we might want to go.[115] It is worth noting in this regard that the alternative of urban cohousing is emerging *within* the mainstream,[116] indicating that we do not have to look very far afield to find other ways of doing things that can provide models of how society in general might move in the direction of greater social and environmental sustainability.

Despite their similarities, Kankanmori and Quayside Village are situated in dramatically different cultures: the one traditionally individualistic in orientation, the other historically oriented to the collective, even as Western forms of individualism are gaining traction. I chose to focus on these two communities in particular in order to trace how cohousing models travel and are translated in diverse contexts. What is similar across contexts? What is altered to fit local cultural contingencies? Comparing communities situated in distinct settings also serves as a reminder that there is no one way of doing urban cohousing: neither Quayside Village nor Kankanmori can stand as *the* model of cohousing. If, as I argued earlier, there is a problem with universalizing what are in fact historically and culturally specific models of the nature of human being, there is also a danger in universalizing one model of urban cohousing. Even within Canada and Japan, neither of which is homogenous, Kankanmori and Quayside Village, like all intentional communities, are unique. My goal, then, is not to provide a singular blueprint for cohousing but, rather, to explore some of the ways that it can unfold, and some of the experiences that residents have, as a way of opening up cohousing as a possibility that can then take any number of forms.

The Project

My goal in this project was not to establish the happiness of Kankanmori and Quayside Village residents by means of psychological measures and comparisons with those who live in single-dwelling households. Instead, I took as my starting point the contrast between cohousing's relative lack of visibility in mainstream orientations to happiness, on the one hand, and evidence, outlined in the studies cited above, that living in cohousing has a positive impact on social and environmental well-being, on the other. Clearly, cohousing has something to contribute—again, not in the sense of proclaiming that everyone needs to live in cohousing but rather in its capacity to help us reflect on how we think about the good life. With existing data on the connections between cohousing and the good life in mind, I set out to explore a particular set of questions: How do residents experience the benefits and challenges of living collectively? How do they put their philosophies into practice? What tensions might be involved in negotiations between connection and personal freedom and autonomy? What practices of environmental sustainability do they engage in? And, finally, how do their visions and practices of community articulate with the different cultural contexts within which they are situated?

The only way to answer these questions—and to complement the primarily quantitative, large-scale approaches of orthodox happiness studies,[117] on the one hand, and the generalized overviews of multiple communities in cohousing studies, on the other—is to spend time in these communities in order to participate in their activities and engage in extended conversation with their residents. This is what I did, between 2014 and 2017, making five visits to Kankanmori, two of which were for two months each and three for ten days each; and six visits to Quayside Village, one of which was for two months, and the others for ten days to two weeks each. With the exception of two of the shorter trips to Kankanmori, during these visits I lived on site; participated in community activities, including not only social activities but also meetings and, at Kankanmori, committee work; collected life histories of residents; and facilitated a series of discussion groups.

The way in which topics for discussion groups were chosen illustrates a keystone of my approach to this project, namely, the idea that if cohousing involves collaboration, research on cohousing also calls for collaboration. A central attraction of collaborative work is that it positions participants as co-researchers, thereby steering research in the direction of what they, as knowledgeable insiders, consider to be most important, relevant, or problematic. Collaborative work also encourages participants to reflect on their values and practices and explore what has become common sense, and thus taken for granted, in their communities.

Collaboration for this project took two forms. First, it took the more traditional form of working with residents to determine the focus of the research, including both the general direction the research should take and the specific topics it should examine.[118] In other words, although I wanted to explore urban cohousing as a model for the good life, I did not determine what this exploration should look like in advance. Rather, orientations and topics emerged over the course of the research, in both formal and informal ways. Formally, I facilitated "brainstorming" sessions during which residents came up with topics for focused investigation; for example, the benefits of cohousing, how to balance personal and community commitments, aging in place, what growing up in cohousing is like, and how to deal with conflict around decision-making. Topics also emerged informally in the course of everyday conversation: for example, residents' rates of participation in running the community, and the future of cohousing. My goal, then, was to collaborate with residents to *coproduce* both the framing for the project and the data and insights generated as a result of that framing.

The collaborative nature of the project also extended beyond my engagements with residents of each community to include collaboration between residents of Kankanmori and Quayside Village themselves. Cohousing, as already described, is part of a global social movement that includes multiple circuits for the mutual exchange of ideas and practices. When, in the early days of the project, I told residents of each community about the other community I was working with, they expressed an interest in learning more; so I sought funding for members of each community to visit the other. The exchange visits provided Quayside Village and Kankanmori residents with an opportunity to reflect on their own orientations and practices in light of what they learned about life in the other community. This learning and reflection, moreover, occurred by means of physical *copresence*—a very different experience from reading about other communities at a distance or discussing them at a conference, however useful those endeavors may be. The exchanges contributed significantly to the collaborative spirit of the project—that is, to a shift in the balance of the ownership of the project from myself, an outside academic, to the residents of Kankanmori and Quayside Village—underscoring my methodological orientation to what it is that *they* orient to in pursuing the good life. It also advanced the overall goals of supporting the circulation of new and deeper understandings of alternative models of the good life, and of enhancing partnerships among intentional communities.

As part of the effort to place the research process as much as possible in the hands of residents, I provided each community with a GoPro so that they could record footage of life in their communities, choosing for themselves what to film and how to frame it. The result is four film shorts: *Life at Quayside Village*, *Life at Kankanmori*, *Exchange at Kankanmori*, and *Exchange at Quayside Village*. Most of the segments were filmed by residents, although in some cases we collaborated on deciding what should be filmed by either myself or the artistic consultant for the project, Don Gill—for example, a tour of someone's apartment or, at Quayside Village, clips of the resident midwife, Vera, meeting with her clients. Given the range of residents involved in filming, the sound and light quality varies considerably. Jamie Lewis, one of the research assistants for the project, worked assiduously to improve the film quality as much as possible and inserted subtitles in Japanese and English for all scenes. Some scenes are accompanied by brief narratives, recorded by residents, while in others the talk of those on film is highlighted. The film shorts (see appendix for URL) can be viewed on their own, to get a sense of the overall feel of Kankanmori and Quayside Village. Alternatively, readers can focus on the specific aspects of life in the two communities that they're most interested in, using the outline provided in the appendix as their guide. The shorts also complement aspects of the text, and so, where relevant, I provide references to particular clips, indicated by a ◊ icon.

Finally, collaboration included discussions about what forms the book and film shorts would take. Over the course of several return trips to each community in 2018 and 2019, I shared drafts of the book and rough cuts of the film shorts with residents so that we could jointly decide what to represent and how to represent it. I also consulted each person involved to make sure they were comfortable with quotes or references to them in the book and/or scenes in which they are included in the films. During these reviews, each participant chose whether they wanted to be referred to by their actual name or a pseudonym.

These processes of collaboration took unique shapes in each community. At Kankanmori, residents decided to form a study group of five to deal with the formal aspects of the project. Brainstorming sessions were conducted with this group, and then all residents were invited to participate in discussions organized around the topics chosen. The study group also made decisions regarding filming and the exchange visits between Kankanmori and Quayside Village. In contrast, the Quayside community wanted all residents to have the opportunity to participate in all phases of the project, from brainstorming, to filming, to choosing exchange participants. As will become clear in the following chapters, these different approaches reflect key patterns in the organizational structures of the two communities.

Outline of the Book

This book positions urban cohousing as an example of the kind of intervention that Charles Montgomery could have had in mind when he wrote that "sustainability and the good life can be by-products of the very same interventions."[119] In light of my strengths and limitations as an anthropologist, and in keeping with Graham Meltzer's observation that "the quality of our social relationships and our 'sense of community' are major determinants of our capacity for pro-environmental behavioural change,"[120] I give primacy of place to social sustainability, weaving in threads of environmental sustainability as they emerge in the visions and practices of the residents of Quayside Village and Kankanmori.

In exploring Kankanmori's and Quayside Village's quest for the good life, I focus in particular on their philosophies and organizational structures, the unfolding of daily life, and the stories and experiences of residents. In chapter 1, I provide general overviews of the two communities, outlining their similarities as well as their unique histories, their spatial arrangements, the goals and desires of their founding members, and the collective processes involved in building community. This is followed by a detailed description of the kinds of people who live in Quayside Village and Kankanmori, including basic demographic data, residents' reasons for moving in, and extended personal narratives of residents' experiences, four for each community.

Chapters 2 and 3 are set up as "conversations" between philosophy and the practices of everyday life; in other words, what are the foundational aspects of each community's governing framework and how do residents put them into practice? In chapter 2, I describe Quayside Village's values, both stated and unstated; the organizational structures built on the basis of these values; and how values and structures play out (or not) in everyday life. I emphasize three orientations in particular: first, *each-according-to-their-strengths, each-according-to-their-desires*, Quayside Village's underlying philosophy of participation in community building and maintenance; second, attention to emotional care; and, third, an emphasis on environmental stewardship. In chapter 3, I apply the same approach to Kankanmori, similarly exploring values, organizational structures, and everyday practices. Kankanmori's key orientations, different from those of Quayside Village, include, first, *everyone is equal*, which translates into sameness in the distribution of contributions to community maintenance and governance; and second, clear divisions between the public and the private, and between official community affairs and spontaneous socializing.

Chapter 4 focuses on the exchange visits between the two communities. In the fall of 2017, three residents of Quayside Village visited Kankanmori for ten days; this was followed by a ten-day visit to Quayside Village by a Kankanmori family of four. In both cases, exchange participants stayed on site. The chapter explores what exchange visitors learned about the other community as well as about their own, and what they brought back—and did not—to their home communities. Follow-up discussions with participants one year after the visits provide insights into the long-term impacts of the exchanges.

Since residents played key roles in determining the direction that the project would take in each community, highlighting sometimes similar and sometimes different concerns and agendas, the comparative aspects of what follows is not tit for tat. Certainly, some aspects of the discussions to follow are directly comparative; for instance, I outline the history and development of each community, compare the built environments of the communities and their philosophical orientations, and, in chapter 4, focus on the similarities and differences noticed by the exchange visitors. But chapters 2 and 3, focused on Quayside Village and Kankanmori respectively, each have a unique flavor, reflecting the specificities of what residents oriented to rather than a list of questions predetermined by an external researcher. Deliberately organizing these chapters to capture the frameworks and concerns of the two communities themselves reflects the deeply collaborative nature of the project, although it does mean that the chapters do not follow parallel trajectories. Another result of this collaborative approach is provided in chapter 1, where the personal narratives of Kankanmori residents are presented in the third person, while those of Quayside Village are presented in the first person.

Finally, in the conclusion, I explore what we can learn about happiness, well-being, and the good life from communities like Kankanmori and Quayside Village. How do such communities transcend individualistic approaches to happiness—the idea that happiness is a primarily internal phenomenon composed of personal satisfaction and positive affect—to approach Community with a capital "C," that is, the community that, as Katsuji, at Kankanmori, put it, "is a basic characteristic of humanity"? How might urban collective housing communities serve as models for both policy-makers and the public at large—as an addition to our "tool kit"[121] for producing the good life that does not eclipse the individual but, rather, serves to enhance individual well-being by means of social connection? Here I argue that cohousing provides insights into how we can increase both social and environmental sustainability, potentially decreasing the patterns of, and various costs associated with, loneliness, isolation, and environmental degradation generated by approaches to life focused on hyperindividualism and overconsumption.

Three Notes on Terminology and Naming
Happiness, Well-Being, and the Good Life

The relationships among these terms are complicated. *Happiness* is often used to refer to a subjective state, in contrast to *well-being*, which is typically used more broadly to encompass physical, economic, and cultural, as well as psychological, factors.[122] Such practices are not consistent, however, and these terms are often used interchangeably, not only with each other but also with other terms, such as *flourishing, thriving,* or *fulfillment*. *Happiness*, furthermore, is often subdivided into different types (for example, the distinction between hedonic and eudaimonic happiness, which may be glossed as pleasure versus virtue). The *good life* is also deployed in various ways, sometimes referring to individuals crafting a desired life for themselves, and sometimes in association with utopic aspirations—that is, with models of how to collectively approach social organization in ways that enhance the well-being of society at large and not just of individuals in isolation. This lack of precise definition and consistency in the use of terminology marks the ambiguous, perhaps elusive, nature of happiness, well-being, and the good life—as well as the reality that the meanings of these concepts, where they exist, can vary enormously. Perhaps it is less useful to pin the terms down than to recognize that they are overlapping pointers, suggesting, without narrowly delimiting, directions in which we might look. In what follows, then, I use the terms *happiness, well-being,* and *the good life* sometimes together and sometimes interchangeably, with the hope that the ways in which they are used will provide some indication of what it is that is being pointed to.

Cohousing and Collective Housing

What is referred to as *cohousing* in Canada is called *collective housing* in Japan.[123] In what follows I use the shorter *cohousing* most frequently, generally restricting my use of the term *collective housing* to discussions of Kankanmori and the Japanese context.

Japanese Names

Typically, Japanese refer to each other by their last names, followed by the honorific *-san*, which translates as Ms./Miss/Mrs./Mr. This is the practice followed at Kankanmori, except in the case of couples who share a last name, when first names are used, with the tag -*san*. After some deliberation, the Kankanmori study group decided that they wanted me to follow the Canadian convention of first names in the English version of this book (in the Japanese version, Japanese convention will be followed), and so this is the practice I have adopted here.

Notes

1. Robert Wright, "The Evolution of Despair," *Time*, 24 June 2001, retrieved 18 December 2020 from http://content.time.com/time/magazine/article/0,9171, 134603,00.html.
2. Anne Allison, *Precarious Japan* (Durham, NC: Duke University Press, 2013); Shu-Sen Chang et al., "Impact of 2008 Global Economic Crisis on Suicide: Time Trend Study in 54 Countries," *British Medical Journal* 347 (2013); Roger Goodman, "Shifting Landscapes: The Social Context of Youth Problems in an Ageing Nation," in *A Sociology of Japanese Youth: From Returnees to NEETs*, ed. Roger Goodman, Yuki Imoto, and Tuukka Toivonen (New York: Routledge, 2012); Sachiko Horiguchi, "Hikikomori: How Private Isolation Caught the Public Eye," in *A Sociology of Japanese Youth: From Returnees to NEETs*, ed. Roger Goodman, Yuki Imoto, and Tuukka Toivonen (New York: Routledge, 2012); Janice Keefe et al., *A Profile of Social Isolation in Canada* (Halifax: Nova Scotia Centre on Aging and the Department of Family Studies and Gerontology, Mount Saint Vincent University, 2006); Junko Kitanaka, *Depression in Japan: Psychiatric Cures for a Society in Distress* (Princeton, NJ: Princeton University Press, 2012); David Leheny, "What's Behind What Ails Japan," in *Critical Issues in Contemporary Japan*, ed. Jeff Kingston (New York: Routledge, 2014); Jennifer McLeod-Macy and Erin Roulston, "3rd Annual Canadian Mental Health Check-Up," *Ipsos Public Perspectives*, April 2017, retrieved 27 February 2020 from https://www.ipsos.com/sites/default/files/2017-08/IpsosPA_PublicPerspectives_CA_April%202017%20Mental%20Health.pdf; David Myers, "Human Connections and the Good Life: Balancing Individuality and Community in Public Policy," in *Positive Psychology in Practice*, ed. P. Alex Linley and Stephen Joseph (Hoboken, NJ: Wiley, 2004); Organisation for Economic Co-operation and Development, *Health at a Glance 2017: OECD Indicators* (Paris: OECD Publishing, 2017).
3. Jackie Tang, Nora Galbraith, and Johnny Truong, *Living Alone in Canada* (Ottawa: Statistics Canada, 2019). This pattern has been noted in the United Kingdom and United States as well; see Helen Jarvis, "Saving Space, Sharing Time: Integrated Infrastructures of Daily Life in Cohousing," *Environment and Planning A: Economy and Space* 43, no. 3 (2011).
4. Michael Hoffman, "Solitude Appears to Have an Image Problem in Japan," *Japan Times*, 11 August 2018, retrieved 27 February 2020 from https://www.japantimes.co.jp/news/2018/08/11/national/media-national/solitude-appears-image-problem-japan/#.XvK7eyOZPq0.
5. Eric Klinenberg, *Going Solo: The Extraordinary Rise and Surprising Appeal of Living Alone* (New York: Penguin, 2012).

6. Julianne Holt-Lunstad, Theodore F. Robles, and David A. Sbarra, "Advancing Social Connection as a Public Health Priority in the United States," *American Psychologist* 72, no. 6 (2017); Ed Diener and Robert Biswas-Diener, "Social Well-Being: Research and Policy Recommendations," in *Global Happiness Policy Report 2018*, ed. Global Happiness Council (2018), retrieved 3 September 2018 from http://www.happinesscouncil.org/report/2018/.
7. Hoffman, "Image Problem in Japan"; Allison, *Precarious Japan*.
8. Justin McCurry, "Concern in Japan over High Number of 'Lonely Deaths' While Living with Others," *The Guardian*, 8 December 2020, retrieved 18 December 2020 from https://www.theguardian.com/world/2020/dec/08/concern-lonely-deaths-japan-dementia.
9. Tim Tiefenbach and Florian Kohlbacher, "Happiness from the Viewpoint of Economics: Findings from Recent Survey Data in Japan," German Institute for Japanese Studies Working Paper 13/1 (Tokyo: German Institute for Japanese Studies, 2013); Tim Tiefenbach and Florian Kohlbacher, "Happiness and Life Satisfaction in Japan by Gender and Age," German Institute for Japanese Studies Working Paper 13/2 (Tokyo: German Institute for Japanese Studies, 2013).
10. Organisation for Economic Co-operation and Development, *How's Life? 2020: Measuring Well-Being* (Paris: OECD Publishing, 2020).
11. Myers, "Human Connections."
12. Barbara Gunnell, "The Happiness Industry," *New Statesman*, 6 September 2004, retrieved 27 February 2020 from https://www.newstatesman.com/node/160445.
13. Robert D. Putnam, *Bowling Alone: The Collapse and Revival of American Community* (New York: Simon and Schuster, 2000).
14. United Nations, *World Urbanization Prospects: The 2018 Revision* (New York: United Nations Department of Economic and Social Affairs, Population Division, 2018).
15. Matthieu Lietaert, "Cohousing's Relevance to Degrowth Theories," *Journal of Cleaner Production* 18, no. 6 (2010): 577.
16. Charles Montgomery, *Happy City: Transforming Our Lives through Urban Design* (Toronto: Anchor Canada, 2013).
17. Ibid., 65.
18. Global Council for Happiness and Wellbeing, eds., *Global Happiness and Wellbeing Policy Report 2019* (2019), retrieved 21 April 2020 from http://www.happinesscouncil.org.
19. Montgomery, *Happy City*, 47.
20. Robert Waldinger, "What Makes a Good Life? Lessons from the Longest Study on Happiness," TED Talk, November 2015, retrieved 20 July 2017 from https://www.ted.com/talks/robert_waldinger_what_makes_a_good_life_lessons_from_the_longest_study_on_happiness?language=en.
21. Diener and Biswas-Diener, "Social Well-Being," 131.
22. Lisa F. Berkman and Leonard Syme, "Social Networks, Host Resistance, and Mortality: A Nine-Year Follow-Up Study of Alameda County Residents," *American Journal of Epidemiology* 109, no. 2 (1979); Lisa F. Berkman and Aditi Krishna, "Social Network Epidemiology," in *Social Epidemiology*, 2nd ed., ed. Lisa F. Berkman, Ichiro Kawachi, and M. Maria Glymour (Oxford: Oxford University Press, 2014); Ichiro Kawachi et al., "Social Capital, Income Inequality, and Mortality," *American Journal of Public Health* 87, no. 9 (1997); see also Holt-Lunstad, Robles, and Sbarra, "Advancing Social Connection."

23. Émile Durkheim, *Suicide: A Study in Sociology*, trans. John A. Spaulding and George Simpson (New York: The Free Press, 1997 [1897]).
24. Roshini Nair, "The Architecture of Loneliness: How Vancouver's Highrises Contribute to Isolation," CBC News, 25 November 2018, retrieved 27 February 2020 from https://www.cbc.ca/news/canada/british-columbia/the-architecture-of-loneliness-how-vancouver-s-highrises-contribute-to-isolation-1.4919548.
25. Joshua Lockyer, "Intentional Communities and Sustainability," *Communal Societies* 30, no. 1 (2010); Graham Meltzer, "Cohousing: Linking Communitarianism and Sustainability," *Communal Societies* 19 (1999); Graham Meltzer, "Cohousing: Verifying the Importance of Community in the Application of Environmentalism," *Journal of Architectural and Planning Research* 17, no. 2 (2000); Graham Meltzer, *Sustainable Community: Learning from the Cohousing Model* (Victoria: Trafford, 2005).
26. Intergovernmental Panel on Climate Change, *Global Warming of 1.5°C: An IPCC Special Report on the Impacts of Global Warming of 1.5°C Above Pre-industrial Levels and Related Global Greenhouse Gas Emission Pathways, in the Context of Strengthening the Global Response to the Threat of Climate Change, Sustainable Development, and Efforts to Eradicate Poverty* (Geneva: World Meteorological Association, 2018); Intergovernmental Panel on Climate Change, "Land is a Critical Resource, IPCC Report Says," *Intergovernmental Panel on Climate Change*, 8 August 2019, retrieved 27 February 2020 from https://www.ipcc.ch/2019/08/08/land-is-a-critical-resource_srccl/; World Meteorological Organization, "Urgency of Climate Action Highlighted for U.N. Summit Preparatory Meeting," *World Meteorological Organization*, 28 June 2019, retrieved 27 February 2020 from https://public.wmo.int/en/media/press-release/urgency-of-climate-action-highlighted-un-summit-preparatory-meeting.
27. Sam Thompson, "Introduction to Happiness and Society," in *The Oxford Handbook of Happiness*, ed. Susan David, Ilona Boniwell, and Amanda Conley Ayers (Oxford: Oxford University Press, 2013), 428.
28. Douglas Keay, "Interview with Margaret Thatcher, September 23," *Woman's Own*, 23 September 1987.
29. Collin van Uchelen, "Individualism, Collectivism, and Community Psychology," in *Handbook of Community Psychology*, ed. Julian Rappaport and Edward Seidman (New York: Kluwer Academic/Plenum Publishers, 2000), 74.
30. Montgomery, *Happy City*, 65.
31. Van Uchelen, "Community Psychology," 68.
32. Martin Seligman and Mihaly Csikszentmihalyi, "Positive Psychology: An Introduction," *American Psychologist* 55, no. 1 (2000); see also Michael Argyle, *The Psychology of Happiness* (London: Methuen, 1987); Alan Carr, *Positive Psychology: The Science of Happiness and Human Strengths* (London: Routledge, 2004); Mihaly Csikszentmihalyi, *Flow: The Psychology of Optimal Experience* (New York: HarperCollins, 1990); Mihaly Csikszentmihalyi, *Creativity: Flow and the Psychology of Discovery and Invention* (New York: Harper Collins, 1997); Shelly L. Gable and Jonathan Haidt, "What (and Why) Is Positive Psychology?" *Review of General Psychology* 9, no. 2 (2005); P. Alex Linley et al., "Positive Psychology: Past, Present, and (Possible) Future," *Journal of Positive Psychology* 1, no. 1 (2006); Martin Seligman, *Authentic Happiness: Using the New Positive Psychology to Realize Your Potential for Lasting Fulfillment* (New York: Free Press, 2002); Martin Seligman, *Learned Optimism: How to Change Your Mind and Your Life* (New York: Vintage, 2006).

33. See, e.g., Tal Ben-Shahar, *Happier: Learn the Secrets to Daily Joy and Lasting Fulfillment* (New York: McGraw Hill, 2007); Paul Dolan, *Happiness by Design: Change What You Do, Not How You Think* (New York: Hudson Street Press, 2014).
34. Gordon Mathews, "Happiness, Culture, and Context," *International Journal of Wellbeing* 2, no. 4 (2012); see also Wolfram Manzenreiter and Barbara Holthus, "Introduction: Happiness in Japan through the Anthropological Lens," in *Happiness and the Good Life in Japan*, ed. Wolfram Manzenreiter and Barbara Holthus (New York: Routledge, 2017).
35. Clifford Geertz, "On the Nature of Anthropological Understanding," *American Scientist* 63 (1975); Catherine Kingfisher, *Western Welfare in Decline: Globalization and Women's Poverty* (Philadelphia: University of Pennsylvania Press, 2002); Catherine A. Lutz, *Unnatural Emotions: Everyday Sentiments on a Micronesian Atoll and Their Challenge to Western Theory* (Chicago: University of Chicago Press, 1988).
36. John Chambers Christopher and Sarah Hickinbottom, "Positive Psychology, Ethnocentrism, and the Disguised Ideology of Individualism," *Theory & Psychology* 18, no. 5 (2008); Mohsen Joshanloo and Dan Weijers, "Aversion to Happiness across Cultures: A Review of Where and Why People Are Averse to Happiness," *Journal of Happiness Studies* 15, no. 3 (2014); Jeannette M. Mageo, *Theorizing Self in Samoa: Emotions, Genders, and Sexualities* (Ann Arbor: University of Michigan Press, 1998).
37. Carolina Izquierdo, "Well-Being among the Matsigenka of the Peruvian Amazon: Health, Missions, Oil, and 'Progress,'" in *Pursuits of Happiness: Well-Being in Anthropological Perspective*, ed. Gordon Mathews and Carolina Izquierdo (New York: Berghahn Books, 2009); Lutz, *Unnatural Emotions*.
38. C. Jason Throop, "Ambivalent Happiness and Virtuous Suffering," in *Values of Happiness: Toward an Anthropology of Purpose in Life*, ed. Harry Walker and Iza Kavedžija (Chicago: HAU Books, 2016).
39. Michael Jackson, *Life within Limits: Well-Being in a World of Want* (Durham, NC: Duke University Press, 2011).
40. Iza Kavedžija, "The Good Life in Balance: Insights from Aging Japan," in *Values of Happiness: Toward an Anthropology of Purpose in Life*, ed. Harry Walker and Iza Kavedžija (Chicago: HAU Books, 2016); Manzenreiter and Holthus, "Introduction"; Yukiko Uchida and Shinobu Kitayama, "Happiness and Unhappiness in East and West: Themes and Variations," *Emotion* 9, no. 4 (2009); Yukiko Uchida and Yuji Ogihara, "Personal or Interpersonal Construal of Happiness: A Cultural Psychological Perspective," *International Journal of Wellbeing* 2, no. 4 (2012).
41. Yukiko Uchida, Yuji Ogihara, and Shintaro Fukushima, "Cultural Construal of Wellbeing—Theories and Empirical Evidence," in *Global Handbook of Quality of Life*, ed. Wolfgang Glatzer, Laura Camfield, Valerie Møller, and Mariano Rojas (New York: Springer, 2015), 823.
42. Hidehumi Hitokoto and Yukiko Uchida, "Interdependent Happiness: Theoretical Importance and Measurement Validity," *Journal of Happiness Studies* 16, no. 1 (2015).
43. Darrin M. McMahon, *Happiness: A History* (New York: Grove Press, 2006); Darrin M. McMahon, "What Does the Ideal of Happiness Mean?" *Social Research* 77, no. 2 (2010).
44. McMahon, *Happiness*; see also Sara Ahmed, *The Promise of Happiness* (Durham, NC: Duke University Press, 2010); William Davies, *The Happiness Industry: How the Gov-*

ernment and Big Business Sold Us Well-Being (London: Verso, 2015); Mark Kingwell, *In Pursuit of Happiness: Better Living from Plato to Prozac* (Toronto: Penguin, 1998).
45. Barbara Ehrenreich, *Bright-Sided: How the Relentless Promotion of Positive Thinking Has Undermined America* (New York: Henry Holt, 2009); Gunnell, "Happiness Industry."
46. Suzanne Moore, "The Self-Care Industry is Peddling Exhausting, Dangerous Drivel," *The Guardian*, 7 May 2018, retrieved 27 February 2020 from https://www.theguardian.com/commentisfree/2018/may/07/the-self-care-industry-is-peddling-exhausting-dangerous-drivel.
47. Ehrenreich, *Bright-Sided*; Catherine Kingfisher, "Happiness: Notes on History, Culture and Governance," *Health, Culture and Society* 5, no. 1 (2013); Matthew McDonald and Jean O'Callaghan, "Positive Psychology: A Foucauldian Critique," *Humanistic Psychologist* 36, no. 2 (2008).
48. Ross Abbinnett, *Politics of Happiness: Connecting the Philosophical Ideas of Hegel, Nietzsche and Derrida to the Political Ideologies of Happiness* (New York: Bloomsbury, 2013); Ahmed, *Promise of Happiness*; Pascal Bruckner, *Perpetual Euphoria: On the Duty to Be Happy* (Princeton, NJ: Princeton University Press, 2010); Luís Fernández-Ríos and J. M. Cornes, "A Critical Review of the History and Current Status of Positive Psychology," *Annuary of Clinical and Health Psychology* 5 (2009); McDonald and O'Callaghan, "Positive Psychology"; Luka Zevnik, *Critical Perspectives in Happiness Research: The Birth of Modern Happiness* (New York: Springer, 2014).
49. Iain Ferguson, "Neoliberalism, Happiness and Wellbeing," *International Socialism* 117 (2007), retrieved 19 July 2017 from http://isj.org.uk/neoliberalism-happiness-and-wellbeing/; Paul Dolan and Mathew P. White, "How Can Measures of Subjective Well-Being Be Used to Inform Public Policy?" *Perspectives on Psychological Science* 2, no. 1 (2007).
50. Roland Robertson, *Globalization: Social Theory and Global Culture* (London: Sage, 1992); see also Ahmed, *Promise of Happiness*; Christopher and Hickinbottom, "Positive Psychology"; Joshanloo and Weijers, "Aversion to Happiness"; Kingfisher, *Western Welfare in Decline*; McMahon, *Happiness*; Zevnik, *Perspectives in Happiness Research*.
51. Wendy James, "Well-Being: In Whose Opinion, and Who Pays?" in *Culture and Well-Being: Anthropological Approaches to Freedom and Political Ethics*, ed. Alberto Corsín Jiménez (London: Pluto, 2008), 69–70.
52. See, e.g., Gable and Haidt, "Positive Psychology"; Seligman, *Authentic Happiness*.
53. Ed Diener et al., *Well-Being for Public Policy* (Oxford: Oxford University Press, 2009), 175.
54. Martin Seligman, *Flourish: A Visionary New Understanding of Happiness and Well-Being* (New York: Free Press, 2012); see also Manzenreiter and Holthus, "Introduction," 8.
55. Shelly L. Gable and Christopher Bromberg, "Healthy Social Bonds: A Necessary Condition for Well-Being," in *Handbook of Well-Being*, ed. Ed Diener, Shigehiro Oishi, and Louis Tay (Salt Lake City, Utah: DEF Publishers, 2018).
56. Diener and Biswas-Diener, "Social Well-Being," 131.
57. Uchida, Ogihara, and Fukushima, "Cultural Construal of Wellbeing," 826.
58. Florian Coulmas, "The Quest for Happiness in Japan," German Institute for Japanese Studies Working Paper 09/1 (Tokyo: German Institute for Japanese Stud-

ies, 2008); Gordon Mathews, "Happiness in Neoliberal Japan," in *Happiness and the Good Life in Japan*, ed. Wolfram Manzenreiter and Barbara Holthus (New York: Routledge, 2017); Yuji Ogihara et al., "Are Common Names Becoming Less Common? The Rise in Uniqueness and Individualism in Japan," *Frontiers in Psychology* 6, no. 1490 (2015).
59. Stefan Klein, *The Science of Happiness: How Our Brains Make Us Happy—And What We Can Do to Get Happier*, trans. Stephen Lehmann (Cambridge: Da Capo Press, 2006), 252.
60. See, e.g., Gable and Bromberg, "Healthy Social Bonds."
61. Diener and Biswas-Diener, "Social Well-Being," 133–34.
62. Aisha Bin Bishr, "Happy Cities Agenda," in *Global Happiness and Wellbeing Policy Report 2019*, ed. Global Council for Happiness and Wellbeing (2019), 119–23, retrieved 30 August 2019 from www.happinesscouncil.org; see also Donia Zhang, "Cooperative Housing and Cohousing in Canada: The Pursuit of Happiness in the Common Courtyards," *Journal of Architectural Research and Development* 2, no. 1 (2018).
63. Edward F. Fischer, *The Good Life: Aspiration, Dignity, and the Anthropology of Wellbeing* (Stanford, CA: Stanford University Press, 2014), 216.
64. Ibid., 215.
65. Mathews, "Happiness in Neoliberal Japan," 231.
66. Mark Cieslik, *The Happiness Riddle and the Quest for a Good Life* (London: Palgrave Macmillan, 2017), 31.
67. Gordon Mathews and Carolina Izquierdo, "Towards an Anthropology of Well-Being," in *Pursuits of Happiness: Well-Being in Anthropological Perspective*, ed. Gordon Mathews and Carolina Izquierdo (New York: Berghahn Books, 2009); see also Gordon Mathews, "Wellbeing," in *The International Encyclopedia of Anthropology*, ed. Hilary Callan (2018), retrieved 27 February 2020 from https://doi.org/10.1002/9781118924396.wbiea1627.
68. Mathews and Izquierdo, "Anthropology of Well-Being," 261–62.
69. Susan Love Brown, "Introduction," in *Intentional Community: An Anthropological Perspective*, ed. Susan Love Brown (Albany: State University of New York Press, 2002), 2.
70. Lucy Sargisson, "Second-Wave Cohousing: A Modern Utopia?" *Utopian Studies* 23, no. 1 (2012): 42.
71. Thomas More, *Utopia*, trans. Paul Turner (New York: Penguin, 1965 [1515]).
72. See McMahon, *Happiness*; Henrietta L. Moore, "'Visions of the Good Life': Anthropology and the Study of Utopia," *Cambridge Journal of Anthropology* 14, no. 3 (1990).
73. E.g., Susan Love Brown, ed., *Intentional Community: An Anthropological Perspective* (Albany: State University of New York Press, 2002); Dan Chodorkoff, *The Anthropology of Utopia: On Social Ecology and Human Development* (Porsgrunn: New Compass Press, 2014); McMahon, *Happiness*; Moore, "Visions"; Melford E. Spiro, *Kibbutz: Venture in Utopia* (Cambridge: Harvard University Press, 1956); Melford E. Spiro, "Utopia and Its Discontents: The Kibbutz and Its Historical Vicissitudes," *American Anthropologist* 106, no. 3 (2004).
74. Brown, *Intentional Community*; Bella DePaulo, *How We Live Now: Redefining Home and Family in the 21st Century* (New York: Atria Books, 2015); Dorit Fromm, *Collaborative Communities: Cohousing, Central Living, and Other New Forms of Housing*

with Shared Facilities (New York: Van Nostrand Reinhold, 1991); Joshua Lockyer and James R. Veteto, eds., *Environmental Anthropology Engaging Ecotopia: Bioregionalism, Permaculture, and Ecovillages* (New York: Berghahn Books, 2013); Sargisson, "Second-Wave Cohousing"; Spiro, *Kibbutz*; Spiro, "Utopia and its Discontents"; Dick Urban Vestbro, "History of Cohousing—Internationally and in Sweden," in *Living Together—Cohousing Ideas and Realities around the World: Proceedings from the International Collaborative Housing Conference in Stockholm 5–9 May 2010*, ed. Dick Urban Vestbro (Stockholm: Division of Urban and Regional Studies, Royal Institute of Technology, in collaboration with Kollektivhus NU, 2010); Jo Williams, "Predicting an American Future for Cohousing," *Futures* 40, no. 3 (2008).

75. Irina Velicu and Gustavo García-López, "Thinking the Commons through Ostrom and Butler: Boundedness and Vulnerability," *Theory, Culture & Society* 35, no. 6 (2018): 56.
76. Ash Amin and Philip Howell, "Thinking the Commons," in *Releasing the Commons: Rethinking the Futures of the Commons*, ed. Ash Amin and Philip Howell (New York: Routledge, 2016); J. K. Gibson-Graham, Jenny Cameron, and Stephen Healy, "Commoning as a Postcapitalist Politics," in *Releasing the Commons: Rethinking the Futures of the Commons*, ed. Ash Amin and Philip Howell (New York: Routledge, 2016); Andrea Nightingale, "Commoning for Inclusion? Commons, Exclusion, Property and Socio-natural Becomings," *International Journal of the Commons* 13, no. 1 (2019); Elinor Ostrom, *Governing the Commons: The Evolution of Institutions for Collective Action* (Cambridge: Cambridge University Press, 1990); Velicu and García-López, "Thinking the Commons."
77. Foundation for Intentional Community, website, 2019, retrieved 4 May 2020 from www.ic.org.
78. This number is likely an underestimate, since communities need to register with the FIC in order to be listed. Kankanmori, for instance, is not included.
79. Yaacov Oved, "The Globalization of Communes," *Social Sciences Directory* 2, no. 3 (2013): 93.
80. Robert Gilman, "Keynote Address: The Dynamic Planetary Context for Intentional Communities (Proceedings of the 11th Conference of the International Communal Studies Association)," *Social Sciences Directory* 2, no. 3 (2013).
81. To give a few examples of English-language sources: Foundation for Intentional Community (www.ic.org), Cohousing Association of the US (www.cohousing.org), UK Cohousing (www.cohousing.org.uk), Canadian Cohousing Network (www.cohousing.ca), Cohousing Australia (https://communities.org.au), *Communities Magazine*, the Communal Studies Association, and the Centre for the Study of Cooperatives at the University of Saskatchewan.
82. Suzanne Bearne, "Totally Together: Could Communal Living Suit You?" *The Guardian*, 3 February 2018, retrieved 27 February 2020 from https://www.theguardian.com/money/2018/feb/03/communal-living-communes-cohousing; "Collective Homes a Solution for Those in Japan Who Don't Want to Live Alone," *Japan Times*, 30 August 2016, retrieved 27 February 2020 from https://www.japantimes.co.jp/news/2016/08/30/national/social-issues/collective-homes-solution-japan-dont-want-live-alone/#.XvLBpyOZPq0; Anna Leach, "Happy Together: Lonely Baby Boomers Turn to Co-housing," *The Guardian*, 15 August 2018, retrieved 27 February 2020 from https://www.theguardian.com/world/2018/aug/15/happy-together-lonely-baby-boomers-turn-to-co-housing; Tom Verde, "There's

Community and Consensus. But It's No Commune," *The Independent*, 10 February 2018, retrieved 27 February 2020 from https://www.independent.co.uk/news/community-consensus-commune-cohousing-retirement-younger-everybody-loves-raymond-a8199316.html. The CBC has also had a number of radio shows on cohousing, e.g., CBC, "Where I Live and Why: Co-housing Development in Edmonton," CBC News, 1 October 2019, retrieved 27 February 2020 from https://www.cbc.ca/player/play/1628975683653 and CBC, "A Closer Look at How Cohousing Works," CBC News, 12 November 2019, retrieved 27 February 2020 from https://www.cbc.ca/player/play/1641455683614.
83. Meltzer, "Cohousing Sustainability," 91–92.
84. Robert C. Schehr, *Dynamic Utopia: Establishing Intentional Communities as a New Social Movement* (Westport, CT: Bergin and Garvey, 1997), 48.
85. Meltzer, *Sustainable Community*; Vestbro, "History of Cohousing."
86. Kathryn McCamant and Charles Durrett, *Cohousing: A Contemporary Approach to Housing Ourselves* (Berkeley, CA: Habitat Press/Ten Speed Press, 1988). Instrumental in the expansion of cohousing in North America, *Cohousing: A Contemporary Approach to Housing Ourselves* was also recommended to me by Ikuko Koyabe, a key architect of Kankanmori.
87. Ibid., 10.
88. Bertil Egerö, "Introduction: Cohousing—Issues and Challenges," in *Living Together—Cohousing Ideas and Realities around the World: Proceedings from the International Collaborative Housing Conference in Stockholm 5–9 May 2010*, ed. Dick Urban Vestbro (Stockholm: Division of Urban and Regional Studies, Royal Institute of Technology, in collaboration with Kollektivhus NU, 2010), 13–14.
89. Lucy Sargisson, *Fool's Gold? Utopianism in the Twenty-First Century* (New York: Palgrave Macmillan, 2012), 175.
90. Susan Love Brown, "Community as Cultural Critique," in *Intentional Community: An Anthropological Perspective*, ed. Susan Love Brown (Albany: State University of New York Press, 2002); Moore, "Visions"; Sargisson, "Second-Wave Cohousing"; Sargisson, *Fool's Gold*.
91. Sargisson, "Second-Wave Cohousing," 44.
92. Ruth Levitas, *Utopia as Method: The Imaginary Reconstitution of Society* (New York: Palgrave Macmillan, 2013); see also Davina Cooper, *Everyday Utopias: The Conceptual Life of Promising Spaces* (Durham, NC: Duke University Press, 2014); Sargisson, "Second-Wave Cohousing"; Sargisson, *Fool's Gold*.
93. Lucy Sargisson and Lyman Tower Sargent, *Living in Utopia: New Zealand's Intentional Communities* (New York: Routledge, 2004), 1; see also Brown, "Introduction," 5–6; Lucy Jayne Kamau, "Liminality, Communitas, Charisma, and Community," in *Intentional Community: An Anthropological Perspective*, ed. Susan Love Brown (Albany: State University of New York Press, 2002), 20.
94. Meltzer, "Cohousing Sustainability," 91.
95. Bjørn Grinde et al., "Quality of Life in Intentional Communities," *Social Indicators Research* 137 (2018).
96. Ibid., 635.
97. Ibid., 636.
98. Amy Lubik and Tom Kosatsky, "Public Health Should Promote Co-operative Housing and Cohousing," *Canadian Journal of Public Health* 110 (2019): 121.
99. Ibid., 121.

100. PBS, "Cohousing Communities Help Prevent Social Isolation," *PBS NewsHour*, 12 February 2017, retrieved 4 May 2020 from https://www.pbs.org/newshour/show/cohousing-communities-help-prevent-social-isolation; see also Berkman and Krishna, "Social Network Epidemiology"; Anne P. Glass and Rebecca S. Vander Plaats, "A Conceptual Model for Aging Better Together Intentionally," *Journal of Aging Studies* 27, no. 4 (2013); Noah J. Webster, Kristine J. Ajrouch, and Toni C. Antonucci, "Living Healthier, Living Longer: The Benefits of Residing in Community," *Generations* 37, no. 4 (2014).
101. Williams, "Predicting an American Future."
102. Sargisson, *Fool's Gold*, 185.
103. Sargisson, "Second-Wave Cohousing," 44–45.
104. Shelley Mallett, "Understanding Home: A Critical Review of the Literature," *Sociological Review* 52, no. 1 (2004); Farhan Samanani and Johannes Lenhard, "House and Home," in *The Cambridge Encyclopedia of Anthropology*, ed. Felix Stein, Sian Lazar, Matei Candea, Hildegard Diemberger, Joel Robbins, Andrew Sanchez, and Rupert Stasch (2019), retrieved 27 February 2020 from http://doi.org/10.29164/19home.
105. Bin Bishr, "Happy Cities Agenda," 121; see also Montgomery, *Happy City*; Geoff Mulgan, "Well-Being and Public Policy," in *The Oxford Handbook of Happiness*, ed. Susan David, Ilona Boniwell, and Amanda Conley Ayers (Oxford: Oxford University Press, 2013).
106. David Clapham, "Happiness, Well-Being, and Housing Policy," *Policy and Politics* 38, no. 2 (2010): 253.
107. Samanani and Lenhard, "House and Home," 9.
108. Ariel Handel, "What's in a Home? Toward a Critical Theory of Housing/Dwelling," *Environment and Planning C: Politics and Space* 37, no. 6 (2019); Mallett, "Understanding Home."
109. Mallett, "Understanding Home," 71.
110. Handel, "What's in a Home," 1052.
111. Janine Brodie, "Social Literacy and Social Justice in Times of Crisis," *Trudeau Foundation Papers* 4, no. 1 (2012): 116.
112. Diana Leafe Christian, *Creating a Life Together: Practical Tools to Grow Ecovillages and Intentional Communities* (Gabriola Islands, BC: New Society Publishers, 2003); Charles Durrett and Kathryn McCamant, *Creating Cohousing: Building Sustainable Communities* (Gabriola Islands, BC: New Society Publishers, 2011); Fromm, *Collaborative Communities*; Claudia Hildner, *Future Living: Collective Housing in Japan* (Basel: Birkhäuser, 2014); McCamant and Durrett, *Cohousing*; Meltzer, *Sustainable Community*; Lee Ann Nicol, *Sustainable Collective Housing: Policy and Practice for Multi-family Dwellings* (New York: Routledge, 2013); Sargisson and Sargent, *Living in Utopia*.
113. Coulmas, "Quest for Happiness," 3.
114. Ibid.; see also Mathews, "Happiness in Neoliberal Japan"; Ogihara et al., "Common Names."
115. Naomi Klein, *No Is Not Enough: Resisting the New Shock Politics and Winning the World We Need* (Toronto: Random House, 2017).
116. Ghassan Hage, "Dwelling in the Reality of Utopian Thought," *Traditional Dwellings and Settlements Review* 23, no. 1 (2011).

117. Mathews, "Happiness, Culture, and Context"; Gordon Mathews and Carolina Izquierdo, eds., *Pursuits of Happiness: Well-Being in Anthropological Perspective* (New York: Berghahn Books, 2009); Gordon Mathews and Carolina Izquierdo, "Anthropology, Happiness, and Well-Being," in *Pursuits of Happiness: Well-Being in Anthropological Perspective*, ed. Gordon Mathews and Carolina Izquierdo (New York: Berghahn Books, 2009); see also Fischer, *Good Life*; Shigehiro Oishi, "Culture and Subjective Well-Being: Conceptual and Measurement Issues," in *Handbook of Well-being*, ed. Ed Diener, Shigehiro Oishi, and Louis Tay (Salt Lake City, UT: DEF Publishers, 2018); Joel Robbins, "Beyond the Suffering Subject: Toward an Anthropology of the Good," *Journal of the Royal Anthropological Institute* 19, no. 3 (2013); Neil Thin, "Happiness and the Sad Topics of Anthropology," Wellbeing in Developing Countries Working Paper No. 10 (Bath: Wellbeing in Developing Countries ESRC Research Group, 2005); Neil Thin, "Qualitative Approaches to Culture and Well-Being," in *Handbook of Well-Being*, ed. Ed Diener, Shigehiro Oishi, and Louis Tay (Salt Lake City, UT: DEF Publishers, 2018).
118. See, e.g., Douglas R. Holmes and George E. Marcus, "Collaboration Today and the Re-imagination of the Classic Scene of Fieldwork Encounter," *Collaborative Anthropologies* 1 (2008); Luke Eric Lassiter, *The Chicago Guide to Collaborative Ethnography* (Chicago: University of Chicago Press, 2005); Joanne Rappaport, "Beyond Participant Observation: Collaborative Ethnography as Theoretical Innovation," *Collaborative Anthropologies* 1 (2008); Stephen L. Schensul et al., "Participatory Methods and Community-Based Collaborations," in *Handbook of Methods in Cultural Anthropology*, 2nd ed., ed. H. Russell Bernard and Clarence C. Gravlee (Lanham, MD: Rowman and Littlefield, 2015).
119. Montgomery, *Happy City*, 253.
120. Meltzer, *Sustainable Community*, 1.
121. Fischer, *Good Life*.
122. Mathews and Izquierdo, "Anthropology, Happiness, and Well-Being," 2–3; see also Thin, *Social Happiness*.
123. Although I have not followed up with research on this issue, Ikuko Koyabe told me that the proponents of collective housing developments in the United States, in particular, felt that the term *collective* would be too closely associated with socialism and communism, and so a decision was made to use the term *cohousing* instead.

1 KANKANMORI AND QUAYSIDE VILLAGE
An Overview

The ideas of collective living and housing are the balance between careers and raising children, men and women's participation, providing space for children and eco-life, and passing on traditions, culture, and creativity. These are the stresses that people are dealing with today, and collective housing is one solution.
—Ikuko Koyabe, key architect of Kankanmori

When I kind of took stock a year or two after [moving in], I looked at things and I thought to myself, well if I had sat down and written down all the things I would like the situation to be in, and all the things I might like in a place to live, if I had sat down and written that, it wouldn't have been nearly as good as this is! And that's true, I mean, I absolutely, I'm getting goosebumps, I absolutely believe that. I could not dream this up. You know? So I'll be eternally grateful.
—Elizabeth, Quayside Village resident

TOGETHER, THE TWO EPIGRAPHS ABOVE capture the more abstract and intellectual framing of cohousing, on the one hand, and the affective experience of it, on the other. As I encountered these features of Kankanmori and Quayside Village, I became curious about how the two communities came into being in the first place. What motivated their creators to put years of effort into building this new kind of housing from scratch, bringing diverse people together to try to form what they imagined as "community"? What goals, desires, and values informed their projects, and how were these inscribed in the design of the buildings themselves? I also became increasingly interested in the motivations of those who live at Kankanmori and Quayside Village now, over fifteen and twenty years, respectively, after they were established. What prompted some of the founding members to stay over the long run and newer members to join already existing cohousing communities—both groups clearly stepping outside of the normal individualized practices of making home in their societies? And how do residents experience collective living? How does the dailiness of living together unfold? In this chapter I begin to answer these questions with an outline of the history and development of each community, and an overview of those who live in them, including their motivations for moving in and staying, and their orientations to and framings of the challenges and benefits of living together in community.

Kankanmori

> We live under the same roof and we greet each other, have conversations, have a meal and tea together, sometimes drink together, go out together sometimes, care for one another's children, watch the children growing, care for the sick together, share happiness together, and of course work together to solve any conflict. Sometimes I receive insight from older people and I receive energy from younger people. (Emiko)[1]

History and Development

Located in Nippori, the "fabric town" neighborhood of Tokyo, Kankanmori is the first urban collective housing community in Japan.[2] The idea of collective housing was introduced to Japan in the late 1980s by Ikuko Koyabe, an architect informally known as the "mother" of Japanese collective housing. When I met with her shortly before her death in 2014, she explained to me that the traditional Japanese culture of collectivity had been lost in the postwar era, as Western-style individualism gained a foothold and people took up educational and employment opportunities in various places throughout the country or overseas. As a result, patterns of lifelong employment in the same company diminished, and extended families became increasingly fragmented and dispersed. Now that the "organic" collectivity of Japanese society had all but disappeared, she continued, collectivity had to be created deliberately, and in forms tailored to contemporary economic and social conditions. Seeking models to consider, Koyabe turned to Sweden, where collective housing had emerged in the 1960s to meet the needs of working mothers.[3] This model made the most sense to her, given that her collaborators in Japan similarly "thought about housing problems in Tokyo through the eyes of working women."[4] Scholars concur with Koyabe's assessment of Japan's decollectivization, which, coupled with recent economic crises, has meant that "the middle-class model of family in postwar Japan, consisting of a salaried white-collar worker/husband, a homemaker/wife, and two children, is [neither] easily attained nor necessarily ideal."[5]

In keeping with her conviction that collective communities should be established from the bottom up, by participants, rather than from the top down, by experts or government officials, Koyabe accompanied eleven potential founding members and several students in 2002 to Sweden to visit a number of its collective communities. The goal was to expose founding members to a range of possible models so that they could then decide for themselves how to organize social and spatial relations in what would become Kankanmori. The idea, in other words, was to use Swedish approaches as a launching pad for a design, both physical and social, that would work in Japan. As Koyabe wrote, "Instead of just taking the ideas of Northern European countries we wanted to adjust their ideas to our lifestyle. We wanted to introduce something new."[6]

The exploratory trip to Sweden was followed by a series of workshops, during which Kankanmori's spaces and frameworks for community living were designed collaboratively. In a narrative written to mark Kankanmori's tenth anniversary, Emiko, who joined Kankanmori a few years after it opened, recounted the surprise she felt when she first discovered how long it took for its creators to plan the community. "Who would do that?" she asked herself. But then, "after I moved in," she wrote, "I understood those planners' passion":

> They probably knew the kind of life they could have with other people. A busy salary man could not work alone on a big garden and there is no guarantee that his family could help him, but living communally he could probably find someone who would work in the garden with him and share their expertise. An individual house cannot have a commercial kitchen but ours at Kankanmori has a big steam oven for professional use and a commercial gas stove. If you want, you could make a professional Chinese meal, bake bread, and invite many people to enjoy your efforts.[7]

In consultation with a real estate developer, Kankanmori's creators settled on Nippori as an appropriate site: it is a reasonably priced, densely urban area with a range of amenities, including schools, grocery stores, restaurants, doctor's offices, and easy access to public transit.[8] Nippori Station is just a short ten-minute walk away, and it takes only twelve minutes, or six train stops, to reach Tokyo Station. Eventually, a twelve-story building was erected on a site across the street from a small park on one side and an elementary school on the other. Opening in 2003, Kankanmori took over the second and third floors of the building, while the top nine floors were dedicated to a retirement community. The first floor holds the administrative offices and cafeteria for the retirement community, along with a kindergarten. The community's creators decided on the name Kankanmori, after the local Kankanmori shrine, around which there used to be a forest (*mori*). As Koyabe wrote, "A forest can only be a healthy forest if there is a variety of trees of all sizes, not just one . . . so I proposed the name with the hope that it would become a forest full of people and greenery."[9]

In keeping with their desire to create a diverse community based on a balance of interdependence and independence, Kankanmori's founders worked closely with Koyabe to design spaces that would accommodate a variety of household types and allow residents to enjoy both privacy and togetherness. The result was 29 apartments, each with its own kitchen and bathroom, ranging from 25 to 61 square meters (269–650 square feet), including a number of one-room and one-bedroom units, several two-bedroom units for larger families, and one apartment designed to be shared by three roommates.[10] Doors to the units are solid and without windows, so residents can have complete privacy when they want it. In addition, the number of internal apartment walls was deliberately kept to a minimum so that residents could have as much freedom as possible to arrange the space to suit their own needs and desires. In order to encourage residents to extend their "private" space beyond the confines of their individual apartments—as a means, in other words, for establishing community—13 percent of Kankanmori is designated common space. This intimate public space[11]—communal, yet for the most part restricted to people who know each other—is dominated by the common room, consisting of a large kitchen and dining/meeting area, a children's play zone, and a lounge and library.[12] Other common areas, including the vegetable garden, laundry room, guest room, workshop, office, and additional play areas for children, are scattered throughout Kankanmori's two floors.

The layout of Kankanmori's first floor (the second floor of the building) illustrates the balance between shared and private space (see figure 1.1). The common room is located at one end of the building instead of in the center, thus maximizing the availability of natural, outdoor light in that area. Sliding glass doors along two walls of the dining/meeting area open onto a wraparound deck, which holds a flower garden and a fish tank and has ample space for tables and chairs so that people can socialize outside. As a means of further expanding opportunities for socializing, the ceiling in the dining area extends up to the fourth floor of the building, with internal windows along one wall that open so that residents on the third floor can speak with the people down below. There is also a second children's play area at the opposite end of the building to the common room, near the door to the vegetable garden. The common bathroom is situated around the corner from the common room, and the laundry room is located a short way down the hall, right in the middle of the building, and across from the workshop, where, for instance, flower boxes can be built. Not pictured in the floor plan are the office, where archives and computer equipment are stored, and the guest room, both of which are located on the third floor. There is also a small recycling building, located outside, which Kankanmori residents share with residents of the retirement community.

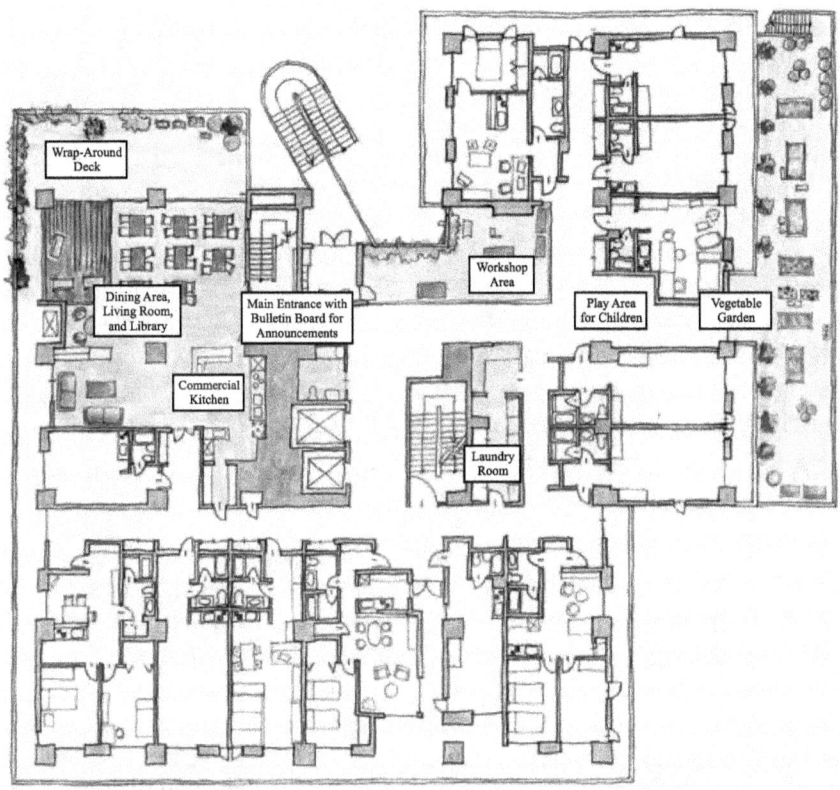

FIGURE 1.1. Kankanmori floor plan, first floor. Reproduced with the permission of NPO Collective Housing Corporation.

While this layout encourages and provides a range of opportunities for social interaction, it also reflects economic and environmental concerns: shared kitchen equipment, a community vegetable garden, and laundry and recycling facilities all contribute financial savings and serve to reduce Kankanmori's environmental footprint.

Peopling Kankanmori

Space is not just a container or stage. It can, of course, both constrain and invite particular forms of social interaction, but it cannot *determine* what these social relations will look like. Designing the building was thus only part of the process of developing Kankanmori as a community. The range of nonarchitectural issues that Kankanmori's creators had to address was enormous, and included everything from devising governing structures to settling on what to eat at common meals. The latter was no small matter. To give just one example: hailing from different regions of Japan, Kankanmori residents were accustomed to eating miso specific to those regions; so what kind of miso to use for common meals became a topic of discussion. Founding members eventually resolved this dilemma by deciding to produce their own Kankanmori miso, which they now do together each year, in late January or February. This was, of course, only one concern among many that had to be considered. Nor were those who established Kankanmori experienced in designing and running collective housing communities. On the contrary, as Koyabe noted, they "became the ones who ran the program for the first time and with no prior experience."[13] Kankanmori was, and is, an unfolding, collective exploration of possibility.

Recruitment

The process of recruiting residents illustrates some of the foundational work involved in establishing and maintaining a collective housing community. Kankanmori is a rental community; residents sign leases for three-year terms, which can be renewed indefinitely. Given this, Kankanmori experiences a fair amount of turnover, averaging four apartments vacated per year. In response, residents have developed a comprehensive set of procedures to efficiently provide prospective residents (as well as researchers and journalists) with a clear sense of what life is like in the community. The monthly general orientation offered by members of the Orientation Committee is a keystone of Kankanmori's recruitment strategy. Anyone can attend the orientation for a fee of five hundred yen (student researchers are charged one thousand yen, and established researchers, developers, and reporters pay three thousand yen). Attendees are given a PowerPoint presentation outlining Kankanmori's history and development, its composition (number of residents, floor plans, types of apartment, common spaces, and so on), its philosophical principles, its committee structure and decision-making processes, and its approaches to common meals and other social events. The presentation is followed by a tour of Kankanmori's two floors and of one of its apartments.

Once someone expresses an interest in moving in, they are invited to attend a common meal so that they can meet some of the other residents and learn more about how the community operates. Before or after the common meal, or during a separate meeting, someone from the Orientation Committee discusses organizational and committee structures with the prospective resident(s) in more detail. In the meantime, the real estate company that oversees the rental contracts for the community checks their finances to ensure that they can afford the rent. Once approved by the real estate company, interested residents can move in as soon as a unit becomes available. Although the financial check comprises the only official vetting process, there have been a few instances when a prospective tenant has been turned away because it seemed clear that they did not have much interest in being part of a community.

It's worth noting that, although not as common, word of mouth does occasionally play a role in recruitment. Shoko, for example, a single woman in her fifties, knew nothing about collective housing before a friend from work who lived at Kankanmori told her about it. Shoko had reached a point in her life where she felt she needed more balance between work, which at the time seemed to take up all her time and energy, and life more broadly; so when her workmate moved to Hakodate, Shoko took over her apartment at Kankanmori.

Within a few days of moving in, new community members are greeted with a welcome potluck. Residents sign up to bring particular dishes, and newcomers often bring drinks and special treats to share. Newcomers also formally introduce themselves at the first monthly meeting after they move in. A similar process happens in reverse when residents move out (see "A Farewell Potluck," chapter 3).

One of the striking features of Kankanmori is the frequency with which former residents return for visits. Those who live elsewhere in Tokyo, having moved out because they had another child and needed a larger apartment, for example, or because they switched jobs and needed to be closer to their workplaces, return regularly for common meals and other social events. Others, living further afield (in Hokkaido or Kyushu, for example), will return for special events, such as the yearly anniversary party, Christmas, or New Year's. One former resident, who now lives overseas, returns with her husband and son for one month each year. There is, then, a far-reaching web of relationships that has been established over time and that continues to radiate outward as residents come and go.

Who Lives in Kankanmori?

Exploring how it is that people end up there in the first place can provide insight into why former residents keep returning to Kankanmori. A key driving force for the development of Kankanmori, and one that continues to inform people's decisions to move into collective housing, was the perceived lack of social connection in Tokyo. This engendered in Kankanmori's creators a desire to establish new kinds of social ties in order to compensate for the now-loosened kinship and workplace ties—the loss of organic collectivity, as Koyabe described it—that emerged after the war. A number of Kankanmori residents told me that they had felt alienated in their previous residences, although they often did not register the full extent of this estrangement until after they had joined Kankanmori and experienced its more convivial atmosphere. Yumiko, for instance, realized in retrospect that the apartment building she had lived in before was impersonal and unfriendly, and several others similarly referred to living in apartment blocks where they didn't know their neighbors and where people never even greeted each other when passing in the hallway. A number of residents had grown up in more communal situations in farming communities or in smaller towns where they had regular contact with extended family and everyone in the neighborhood knew each other. After moving to Tokyo, they found themselves suddenly feeling cut off and isolated. This motivated them to search for something better.

Some residents decided to investigate Kankanmori after learning about it at university or encountering it by chance when attending public events, surfing the net, or watching TV. Others had lived in some form of collective community before and were actively searching for a place like Kankanmori. Yet others were encouraged by friends or family to join Kankanmori. Katsuji, for instance, who worked for a diamond company before he retired, lived with his mother, who did everything—meals, laundry, cleaning, etc.—until she died at the age of eighty-nine. His brother decided that Katsuji couldn't live alone, and so he suggested that Katsuji move to Kankanmori. Now in his early eighties, Katsuji has been at Kankanmori for well over a decade and is very happy to be there: there is always someone around with whom to share afternoon tea, drinks in the evening, common meals, or excursions to restaurants. "It's a big family here," he says. Mayumi, in her early fifties, also moved in after a death:

> Just over five years ago, my husband died. Up until then I had been able to exchange energy with him pretty well, but I had no one else to do that with, and I wasn't connected to the community. I was on my own. I had more energy than I knew what to do with, and when I saw this place on TV, I was intrigued. It looked like a place where I could have that mutual exchange of energy.

Finally, a number of residents joined Kankanmori so that their children could benefit from community living. In cases of couples with children, it was most often the mothers who did the research on Kankanmori and who took the lead in making the decision to move there. This was the situation with Junko, who had a strong desire to raise her daughter in a community environment. She did some research on collective housing on her own and then told her husband, Hideki, about Kankanmori. Together, they decided that their daughter would benefit from interacting with diverse children and adults in an informal environment rather than only in an institutional daycare setting. Indeed, within a few months of their move to Kankanmori, they found that Yuho was opening up and becoming less shy. This desire for exposure to a range of people was shared by most residents. In her chapter in Kankanmori's self-published 2014 book, Yoshie wrote,

> A prosperous resident in his seventies used to drive a red car and I, who was busy doing protesting about government policies, would not usually become friends with someone like him but because we both lived in Kankanmori we did.[14]

Tables 1.1 and 1.2 provide a snapshot of the ages, genders, and years in residence of Kankanmori members in 2017. Among the adults, there are notably more women (eighteen) than men (seven)—a fairly common pattern in intentional communities. With the exception of the under-thirty adults, the age range is fairly evenly spread, although there are slightly more in the thirty to thirty-nine range than in the other cohorts. All the children are under ten. Members' professional backgrounds are mostly middle class: residents in 2017 included two each of TV producers, NGO staff, engineers, and professionals involved in the agriculture sector; four people who worked in various positions for newspapers; and others who worked in translation, editing, architecture, library science, finance, business training, academia, and advertising.

TABLE 1.1. Adults at Kankanmori, by age and years in residence, 2017. Table created by Jamie Lewis (research assistant for the project).

Years at Kankanmori	Adults at Kankanmori									
	Age									
	20–29		30–39		40–49		50–59		60+	
	Female	Male	Female	Male	Female	Male	Female	Male	Female	Male
Less than 1 year	1		2				1			
1–4 years			2	2	1	1	2		1	1
5–10 years			1		3	1		1	1	
11–15 years							1		2	1

TABLE 1.2. Children at Kankanmori, by age and years in residence, 2017. Table created by Jamie Lewis (research assistant for the project).

Years at Kankanmori	Children at Kankanmori							
	Age							
	0–5		5–10		10–15		15–20	
	Female	Male	Female	Male	Female	Male	Female	Male
Less than 1 year		👤						
1–4 years	👤👤	👤👤						
5–10 years			👤	👤👤				
11–15 years								
16–20 years								

Four Stories

While a demographic overview provides a big-picture view of the community, it does not lend much insight into the lives and stories of those who live at Kankanmori. As a means of fleshing out this snapshot, then, below are the personal narratives of four residents. In keeping with the desires of the study group established for this project, the stories are based on life history interviews I conducted with residents, during which we discussed how and why they came to live at Kankanmori and what they found most notable about their experiences there. The study group chose these four residents in order to represent a cross-section of the community. They include Yoshie, a founding member; Keiichi, one of the few single male residents; Natsuko, a relatively new resident; and Yui, a younger former resident.

Yoshie's Story

Yoshie, an eighty-year-old TV producer, has been involved in Kankanmori from the start. When she and others were beginning to plan Kankanmori, she was living with a group of people in an old house, in a kind of organic collective housing situation. It was, in her view, a trial run for Kankanmori.

It took ten years to establish Kankanmori—to find the land for it, develop the plans, get it built, and recruit other interested parties, which they did by advertising to the city government and public housing organizations and by holding informational meetings at a public facility. Over the course of two years, potential residents and architects held a number of workshops. Yoshie was involved in many of these workshops, and then she moved into Kankanmori one year after it opened. She has been here ever since.

Yoshie's interest in collective housing goes back over thirty years. She was inspired by two pioneers: Ikuko Koyabe, who brought the Swedish model of collective living to Japan, and Yasuhiro Endoh, who was involved in the development of U-Court in Kyoto.[15] She visited U-Court, read Endoh's writings, and collaborated with Koyabe in holding symposia to discuss the planning and development of collective housing in general, and of Kankanmori in particular. Her interest was also informed by her experiences with pregnancy and motherhood: living in a public apartment block[16] while pregnant, she couldn't find a nursery, and she had no access to reasonable maternity leave. So she made her own nursery, recruiting eight people who together provided mutual support.

Given these experiences, as well as her observations of emerging social trends, Yoshie's focus has always been on the practical. Not only is there a range of family forms, including those in which both parents work as well single-parent families, but in Tokyo today more than 40 percent of people are single, and 30-35 percent are elderly. There is thus a real risk of isolation—a risk she experienced firsthand after her partner died. In Yoshie's view, what collective housing does is draw on certain aspects of traditional Japanese values to create new living situations that respond to the contemporary context. Although community in Japan has a long history, things have shifted, and there is a need for collective housing.

In addition to issues related to childcare, Yoshie's involvement in collective housing reflects her political orientation: she is interested in diversity (rather than in groups of narrow, similarly oriented people) and has a long-standing concern with the problem of domestic violence. She was part of a group that started a new TV production company when she discovered that the broadcasting company she used to work for was not amenable to covering political issues, such as the Vietnam War, the building of Narita Airport, or student protests. Post-Fukushima, she has also been involved in the anti–nuclear energy movement. In many ways, Yoshie sees collective housing as a political phenomenon, and when she goes to protests, she sometimes runs into other Kankanmori residents.

There have been many changes in Kankanmori over its life. At first Kankanmori was run by an NPO (nonprofit organization), but then it broke away so that it could govern itself. Although the original residents were very active, a number of them moved away due to employment or parental issues, and they went through some difficult periods of high vacancy rates. They responded by setting up their own company, constructing a homepage, hosting symposia, and focusing on recruiting families with children, with the result that they now have a robust community.

There are, of course, challenges. People have long working hours, especially some of the men, and so it's not always easy for people to be involved in collective activities. It can also be difficult to balance the communal and the personal. Kankanmori is a busy place, it can often be noisy, and residents have many responsibilities and commitments (committee work, etc.). It is a constant balancing act.

The benefits, however, outweigh all of the challenges. Yoshie finds that she can enjoy spending time with kids—time that she wishes she had had when her son was young and she was busy with work.

In Yoshie's view, the model of collective housing clashes with a business model. She would like to see collective housing be public and supported by government. This is the next stage, which would bring collective housing in Japan closer to the Swedish model, in which city governments are heavily involved. The next stage will also have to deal with aging, with the huge demographic shift currently unfolding in Japan. When all is said and done, however, Yoshie doesn't worry about Kankanmori: it will be OK.

Keiichi's Story

Keiichi, a fifty-year-old correspondent for a farming equipment newspaper company, has been living in Kankanmori for over a decade. He grew up in a rural area with his parents, younger brother, and grandparents, moving to Tokyo when he was eighteen.

Several years before joining Kankanmori, Keiichi serendipitously encountered a book written by Ikuko Koyabe, read it, and got interested. He then attended an orientation. He was more curious than determined to live in collective housing, but he put himself on the waiting list anyway. When he later attended Kankanmori's third anniversary party, he discovered that they had a vacancy. Since the contract for his apartment was running out, he decided to give Kankanmori a try, reasoning that he could always leave if things didn't work out.

When he first moved in, Keiichi was very busy with his work at an event-planning company, and so he wasn't an active participant in Kankanmori life, in terms of either committee work or social activities. His work colleagues also did not respond well to his decision to move into collective housing. After a while, he started to think about his long work hours—especially after observing people at Kankanmori involved in various activities—and decided to "treasure my life more" than work. He quit his job and took up his current position, which provides greater flexibility and more free time.

Once in his new job, Keiichi became increasingly involved in Kankanmori affairs: he joined the board and started participating in planning events. He needed to give up some of his private time to do this, but he eventually figured out where to draw the line in terms of exactly how much he could dedicate to participating in common events and how much he should keep to himself. Other than that, he had no real problems adjusting.

Keiichi's family doesn't really understand collective housing, although they do understand the idea of community, and his mother regularly sends boxes of fruit for him to share with others. Some of his friends had a negative response to his decision to move to Kankanmori, so he ended up making new friends who better understand his approach to life.

Although Keiichi claims that Kankanmori is not a utopia, he very much likes his life here and has no plans to move out. Things could change, of course, if, for instance, he got married, but if things stay as they are, he will stay here. He likes to drink with people at Kankanmori, and he especially enjoys the social aspect of living in the community. Although he didn't think that he cared much for children, he has discovered that he really enjoys them.

Keiichi feels that collective housing is unfortunately not very popular in Japan at this time, although perhaps it should be. Most Japanese, he said, were at one time farmers. Even during Japan's periods of economic growth, the close bonds typical of farming communities remained. Neighbors would just show up and hang out. When he started to live alone he was happy at first—he felt free from those relationships. But then he realized that he barely had any community. Moreover, it also used to be the case in Japan that people would remain at a particular job or company from the time they started working until they retired, and that lifestyle provided its own sense of community. The farmer relationship and the company relationship were the same in Keiichi's view: they both provided foundational connections. Now that people have lost these two sources of community, they are starting to realize that this is not such a good thing. People no longer know how to maintain community, and there is a need for much discussion around this topic. The younger generation in particular is trying to figure out how to make and maintain community. Perhaps they will someday see the value of collective housing.

Natsuko's Story

Natsuko is a thirty-two-year-old mother of two boys, aged two and five, who works in sales promotion and planning for a newspaper company. Natsuko grew up in Nagano, and she came to Tokyo to study music at university. Her husband, also thirty-two, works for an agricultural company. They have lived at Kankanmori since 2015.

Neither Natsuko nor her husband have any family in Tokyo, nor do they have a wide range of friends in the city. This was in contrast to Natsuko's childhood: she grew up in an extended family, with numerous cousins, in the countryside. She was never lonely, and she didn't want her children to be lonely either. She also wanted them to interact with different adults outside of daycare and school, to learn that there are different people with different values, and to not be overly influenced by their parents. She, too, enjoys interacting with many people. This was her experience in school, when she shared living spaces, as well as growing up.

Natsuko learned about Kankanmori on a website for working parents. She immediately contacted Kankanmori to see if there were any vacancies, and she received an invitation to visit. When she arrived, she found that Kankanmori was exactly as she imagined, and she felt drawn to the garden in particular. Although her husband is less socially inclined than she is, Natsuko was able to convince him to make the move. Since he would not be able to spend much time at home because of his job, he thought it would be helpful for her to be in a place like Kankanmori.

Despite being what she imagined and desired, she nevertheless had to make some adjustments when she and her family first moved in. It took her some time to figure out how to sign up for activities, like cooking a common meal. In other words, she had to find her place in an already established community. She decided that she would not decline any invitation to join in activities, and she also volunteered to do things that she wasn't initially interested in, like polishing the tables in the common room. After about a year and a half, she now finds no shortage of things to do, and Natsuko feels part of the community.

Things have been a little more difficult for her husband, who is less likely to initiate relationships or activities—and who wouldn't have even been aware of events at Kankanmori had she not pointed them out to him. But he, too, has adjusted to life at Kankanmori, especially now that he has switched jobs.

For Natsuko, one of the highlights of living at Kankanmori is participating in common meals. Not only does she and her family get to try a variety of different foods, but there are always people around to help her with her two children. Because of this, she sees common meals as her "relax time." She also finds it hugely beneficial that her children have other children in the community to play with. They're safe, playing inside the building (since, given their ages, Natsuko would not let them go to the park across the street on their own). In addition, when it is raining, Haruko, another resident, can pick up her son from daycare by car; and when Haruko is busy with work, Natsuko can pick up Haruko's daughter after daycare. So, parents help to look after each other's children. Natsuko is very grateful for this assistance.

Living at Kankanmori is not without its challenges, however. Two stand out for Natsuko. The first has to do with how quickly personal information travels—with how much people know about each other's personal lives. For instance, when her older son, Taichi, fell and was taken to the hospital, news traveled so quickly that the entire community was aware of it by the time she and Taichi returned home. A similar process occurred when her husband found a new job. Not everyone is comfortable with that level of information sharing (especially her husband). The second challenge has to do with aging: with more and more older people living at Kankanmori, they need to figure out how to cover the tasks of those who are no longer able to contribute as much. They have yet to create a system for this.

All in all, though, and despite sometimes feeling a little too busy with events, Natsuko and her family are very happy at Kankanmori. Some of her extended family and friends have expressed curiosity about the community. Although one friend said he would never want to be in a situation where he had to communicate with other people while at "home," others have had good impressions of Kankanmori. And depending on her and her husband's work situations, they plan to stay at Kankanmori for the foreseeable future.

Yui's Story
Yui is thirty years old, and she lived at Kankanmori for eight years. She grew up in Toyama with her parents and younger brother, and she has experienced both rural and urban living.

Before going to university, Yui had never lived alone: she always lived either with family or, in high school, with roommates in a dorm. When she moved to an apartment block to attend university, she encountered a total lack of community: people wouldn't even say hello to each other in the hallway. There was no one to talk with, and she felt lonely and uncomfortable. She also found the idea of living only with people in her own age group unsettling: she likes older people as well as younger children. She had started to think that she would like to find a different way of living, perhaps in a sharehouse or guesthouse, when a TV segment about Kankanmori caught her eye. She was attracted to the images of the garden as well as to those of collectivity. She immediately made up her mind to move in.

Yui moved into a share room (designed for several roommates who share a kitchen and bathroom) with two women. She got along very well with one of the women; the other was busier and wasn't around as much. Over time, she experienced a number of ups and downs with roommates, including one, a man, with whom she found it difficult to live. Although she never developed deep friendships with any of her roommates, she was very satisfied with her living situation at Kankanmori.

Kankanmori had everything that Yui wanted—in particular, social relationships. When she first moved in, she was afraid of getting fat, and she also had an aversion to many kinds of food, and so she hoped that participating in regular common meals would give her access to better food and produce healthier eating habits. Although she didn't attend common meals when the menu wasn't to her liking, or when she lost track of time (she likes to read and listen to music by herself), she did enjoy eating and drinking with others.

Yui's capacity to balance the individual with the collective aspects of living at Kankanmori waxed and waned. She sometimes found herself feeling guilty when she chose not to participate in a collective activity, especially when the others who were more involved were juggling childcare as well as work. Although she felt that this guilt was self-imposed, since no one ever said anything to her directly, she did occasionally overhear Kankanmori residents criticize other residents for not participating enough, and so she feared that others might talk about her behind her back. As a result, she went through a phase of trying to follow the lead of others when it came to participating in community activities. However, at some point she decided to just "be myself"—to do what she wanted—with the hope that others would "forgive my lack of participation." That, she said, is how she finally managed to balance things out. For the most part, she felt accepted by others for who she is, and once she decided to just be herself, the guilt disappeared.

Although Yui was happy with the space at Kankanmori and felt that the rent was reasonable, she valued above all the relationships she developed with other residents. However, after changing jobs, she found herself getting busier and busier. To stay at Kankanmori would have meant giving up one of her weekend days each week, since she couldn't fulfill her Kankanmori duties during the week. She also began to feel that she needed to live like any ordinary worker in her thirties living in Tokyo, without the social benefits of living in collective housing, and so she moved out of Kankanmori. She returns frequently, however, to attend Kankanmori events or just to visit.

Although each narrative is unique, there are nevertheless several common threads running through them. Yoshie, Keiichi, Natsuko, and Yui all express concerns about loneliness and isolation and desires for companionship, harkening back, in some cases, to childhoods marked by close ties with numerous others. Yoshie and Natsuko extend this need for connection to the care of children. First is the need for help in raising them. Thus, when her son was young, Yoshie established a nursery so that she and the other mothers in her apartment block could collectively care for their offspring, and this fed her desire to participate in creating Kankanmori. Natsuko, for her part, underscores both the practical benefits of sharing childcare duties with others and the "relax time" she experiences when others help look after her sons during common meals. The two women also highlighted the need for safe spaces in which children can play, and for others with whom they could play. Finally, both emphasized the importance of exposing children to a range of diverse others: as Natsuko explained, she wanted her children "to interact with different adults outside of daycare and school, to learn that there are different people with different values, and to not be overly influenced by their parents." Whether with regard to their children or themselves, these residents stressed the fundamental importance of mutually caring connections with others.

Balance is another theme that runs through the narratives, in both positive and challenging ways. On the side of challenge is the effort it takes to harmonize the communal and the personal: Yoshie notes that many residents have long work hours, Keiichi describes the time it took for him to learn where to draw the line between his participation in community activities and his personal time, and Yui describes feelings of guilt and having to learn to "just be myself" and so make peace with her lack of participation relative to that of some of the other residents. Part of this challenge of balance concerns issues of privacy, which Natsuko struggled with when she discovered that news about certain events (her son's injury, her husband's new job) traveled through the community in ways that were outside of her control. After periods of adjustment, however, Keiichi, Yui, and Natsuko all managed to produce some kind of equilibrium, albeit fluid and malleable, between their personal and collective lives, and they all eventually came to feel "part of the community," as Natsuko put it.

Living in community also had beneficial impacts on issues of balance. Keiichi, in particular, describes how moving to Kankanmori prompted him to realize that he needed to adjust the weighting of his life between employment and everything else. Moving into collective housing brought this need to the surface, and he ended up reevaluating his job as well as his friendships, in the end changing both in his project of learning to "treasure my life more." From his perspective, as well as from the points of view of Yoshie, Natsuko, and Yui, the benefits of living in community more than compensate for its challenges.

It is worth noting that the emphasis on community and mutual care that runs through all four stories is positioned by Yoshie and Keiichi in a wider social and political context: both see collective housing as not only a personal option but also a *social* one that mitigates the structural forces of fragmentation. Yoshie in particular sees collective housing as an explicit political and policy-relevant intervention designed to address the problems generated by the postwar erosion of traditional Japanese forms of community—such as childcare shortages, domestic violence, and social isolation—as well as issues associated with a rapidly aging population. Keiichi, for his part, implicitly points to postwar redefinitions of the good life in which commitments to work and extended family began to take on increasingly negative valence in relation to valorizations of privacy, individualism, and consumerism.[17] He predicts that people will increasingly recognize the disbenefits of these shifts and hopes that the younger generation will "someday see the value of collective housing."

Quayside Village

> I was living on my own—my son was with me at the time but had moved out—and I just thought, "How do I wanna live?" And the answer was I didn't really wanna live in just a regular apartment. I liked the idea of being with other people. I liked the idea of a multigenerational community. (Carol)

History and Development

Quayside Village, which celebrated its twentieth anniversary in 2018, is the first urban cohousing community in Canada. It is situated in North Vancouver, five blocks up from Lonsdale Quay, where residents can catch the fifteen-minute sea bus to Gastown and then walk an additional ten minutes to arrive in Vancouver city center.[18]

The development of Quayside Village was initiated by a small group of people who attended a public meeting on cohousing organized by members of the Canadian Cohousing Network and residents of WindSong, a suburban cohousing community located in Langley, British Columbia. The idea was to create a specifically *urban* cohousing community—what is currently referred to as "urban-walkable." Three women, dubbed the "three blind mice" in light of both their relative lack of knowledge of and bravery in entering this new territory—one of whom, Carol, still lives at Quayside—were instrumental in pushing the development forward. Investing their own funds to launch the project and challenging lawyers who questioned their competence, they proceeded to secure financing, form a company of shareholders, hire architects and contractors, locate a site for the building, and recruit members. Very early on—three years before the building was completed—the "three blind mice," along with the fourteen collaborators they had recruited, articulated their mission: to create "a safe, friendly community which is affordable, accessible and environmentally conscious."

Four months before the 1988 completion of the building, one of Quayside's founding members, Stacy, wrote a series of reflections on what it means to live in cohousing. Her goal was to provide a sense of the community for potential residents, since some of the units remained unsold at the time. The following excerpts from her reflections capture the orientation of Quayside's creators:

The best way to understand Quayside Village is by understanding how it came to be. Like any real community, Quayside Village is a crossroads where people with different personalities, convictions, habits, priorities, quirks, gifts, and goals encounter each other. What makes us a community is that our lives intersect. What makes us different from "naturally occurring" communities such as a village is that we have intentionally chosen to work together to create a housing situation that will foster neighborliness. We are self-conscious about the processes (such as consensus decision-making) that we are using to make this happen. Cohousing, for us, refers to this process, and the intent behind it, more than anything.

What draws us together is not a belief in cohousing as some abstract ideal, but a belief in what cohousing, as a process, can do. . . . Though we in this society tend to think of rooms, condominiums, apartment buildings, and neighborhoods as merely the physical stage on which we act out our lives, a closer look shows that the characteristics of these spaces actually set much of the script we live out in our daily practices.

Quayside Village has always had two sides, one visionary and idealistic, the other eminently practical and down-to-earth. It requires vision, dreams, and commitment to do something that goes against the grain: normally people shop for housing rather than undertaking the responsibility for designing and managing it. Moreover, making Quayside Village into a reality has required each of us as individuals to cast our lots in with a group of people. We have entrusted not only some of our hopes but also some of our money in a fundamentally collective activity. To do so required overcoming the everyman-for-himself attitude in favor of a faith that we can better achieve what we individually want and need through cooperation.

We are part of this project because we see practical advantages for ourselves in it. We look forward to some shared meals because many of us like the idea of less cooking in our own kitchens and more conversation over dinner tables. We want to really know our neighbors because we know that we are safer if we do. We also recognize that we all need a little help sometime, whether it is someone to take care of the cat while on vacation or someone to give [us] a ride to a store. We think, in general, that we can "get" more for ourselves by sharing more with others.

The principles expressed by Stacy, both idealistic and practical, informed the design of Quayside's building. As at Kankanmori, planning meetings were held regularly over the course of several years. Working closely with architects and contractors, Quayside's creators, like Kankanmori's, designed a building that would attract a diversity of people and allow for a balance of interdependence and independence. Both environmentally conscious and respectful of the buildings that were demolished to build Quayside Village, founding members incorporated wood and stained glass from the old buildings into their common room. In addition, one of the buildings formerly on the site had a dome, and so, in honor of this, Quayside Village has a dome room on its third floor that residents can use for yoga and meditation, small meetings or social gatherings, or as a quiet place to work.

The result of the planning process was a stand-alone four-story building consisting of nineteen residential units and one commercial unit. Reflecting the principle of diversity as well as negotiations with the city regarding density, four of the apartments are designated "affordable" (priced at 80 percent of market rate), and one is an affordable rental unit. The residential units range from a 449-square-foot (41.7-square-meter) "bachelor" unit to a 1,062-square-foot (98.6-square-meter) "townhome."[19] For twenty years the commercial unit was occupied by a convenience store; at the end of 2018 it was converted into a coffee shop that attracts residents from throughout the neighborhood.

The layout of Quayside Village's first floor illustrates how ideas of independence, interdependence, and community were inscribed in the building. Most notable, the units and common spaces are organized in horseshoe-like fashion around a central courtyard, serving to spatially orient residents to others in the community. Although not clearly visible on the floor plan, all units have doors facing the courtyard, with only one exception; and the doors are not solid but have windows, which also function to orient residents toward each other (many have window coverings that they can raise

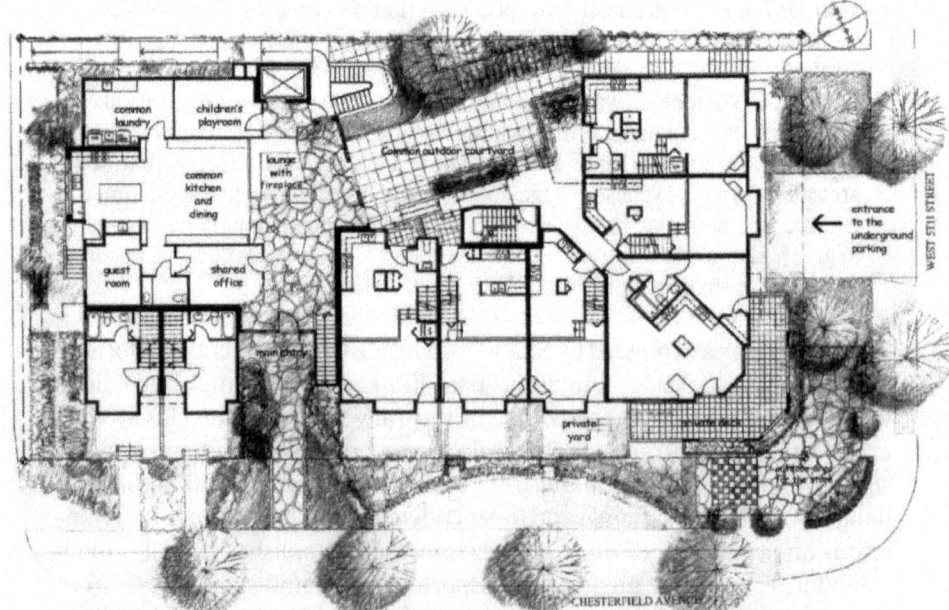

FIGURE 1.2. Quayside Village floor plan, first floor. Reproduced with the permission of the Quayside Village community.

or lower depending on their desires for privacy). Finally, not pictured in the first-floor layout are the additional common spaces on the third floor: the dome room, as already mentioned, and a large deck where residents may lounge on benches or host small dinner parties. The third-floor common space also has clotheslines for drying laundry and a small raised bed for growing vegetables. Altogether, common spaces, which include a kitchen, a large dining and meeting room, a lounge, a guest room and bathroom, a laundry room and children's playroom, an office, and the third-floor dome room, comprise 2,500 of the building's 20,475 square feet, just over 12 percent. Gardens, which surround two sides of the building, are used for growing vegetables and decorative plants, and a large composting area takes up much of a third side of the building.◊[20]

Peopling Quayside Village

With the exception of the one rental apartment, residents at Quayside Village own their units, although, in accordance with strata regulations,[21] they pay monthly fees, depending on the square footage of their units, to cover utilities and the maintenance of shared property. Recruitment was important during Quayside's development phase, but it has not been an issue in many years, and turnover, averaging 1.36 move-in/move-outs per year, is relatively infrequent. Owners are of course free to sell their units on the open real estate market, and there is an official waiting list of people interested in moving to Quayside Village, but when someone decides to move out, new residents are often found by word of mouth. Yuki, for instance (as she describes in her narrative, below), learned about Quayside Village when she was a client of Vera's, Quayside's resident midwife; and Juhli made her way to Quayside through her mother, who was already a resident.

Processes for introducing prospective residents to the community are informal: they are given a tour of the building and invited to attend a common meal so that they can meet some of the residents and get a feel for community life. Although there are no formal interviews or orientations, existing community members nevertheless remain concerned about new residents' commitment to cohousing. There is, then, a kind of informal vetting process. Potential buyers may of course opt out on their own if they discover, in attending a common meal, that the spirit of cohousing does not suit their temperament. But community members may also put pressure on sellers, who, after all, have been living in cohousing and thus have some loyalty to its philosophy. In one case, for instance, after a couple interested in purchasing a unit attended a common meal, some Quayside residents approached the owner and asked them not to sell it to the couple in question because they seemed more interested in purchasing an investment property than in living in a community. The owner complied and eventually found a buyer who had never encountered cohousing before but was keen to try it—and who in fact quickly became an active participant in community affairs.

When they move in, new residents are greeted with a welcoming common meal or potluck, and they are told that they can ask anyone, at any time, for information on how things work. There is no official orientation process, so newcomers learn about the community gradually, via word of mouth, as issues or questions arise. This has led to confusion on occasion, and some residents told me that when they first moved in they struggled to understand how things operated and felt unsure of what they should be doing to contribute to the community. In recognition of this, toward the end of the research period for this book, several residents undertook the task of compiling an orientation manual.[22]

Who Lives at Quayside Village?

Many of its residents chose to move to Quayside Village because they were worried about loneliness and isolation, either current or future, and wanted to live in a place where they would have others to depend on—and enjoy—while still being able to maintain privacy and independence. Linda, for instance, one of the five founding members still living at Quayside on its twentieth anniversary, had lived in an intentional community on Quadra Island for almost five years. When she heard about plans for Quayside Village, she and her partner Brian immediately got involved. Linda once told me that, in her view, people who live at Quayside are less depressed in winter (which, in Vancouver, tends to be gray and overcast) because they have regular opportunities to interact with others. For her part, Elizabeth, who joined Quayside Village in 2005, did not want to live an isolated life in a high-rise apartment building, and also wanted to live in a place that allowed pets. She found out about Quayside through her daughter, whose midwife, like Yuki's, was Vera. Yet another resident, Marylee, once said during a discussion group that moving to Quayside saved her life: she needs company, as well as the varied life experiences and skills that Quaysiders share with each other.

As I noted in my discussion of Kankanmori, it was usually mothers, rather than fathers, who took the first steps in moving nuclear families into the community. Women were also key movers at Quayside Village in another respect: four of the nine men in residence during the course of this study had moved in specifically to be with their partners. Once there, however, and despite some initial confusion regarding what cohousing actually was, let alone how to live in it, all were converted. Phil, Donya's husband, put it this way:

> I can't imagine going back to a life with neighbors I don't know, neighbors that don't wanna know me, neighbors that I look at the ground when I walk past 'cause I don't want an awkward conversation, neighbors that aren't lookin' out for me.

As he summarized: "Come for the significant other, stay for the community."

Tables 1.3 and 1.4 provide an overview of Quayside Village residents in 2017 according to age, gender, and years in residence. As table 1.3 indicates, most Quaysiders are long-term residents. As at Kankanmori, they are predominantly female; and, also as at Kankanmori, they tend to have middle-class backgrounds: residents in 2017 included two academics, two business managers, and one each of a college instructor, cohousing consultant, business coach, architect, carpenter, naturopath, childbirth coach, midwife, and holistic nutritionist. Those who were retired had previously worked in mechanical engineering, psychiatric nursing, and community planning. There is, in addition, a strong emphasis in Quayside Village on the arts, with four residents professionally involved in music and one in storytelling and the visual arts. Quayside Village's children (table 1.4) are grouped in the ten to fifteen age range (the two women who grew up at Quayside, Elise and Jana, are included in table 1.3, since they are now adults).

TABLE 1.3. Adults at Quayside Village, by age and years in residence, 2017. Table created by Jamie Lewis (research assistant for the project).

Years at Quayside Village	Adults at Quayside Village									
	Age									
	20–29		30–39		40–49		50–59		60 +	
	Female	Male	Female	Male	Female	Male	Female	Male	Female	Male
Less than 1 year										
1–4 years		♀	♀			♀♀♀		♀	♀♀	
5–10 years			♀		♀		♀		♀♀	♂♂
11–15 years			♀		♀	♂			♀♀♀♀	♂♂
16–20 years	♀♂						♀♀		♀♀	♂

58 COLLABORATIVE HAPPINESS

TABLE 1.4. Children at Quayside Village, by age and years in residence, 2017. Table created by Jamie Lewis (research assistant for the project).

Years at Quayside Village	Children at Quayside Village							
	Age							
	0–5		5–10		10–15		15–20	
	Female	Male	Female	Male	Female	Male	Female	Male
Less than 1 year								
1–4 years						♂		
5–10 years						♂		
11–15 years						♂		
16–20 years								

Four Stories

A more nuanced view of the lives and experiences of Quayside Village residents is provided in the detailed stories of four of its members: Kathy, a founding member; Peter, one of the men at Quayside; Yuki, who has lived in the community for over five years and has also visited Kankanmori; and Elise, Kathy's daughter, who has lived at Quayside Village since she was four months old. Together, they are representative in terms of years at Quayside Village, gender, and ethnicity. In contrast to Kankanmori, where I drafted narratives based on life history interviews, Quayside residents wanted to write their own stories, so they appear here in the first person rather than the third.

Kathy's Story

KATHY: My decision to join three women who were determined to start a cohousing project in North Vancouver was one of my best life decisions so far. Those three wise women were in their sixties, and I was approaching forty and wanted to have a baby as a single woman. I knew I would need "a village to raise a child," and cohousing sounded like an ideal scenario. Shortly after joining them, I was accepted to a master's program in Toronto and left Vancouver for a year. Immersed in my studies and the intricate planning and logistics of how to get pregnant by self-insemination, I was far from the world of North Vancouver and cohousing. After a year, with studies completed and one month pregnant, I was planning for my return home. I called Carol, the feistiest of the three women, to check if they were still thinking about a cohousing project. I had seriously underestimated the determination of these three. In my absence they had gathered together fourteen households of interested people, formed a company with fourteen shareholders, hired a consultant, found an ideal site, hired an architect and a building contractor, and got construction financing. Over the phone that day, Carol reported that there was currently a big hole in the ground for the underground garage and that they were pouring concrete.

I have now been living happily at Quayside Village Cohousing with my twenty-year-old daughter since she was a newborn. Raising a child in cohousing has been a wonderful experience. My daughter, as an only child, has had the opportunity to develop very sibling-like relations with other kids in the building. She has also been blessed with many caring adults in her daily life and all sorts of different role models, which I think is sadly missing in our isolated nuclear family model of living. In a world where parents often feel that they need to be aware of their child's safety at all times, Elise has wandered freely all over our community since age three. I had to teach her to leave her shoes outside the door of whatever home she was in so I could go around and find her eventually.

I wanted to start my own daycare so I could stay home with my daughter. Before finding the three dynamos, I had checked out many potential strata developments about the possibility of a home daycare. Not one was open to the idea. When I ran the idea by the three Quayside women, they were thrilled by the possibility of more kids coming to the community each day. I started Quayside Kids Licensed Family Child Care the month after I moved in. My first client was my neighbor's three-year-old daughter. The daycare quickly grew to the maximum of seven children, whom the community embraced as members. They played in our courtyard on a daily basis, and their families attended all the kid-centered community celebrations for Halloween, Easter, or whatever. I started out thinking I would run the daycare for five years, until my daughter went to school. I ended up carrying on for twelve years. One of the biggest issues for home daycare providers is the adult isolation of being alone in your home with the kids. At Quayside Village, I never felt a single minute of isolation from other adults, who were always just outside my door. This same lack of isolation is something I look forward to as I gradually get closer to thinking about my eventual needs for aging in place.

Each cohousing community has its own unique flavor. At Quayside Village, we are known for attention to sustainability and encouraging some degree of housing affordability. Since our inception, we have strived toward zero waste, with an extensive recycling program well beyond municipal programs. Our entire twenty-unit building produces less than two small bins of garbage per week; each household less than one shopping bag per week. The City of

North Vancouver has often used us as an example of moving toward better attention to waste management. At construction, we chose to install a gray-water recycling system where the water from sinks, showers, and laundry is recycled back for toilet use after filtration. Unfortunately, the pioneering system we installed has never been very effective, and we are currently looking to replace it. Early on, in collaboration with the City of North Vancouver, we decided to offer one affordable rental unit in the community and four below-market units that sell in perpetuity at 20 percent below market value.

Most cohousing in North America is based on a strata ownership model, as it is a familiar model for municipalities, for lending institutions, and for buying/selling units. Cohousing gets around some of the downsides of stratas by changing the bylaws so that all residents are on the strata council and decisions are made by consensus. After several years of living at Quayside, Carol had a friend who was upset because her strata building would not let her change her window coverings; the justification being that they needed "uniformity." At our subsequent monthly community meeting, Carol put forth a proposal that each unit at Quayside Village paint their currently white front doors to be any different color of the rainbow, with the justification that it will be a daily reminder that we are free and don't live in an institution. The proposal passed unanimously.

Living in cohousing is not without challenges. People lead busy urban lives in North Vancouver, and sometimes residents are pulled in many directions and struggle to participate or keep community needs as a priority. Also, in North America, we have a population somewhat deskilled in living closely with others beyond one's nuclear family. Each cohousing resident can encounter neighbors that they find difficult. Interestingly, the ones you find difficult may not be the same ones I find difficult. We all have different buttons that get pushed. We must remain conscious of the many benefits there are to living in close contact with our neighbors when we come across situations that are difficult. We have much more motivation to work through the difficulties and push through to the other side when we know we share a community with that person. One of the people at Quayside whom I found the most difficult and pushed most of my buttons the most frequently has now become one of my dearest friends. In having to discuss with her the difficulties I was experiencing that I was attributing to her behaviors, I came to understand a whole different experience of the world through her eyes/history, and the ongoing exchange of ideas that has resulted has made my world richer.

Peter's Story
PETER: I moved to Quayside Village Cohousing roughly seven years ago, as of this writing. I was acquainted with other "intentional" communities in my personal and professional life. My work as a community planner with the City

of Vancouver took me around Vancouver's neighborhoods, discussing and setting local policy. Some of the policies included responding to housing issues—questions of density and height figuring prominently. But people were very interested in looking at affordable housing, and housing appropriate as one ages, so cooperatives and cohousing initiatives in the city and region were often discussed. In my personal life I had purchased shares in an "equity housing cooperative," which was in the early stages of being developed for and by prospective residents (including myself). This led to roughly fifteen years of co-op living, giving me a perspective on intentional communities that led me in part to becoming a member of Quayside Village.

At the risk of being cute with the text that follows (which really just unfolded when I was asked to write about Quayside), I propose some personal attributes (and by extension community attributes) that would come in handy when seeking to become a happy and thriving member of a cohousing community:

1. **C**ommunicate your hopes, interests, concerns, and appreciation for those small triumphs that seem to regularly occur within a cohousing community. It is the only way to get to know others within the community, opening up opportunities for connection. Silence of course is sometimes necessary to retain one's sanity when living in close quarters with your neighbors—perhaps to facilitate meditation or enable afternoon naps, for instance—and open communication can sometimes lead to misinterpretations, misunderstandings, and hurt feelings. But these things always happen in any relationship and are always reparable with effort and goodwill—and good communication is well worth the risk, given that the payoff is a developing closeness with others.
2. **O**utgoing people are the heart and soul of a cohousing community, not simply at a "performance" level to keep people amused but more as a conduit to create connections to and between members. This point is of course related to the first. Beyond the simple directive to "communicate," exhibiting the skills and interests that often remain hidden with the larger community can lead to all sorts of activities that members can easily participate in (I've parlayed my interest in contract bridge and Shakespeare into regularly occurring bridge and theater evenings at Quayside). Members need to be "out there," taking the lead in their small way, and nurturing community interests and connections.
3. "**H**umility" is something to practice when living together with others and taking part in making decisions for the community. Living in single-family homes can enable people to become the "king" or "queen" of the household, whose word is law (at least until the kids become teenagers); this is not possible or wise in a cohousing community. Empha-

size your knowledge, skills, and abilities, make best use of them for the betterment of the community, but recognize that others have their own knowledge base, their own set of skills and abilities, that may be equal to or, even better, may improve upon your own when addressing community issues.

4. **O**pportunities should be taken advantage of when living in situations where there are strong connections between people. This relates to point two above. But it is much more than that. There are a host of things that can be better, and more enjoyably done when working together rather than alone—difficult jobs around the apartment or building of course, but also heading out to a concert or movie or lecture, taking care of children and pets, commuting to work or school, etc. These arrangements can be made with workmates or next-door neighbors, but it is so much easier when living in a situation where everyone is close by and knows each other well.

5. **U**nderstanding of other community members (and yourself) is of vital importance. We all have "triggers" or "hot buttons" regarding issues related to politics, sex, religion, and sport (e.g., some people actually support the New York Yankees, can you believe it??!!). These triggers can also be pulled when making collective decisions about the cohousing community. Holding strong views does not make them right, for yourself or for others, but we continue to express them—we actually *need* to express them in order to dissect issues and decide on courses of action. These discussions often generate some "heat," and if you or others respond with strong emotions, it is vital to respect those feelings. We can also offer some solace and comfort because we understand where those feelings came from, and we hope for the same understanding when we "lose it" over a decision that is not going our way.

6. **S**haring of "resources" is often an efficient and effective way of getting things done. This is related to point four above. But, again, it is more than that. Within a single isolated household, people require all the tools and skills needed to pursue interests and complete household tasks. Books, wrenches, extra chairs (when the extended family comes to dinner), vacuums, and other appliances are examples that come to mind. At Quayside, we have a large inventory of all of the above that gets circulated around the village—the stuff that is shared is *not* stuff that you need to buy or find a place to store.

7. **I**gnore the times you may feel slighted or disrespected, when people seem to be stepping out of line. This relates to points three and five but emphasizes the need to "let things go." Life goes on after losing a fight over a community decision, maybe one that you are sure was unwise or ill considered. Life is full of such situations, not just in cohousing but

also at work and within the family. Yet we generally don't leave work or abandon the family because one decision didn't go our way. On balance, in our working, family, and community life, there will be many more opportunities to express our point of view, experience respect and solidarity, and confirm relationships.

8. *N*egotiate, don't "fight or take flight," when faced with serious disagreements with other community members. Explore the values and interests that underlie people's positions (including your own). Is there an approach that can satisfy the key interests expressed by members without giving too much away of what you really want or need? When living in a cohousing community, what you gain in connection, friendship, and support you lose in control. Have the patience to figure things out together.
9. *G*enerosity goes beyond point six; it is an active effort to give something to others in the community, with no sense of being compensated or seeing some form of reciprocation. This admittedly is the gold standard of community living that we cannot live up to all the time, but if exhibited on occasion, it generates the greatest impact on members, and it can trigger the feelings of warmth that confirm the wisdom of living in a cohousing community.

There you have it, an "off-the-cuff" psychological portrait of the ideal cohousing community member. Really, the points expressed above are important in any relationship, not just in a cohousing living situation. They underline the importance of people living together and the opportunities for comfort and joy that this affords.

Yuki's Story

YUKI: I am a fifty-four-year-old mother of one daughter, Mirai, who is seven years old. I was born and raised in Japan. I first visited Canada on a working holiday visa in 1988 when I was twenty-five years old, and I stayed for two years. I fell in love with the nature in Canada through my experience living in Banff, Alberta, and Prince Edward Island. I was touched by the kindness shown by Canadian people and also impressed by their diversity. I determined to return to Canada and did so three and a half years later in 1994. For the next six years, I lived in both countries back and forth, but I finally settled in Canada in 2000. I lived in Ottawa, then moved to Vancouver in 2005, and I have been living here since then.

I worked for the Canadian Tourism Commission, which promotes Canada as a tourist destination, from 2000 to 2014. I enjoyed my job, although it could at times be quite stressful. My life was centered on my career advancement for a while. The turning point occurred when I started feeling dissatisfaction with my everyday life and experiencing a feeling of emptiness. I wanted to have a purpose for my life, and I realized that my desire to have my own child was growing inside my heart. With a couple of years' research and preparation, I decided to become a single mother by choice. I knew becoming a single mother would not be an easy road and would involve many challenges, but my desire was strong enough to make it happen. I felt lucky that I received support from my friends.

There were many incidents that made me think Quayside Village must be my future home. I feel it was almost my destiny to become a member of Quayside Village, and it wasn't just a coincidence. With my friends' support, I got pregnant in 2009. I was given a choice of having either a medical doctor or a midwife. As all my family lived in Japan, I wanted to have a midwife, who I believed would be willing to spend a little more time with me than a medical doctor. I don't remember how I chose Midwifery Care North Shore, but I met with Vera, a wonderful midwife and a Quayside Village resident. She accepted me as her patient, which I was very happy about. Then I decided to take a prenatal class that I found through the internet. I didn't know the instructor until I met her on the first day of the class: Heather, another lovely Quayside Village resident. Then I met with Kathy (yet another resident) through Vera, and Kathy became my role model as a single mother by choice. All those amazing connections already made me feel at home at Quayside Village. It took almost three years before I could finally move to Quayside Village, as no two-bedroom units were listed for sale for a long time. I remember that I was extremely happy when Kathy called me and said, "There is a sale for a two-bedroom unit." Without a hesitation, I said, "I am in!!"

My daughter and I have lived in Quayside Village since 2013, and we truly enjoy the life here. For the first two years after we moved in, I found it difficult to contribute my time to community activities as I had a full-time job and was also raising a child all by myself. I felt somewhat guilty; however, my neighbors all told me that I only needed to contribute what I could. I was appreciative of the flexibility that Quayside Village offered, and residents' understanding lifted the weight and lightened my stress. I am now a member of the finance team and take care of everyday payments (issuing checks) as I have a little more spare time.

The people at Quayside Village became our family, and my daughter calls one woman her Canadian grandmother and two older girls her sisters. It has been wonderful to see my daughter visiting neighbors on a regular basis and having frequent interactions with other adults in the community. She enjoys visiting Carol (her Canadian grandmother), and they read books together. It is such a safe environment that I can feel comfortable letting her walk alone in the complex without my supervision.

One of our favorite parts of living at Quayside Village is the festivities during the holiday seasons. The community celebrates Christmas, Thanksgiving, and Easter together and often has potluck dinners in the common house. I remember that those holiday seasons could be very lonesome for immigrants like myself, as we are living away from our families. I am very grateful that my daughter doesn't need to have that feeling; rather, she is surrounded by the warmth of people who care about her.

I understand there are challenges in living in the tight community of cohousing; however, I value the benefits of living in cohousing more. I had to make some adjustments, and I am still making more, but I choose those adjustments over feeling isolated and lonely; therefore, my plan is to stay at Quayside for a while.

I had the privilege of visiting Kankanmori in 2016 and learning how they operate. Their systems are well structured, somewhat unlike Quayside Village, which is more loosely structured. It seemed that residents in Kankanmori were participating in several different committees and carrying almost equal responsibilities, which could be a good solution in avoiding conflicts between residents. Their common house has an open feeling and is very functional. I would love to visit them again and join their common meals someday.

Elise's Story
ELISE: I have lived at Quayside Village Cohousing for twenty years, since I was four months old. Cohousing was, and is, the perfect environment for me to grow up in as I am an only child of a single mom. There were always children and adults around that I could hang out with or talk to. I grew up very social and have always loved having conversations with adults, even as a child. This helped me immensely in high school in speaking with teachers and other adults in my life. I have two best friends, whom I call my sisters because of cohousing. We all grew up together and despite all being only children we still have sisters. As a kid I would describe all my neighbors as my uncles, aunts, and grandparents. I was always supported in everything I did by the community, and that gave me great confidence in myself and everything I was passionate about.

In high school I was super involved in my school and loved organizing events to help out the community. I was a part of the student council for all five years of high school, and I realize now that my participation was influenced by my cohousing experience. I grew up with amazing role models around me, as everyone has their own role in helping the community. I learned that when everyone contributes a little bit, big things can be achieved.

I grew up with a lot of empathy and understanding as I was surrounded by people, all with different personalities. I learned about conflict management and community values just by the influence of my neighbors. All of this has greatly impacted my life, and I'm coming to realize this even more as I get older. From children to seniors, everyone has an important role in developing the community not only within the cohousing but also with its neighbors. I feel very lucky to have grown up in such a community-oriented environment; I know that it has shaped me as a person, and I will always be proud to call Quayside my home.

A number of the themes that run through these narratives overlap with those expressed in the Kankanmori stories. Both Kathy and Yuki refer to issues of isolation and loneliness, and both stress the importance of social connection and mutual care. Kathy, for instance, refers to "isolated nuclear families," while Yuki underscores how the multiple relationships she forged with people at Quayside Village "made me feel at home." Cohousers support each other in myriad ways: there are always people around—other adults "just outside my door"—so Kathy was able to run a daycare out of her unit without feeling like she was the lone adult, and she can now look forward to similar backing as she contemplates growing older. Yuki, for her part, finds support in raising her daughter at Quayside Village—support that takes the form not only of help in looking after Mirai but also of the advice she received, when Mirai was younger, to minimize her engagements with community affairs as needed, which meant that others in the community were willing to do more. Elise points to the advantages of having multiple "siblings" to play with and adults to turn to as she was growing up, a benefit that Yuki also mentions in reference to Mirai, who calls one resident, Carol, her "Canadian grandmother," and two of the other children, Jazzy and Jade, her "sisters." These connections are not just about mutual care and support but also about the pleasures of a rich social life, of the constant interactions with others that provide a sense of the warmth and at-homeness that Yuki mentions.

Peter's narrative brings out a key theme mentioned in the introduction: namely, that living in cohousing involves "a circular process . . . in which the group intentionally designs" spaces and procedures "that will shape their own behavior."[23] In this case, as Peter advises, the "procedures" concern the need to cultivate particular personal attributes and practices: communication skills, openness and outgoingness, humility, a willingness to make the most of whatever opportunities present themselves, a focus on understanding (both oneself and others), a desire to share resources, a capacity to ignore slights and accept that one's priorities are not always shared by others, an openness to negotiation, and the practice of generosity. These attributes, which enable the cooperative decision-making that Kathy refers to, are ideally the personality characteristics that residents develop as they live in cohousing. As Kathy notes, "In North America, we have a population somewhat deskilled in living closely with others beyond one's nuclear family." Skill in collective living—in collaborative decision-making, conflict resolution, and in balancing the collective aspects of life with individual expression (e.g., the color of the doors)—is thus learned over time, by adults who move into cohousing after growing up in more individualistic-oriented settings, and by children who grow up in cohousing, as Elise so eloquently demonstrates. The challenges of living in cohousing—recognizing that different people participate in community maintenance at different rates, and learning to live with others who might have conflicting approaches to life—thus provide the means to learn the skills Peter outlines, which, as he puts it "underline the importance of people living together and the opportunities for comfort and joy that this affords." These are all benefits that Yuki, Kathy, and Elise highlight, and these clearly override the challenges and adjustments that they also refer to.

Constructing the Good Life in Urban Cohousing Communities

There are of course differences between the narratives of Quayside Village and Kankanmori residents. The wider political aspects of cohousing referred to by Yoshie and Keiichi—structural, society-wide patterns of fragmentation and isolation—do not come through as explicitly in the Quayside narratives, other than in the emphasis on environmental sustainability mentioned by Kathy, which, in turn, is not present in the Kankanmori stories. There is also a stronger flavor of individualism running through the Quayside Village narratives, particularly with regard to personal development, although Yoshie and Natsuko point to issues of personal development as well when they highlight the importance of children's exposure to diverse adults.

I return to these differences, which reflect cultural context as well as the unique temperaments of individual residents, in later chapters. Here I wish to briefly reiterate several shared patterns of experience. Together, the anecdotes and stories presented in this chapter make the point that while everyone may have their own individual reasons for joining a cohousing community—and personal agendas in remaining—they also share many desires: for connection, mutual care and support, safety, autonomy, and fun. It is also important to note that, as these stories illustrate, the perspective of collective housing residents always seems to expand outward: Yoshie points to social issues such as domestic violence and shortages in childcare; Keiichi underscores problems with social fragmentation; Kathy, Yuki, and

Natsuko all refer to the importance of exposing children to diverse others so that they can grow up to be well-balanced and community-minded adults; and Peter and Kathy both outline how cohousing residents can learn to live with others, in the process becoming less self-centered—with all the benefits of connection that stepping outside of oneself can bring. Living in cohousing thus encourages residents to engage in ever-widening sets of relationships, moving beyond the kind of self-centeredness that can be engendered by some mainstream and popular culture approaches to well-being—which, albeit often unwittingly, can give rise to the kind of isolation that produces distress and the need for personal happiness in the first place. It is thus the *collaborative* nature of living in cohousing, including the collaborative processes involved in producing spaces of independence and privacy, that produces the good life.

The benefits of diversity and learning to live with others that many of the narratives underscore tells us something not only about the kinds of people who choose to join cohousing—that is, people who are interested in connecting with and learning from a range of others—but also what living in cohousing does to those who reside there: it supports the collectivist orientations of those who grew up in or have experience in cohousing, and, in the case of those who don't have much experience in coliving, it feeds aspirations to become more community minded. Peter's COHOUSING mnemonic provides a clear outline of this. This is one pillar of cohousing: work on the self as part and parcel of work on community. As Peter put it, "I propose some personal attributes (and by extension community attributes) that would come in handy when seeking to become a happy and thriving member of a cohousing community." The individual and the community here spill over into each other. This orientation to cooperation, mutual care, and joint pleasure is encouraged by the kinds of communal spaces that the creators of the two communities co-designed—a second pillar of community development. A third pillar entails outlining particular values and policies (with a small "p") to guide community life, including approaches to everything from decision-making and governance structures to how to deal with common space and equipment, visitors, and pets—and, in the case of Kankanmori, what kind of miso to use for common meals. At the foundation of such value orientations and policies lie the answers to the question, *How do we envision the good life, and how can we go about producing it?*

The policies a community devises—its organizational frameworks and structures of participation—are charters for social action: they reflect particular perceptions of the world and tell residents, in accordance with those frameworks, how to think and how to act.[24] As such, they provide the scaffolding for the community, the (ideal) skeleton on which everyday life hangs. Like the built environment, however, they do not determine action in any kind of mechanistic way. Rather, they are interpreted, responded to, abided, challenged, and modified by those who have constructed them and are attempting to realize them in their everyday lives. Statements of value and explicit policies thus represent the ideal, the *vision* that members have of their community—what could be called their utopic imagining. These visions are in constant conversation with *practice*, with efforts to realize the ideal in concrete, everyday reality. The questions then become: How are ideas mobilized through practice? How is the relationship between philosophy and daily life negotiated? In the following two chapters, I focus on this "conversation" between philosophy and practice that marks everyday life in Kankanmori and Quayside Village.

Notes

1. Kankanmori Residents, *The Collective House, Kankanmori: This Is the Alternative Way of Living in Modern Japan* (Tokyo: Domesushupan, 2014), 162.
2. Recall that I am using the term "collective" in the Japanese context.
3. Vestbro, "History of Cohousing"; Alison Woodward, "Communal Housing in Sweden: A Remedy for the Stress of Everyday Life?" in *New Households, New Housing*, ed. Karen A. Franck and Sherry Ahrentzen (New York: Van Nostrand Reinhold, 1989).
4. Kankanmori Residents, *Collective House*, 129.
5. Satsuki Kawano, Glenda S. Roberts, and Susan Orpett Long, "Introduction: Differentiation and Uncertainty," in *Capturing Contemporary Japan: Differentiation and Uncertainty*, ed. Satsuki Kawano, Glenda S. Roberts, and Susan Orpett Long (Honolulu: University of Hawai'i Press, 2014), 2.
6. Kankanmori Residents, *Collective House*, 12.
7. Ibid., 163.
8. See *Life at Kankanmori*, "Walk through the Neighbourhood," 0:00.
9. Ibid., 131.
10. See *Life at Kankanmori*, "Haruko Giving a Tour of Her Family's Apartment," 1:06. See also *Exchange at Kankanmori*, "A Tour of Shoko's Apartment," 0:45.
11. I thank Hulya Demirdirek for suggesting this term.
12. See *Exchange at Kankanmori*, "Quayside Visitors Tour Kankanmori," 0:05.
13. Kankanmori Residents, *Collective House*, 133.
14. Ibid., 3.
15. U-Court, which opened in 1985, has forty-eight units in three buildings arranged around a U-shaped courtyard, a design intended to increase possibilities for interaction among residents. Although there is a common meeting room, there is no common kitchen or means for sharing meals; it is thus a precursor to communities such as Kankanmori rather than a full-blown collective housing community.
16. Public housing in Japan differs from the public/social housing in Canada that targets low-income people in particular. The Public Housing Act and the Japan Housing Corporation Act were developed in the early 1950s to address housing

shortages stemming from the war and postwar urbanization. Now administered by the Urban Renaissance Agency, public housing rents at market rates but eliminates the range of expenses associated with living in apartment blocks owned privately.
17. Allison, *Precarious Japan*; Coulmas, "Quest for Happiness"; Gordon Mathews, *What Makes Life Worth Living? How Japanese and Americans Make Sense of Their Worlds* (Berkeley: University of California Press, 1996); Yoshio Sugimoto, *An Introduction to Japanese Society*, 4th ed. (Cambridge: Cambridge University Press, 2014).
18. See *Life at Quayside Village*, "Walk through the Neighbourhood," 0:00.
19. See *Life at Quayside Village*, "Jazzy's Tour," 0:51.
20. See *Exchange at Quayside Village*, "Haruko Explores Quayside Village," 0:07.
21. *Strata* refers to a legislated provincial framework for organizing and regulating shared properties, such as condominiums, townhouses, and, in this case, cohousing.
22. See chapter 4 for discussion of the role played by the exchange visits in jump-starting this effort.
23. Sargisson, "Second-Wave Cohousing," 44.
24. Bronislaw Malinowski, *Myth in Primitive Psychology* (London: Norton, 1926); see also Cris Shore and Susan Wright, "Policy: A New Field of Anthropology," in *Anthropology of Policy: Critical Perspectives on Governance and Power*, ed. Cris Shore and Susan Wright (New York: Routledge, 1997).

2 QUAYSIDE VILLAGE

> We are a multi-generational community comprised of couples, singles and families with children ranging in age from infants to young adults. Our nineteen households are racially, culturally and spiritually diverse but we all appreciate the joys and challenges of living together in cohousing. Cohousing provides personal privacy as well as the benefits of living in a community where people know and interact with their neighbors.
>
> —Quayside Village Overview

ONE EVENING I MET WITH some of the younger residents of Quayside Village to discuss what it was like to grow up in cohousing. When I asked how they explained their community to people unfamiliar with cohousing, Jana, who moved to Quayside Village with her parents when she was two and had no memories of living anywhere else, said, "I always try to explain it like if you lived in a really friendly neighborhood but somebody instead decided to build an intentionally really friendly neighborhood all in one building, instead of along one street, like that's what it is." Elise, whose narrative is included in chapter 1, and who has been a Quayside resident since she was four months old, recounted the simple explanation she gave her friends: "I would describe it as, like, I have sisters and, like, a ton of aunts and uncles." Later in the conversation, Aiden, a nine-year-old who was born at Quayside, imagined the loneliness he would feel were he not living in cohousing: "Whenever I go to other people's houses there's no neighbors, right, you're like the only house, no one around you, that's the only people." Together, Jana, Elise, and Aiden embodied the realization of some of what Quayside Village's founding members had been trying to create: a "friendly neighborhood" where children would have many "relatives" to turn to or play with and in which no one would have to experience having "no one around you."[1]

How Values Unfold: A Conversation between Philosophy and Practice

Even before the building was constructed—indeed, as part of the design process—Quayside Village's founding members articulated their aspirations:

To have a community which is diverse in age, background and family type, that offers a safe, friendly living environment which is affordable, accessible and environmentally conscious. The emphasis is on quality of life including the nurture of children, youth and elders.

As described in chapter 1, possibilities for diversity of household type, age, and economic status were inscribed in the building itself, with units ranging from a "bachelor" apartment to multiple-floor townhouses, and including designated affordable as well as market-price units.[12] Recognizing that the built environment could set the stage for but not determine the feel of social life, Quayside Village's creators included in their mission statement a set of orienting principles for the social milieu they wanted to construct: one marked by safety, friendliness, nurture, and an emphasis on environmental sustainability.

In 2018, as Quayside Village approached its twentieth anniversary, residents decided to revisit and expand on this original mission statement. After several meetings, the Thriving Committee came up with the following set of complementary principles, which were subsequently unanimously approved by the community:

Environmental Stewardship: We value acting as stewards of all elements of our environment. We educate ourselves to do so and take direct actions where we can. These actions include extensive recycling, minimizing waste, and reducing polluting practices and products. We garden for both food and beauty.

Trust: We trust the wisdom of our collective diversity of attitudes, beliefs, and cultural traditions. Through this approach we create a community that is safe—physically, emotionally, socially, and spiritually. We aim for:
- Respect for the privacy of all
- Actions that enhance the collaborative, cooperative spirit of living in community
- Adults and children having positive relations within the community
- Celebrations of milestone life events
- Maintaining a healthy community by seeking solutions to problems that may arise for individuals or for the group
- Safely working through disagreements knowing that differences make our community and our collective decisions stronger

Communication: Open communication is key to a thriving community. Meeting this standard calls for skillful, conscious action by all, including:
- Listening with an open mind
- Respecting opinions even if they are different from our own

- Welcoming new ideas for the community to consider
- Assuming others have good intentions and they are doing the best they can
- Inspiring others through positive action and example
- Expressing gratitude for others' efforts to sustain our community
- Recognizing the diversity of communication needs and styles
- Supporting each other in working through challenging communication issues for the purpose of resolving them
- Having the courage to raise difficult issues

Camaraderie: We value camaraderie for creating and sustaining a positive, healthy community. Examples include:
- Expressing kindness
- Cooking and eating together
- Sharing individual interests with others
- Completing tasks and taking on responsibilities necessary for a functioning and thriving community
- Fostering creativity and fun with simple, easy organization

Community Engagement: As individuals and groups, we value participation in the wider community to build a better world.

Both the original and expanded statements, posted on the wall in the lounge just above the architectural model of the building, are living documents, frameworks for going about the business of building and maintaining community. They help to keep residents attuned to what is most important as they navigate the ever-changing landscape of shifts in society, including not only those of general attitude, or ethos, but also those related to the availability of resources, government policies, and the state of the environment.

Quayside residents draw on these mission statements in a variety of ways. In some cases, values are discussed, planned around, and formally put into practice. Environmental stewardship, for instance, is frequently on the agenda of community meetings: what and how to recycle, the division of labor in caring for the gardens, whether or not funds should be allocated for a graywater system, and so on, are common topics of both discussion and action. Environmental stewardship, in other words, is a value that lends itself to concrete intervention. Other ideals, such as diversity in age, background, ethnicity, or ability, do not lend themselves to practical management in the same way (aside from the possibilities for diversity inscribed in the building itself in the form of a range of unit types and sizes). Diversity in age provides a case in point. For many years, Quayside Village had a number of younger residents: three of its founding members, Kathy,

Stacy, and Nina, raised their daughters there (Jana and Elise, mentioned above, still live at Quayside), and as time went by, other residents brought children into the community. Kathy's daycare added a number of children for the first twelve years of Quayside Village's life, and Vera's midwifery practice, which has been a part of Quayside for more than half of its existence, means that babies and young children are a more or less constant presence in the community. By the end of 2018, however, Quayside Village found itself with only three youth, one close to ten years old, and two on the cusp of their teens. This was troubling to some residents, who worried about an aging community and pined for the energy and liveliness that children bring to everyday life. Given the relatively low turnover in residents, some Quaysiders began directing jokes at one of the couples of child-bearing age living there at the time—subtle hints about how wonderful it would be to have a few new babies on the premises, along with guarantees that the community as a whole would pitch in to help. There was also regular talk of the need to bring in younger adults and increase the ethnic and class diversity of the community. These kinds of concerns may not make their way onto official meeting agendas, but the awareness is there, and if a resident decides to sell their unit it could influence their thinking when choosing among potential buyers.

Stated values, then, travel through the community and take shape in various ways: sometimes official and sometimes unofficial, sometimes practical and other times aspirational. There are, in addition, two orientations—reflecting, perhaps, widely held cultural assumptions—that have a significant influence on everyday life at Quayside Village even though they are not explicitly articulated in its value statements. The first relates to beliefs about the key role of emotional expression in social life, and the second concerns the relative place of volunteerism versus obligation in building and maintaining community. I discuss both values in the sections on "Trust and Communication" and "Camaraderie" below, but I begin here with the first principle articulated by the Thriving Committee on the eve of Quayside Village's twentieth anniversary: environmental stewardship.

Environmental Stewardship: We value acting as stewards of all elements of our environment. We educate ourselves to do so and take direct actions where we can.

Brian, a founding member and the acknowledged "composting king" of Quayside Village, got the community involved in recycling programs from the start, including during the construction phase of the building, when he arranged for building materials to be recycled—a first in Vancouver's construction industry. Throughout his years at Quayside, he has been a tireless promoter of the concept of "zero waste," which involves recycling and composting to the point that conventional garbage is no longer produced. Although some residents fear that zero waste might be unattainable (during the course of the research for this book there were four regular-size garbage bins that got picked up by the city every other week), most are in agreement with the principle and work hard to achieve this goal. To assist in this endeavor, each household has its own recycling system, consisting of containers for different categories of item (cardboard, stretchy plastic, nonstretchy plastic, metal, etc.); when full, residents empty them in the appropriate containers in the recycle room in the parking garage. Various industries collect the paper, cardboard, glass, and plastic containers, and residents volunteer to take other recyclables, such as batteries, wood, electrical appliances, foil, and so on, to drop-off points as necessary. The space under the main kitchen sink in the common room also has a series of containers for recycling, which residents empty in the recycle room whenever they notice that they're full.[13]

Each household, as well as the common kitchen, also has a composting bucket, so that no organic waste goes into the trash. Residents deposit their waste into an elaborate composting system located just outside the back door to the common room. This system consists of two large custom-built triple-bin containers through which organic waste moves in sequential order to be transformed into compost, which is then used in the vegetable and flower gardens. Meat bones are placed in bags in the common freezer, which volunteers periodically empty into a designated bin that is then picked up by a private recycling company.[14]

One afternoon, Brian summed up for me Quayside's successes in recycling and composting:

> So we set a goal to see if we can reduce garbage by 90 percent. And it took about ten years to slowly go from about 50 percent to about 90 percent. And at that point we did this incredible [thing: got rid of the dumpster]. As far as I know there isn't a building that has been about to get rid of their dumpster—[that] recycles so much stuff that their garbage can is basically empty.
>
> We probably develop about ten cubic yards of compost, which is half a dump truck per year. The compost we produce is enough for the container gardens that are up on the third floor deck and the raised beds, so that we produce enough compost for really all of that kind of food growing. But, oh man, all the plants, you know, the entire property is surrounded in plants and you know, it's amazing how if you spread a two-inch thick layer [of compost] over the whole property, that's a dump truck load!

Initially, a graywater system, designed to recapture water from kitchen sinks and washing machines for toilets and irrigation, was constructed in the parking garage. Due to municipal regulations and high costs, the system was never completely functional, and periodic efforts to revive it have been unsuccessful. Nevertheless, many residents would like to see Quayside Village continue to work to become more environmentally efficient. During the course of this study, for instance, drying racks were installed in the laundry room to encourage residents to forego use of the clothes dryers, and other measures, such as installing triple-glazed windows and water-efficient toilets and showerheads, are on the long-term agenda.

Environmental stewardship also entails growing food, which puts the compost produced by the community to good use and works to diminish the community's contribution to the damages caused by industrial agriculture and the long-distance transportation of produce.[95] There is no grass in the front gardens at Quayside Village; instead, residents use these spaces to grow various kinds of vegetables (greens, carrots, and sometimes even corn), interspersed with fruit trees, flowers, and other decorative plants. These are attended to by members of the Gardening Committee, along with others who volunteer to take on some of the watering duties in the summer. Linda, the "gardening queen" (and Brian's partner), also has a set of raised beds on the south side of the building, where she cultivates greens and beans, among other vegetables. She describes herself as "a year-round gardener, I always have food that's growing." Finally, there is a small container garden on the third floor patio where Peter cultivates cherry tomatoes. Most of the vegetables are shared with the community, either by being incorporated into common meals or set out in baskets in the lounge for residents to help themselves to as they wish. When there is not enough of a particular vegetable to go around, Linda will distribute it to those who favor it: "Sometimes I know certain people like certain food, and I won't have enough for everybody, but I'll say, 'Oh, I know that this person really likes zucchini,' so I'll just take them to their door [and] hang it [in a bag] on their door handle." A number of residents cultivate pots of herbs, such as basil, for their personal use, although there are potted herbs in the courtyard as well.

Last but not least is beautification: *We garden for both food and beauty.*[96] Beautification is Elizabeth's territory: she takes care of all the plants on the second floor walkway and in the courtyard, a task she assumed when she arrived in 2005. She began by creating a Zen garden in a section of the courtyard that receives little sun, and then expanded to plant and tend flowers, leafy plants, and herbs in the rest of the courtyard, on the second floor walkway, and in some areas around the perimeter of the building. The community gave her "complete free hands" to do this, even providing some funding; and, she says, "it's wonderful. And for them it's wonderful too, they don't have to pay a gardener." By her reckoning, she puts in about twenty hours a week in the summer months; and in the fall, she distributes plants that need to winter indoors to other residents, reclaiming them—at least the ones that residents are willing to relinquish—in the spring. Elizabeth also took it upon herself to construct two mosaics, each composed of bits and pieces of broken keepsakes donated by residents. The larger mosaic adorns the walls of the courtyard's fish pond, and the smaller one sits on the bottom wall in front of the unit directly across from the pond.

Quayside Village's groundbreaking contributions to environmental stewardship have been recognized by the city. In 2004, the community received an award for leadership in waste reduction and recycling and also won first prize in the North Shore Gardens Contest for its environmentally sustainable garden. These were followed by recognition in 2008 for its contributions to community environmental stewardship, and in 2013 by an award for urban agriculture and energy conservation. Earlier, in 2003, Quayside Village was a finalist for the World Habitat Award, a UN initiative, and in 2010 it won a Heart of the Community award. Both awards link environmental and social sustainability.

Trust and Communication: We trust the wisdom of our collective diversity of attitudes, beliefs, and cultural traditions. Through this approach we create a community that is safe—physically, emotionally, socially, and spiritually.

Open communication is key to a thriving community. Meeting this standard calls for skillful, conscious action by all.

In Quayside Village's framing, the values of trust and communication reflect a central concern for the emotional well-being of community members, and residents work together to create safe spaces and fair procedures for people to express their views and feelings and to have those views and feelings respected. An emphasis on emotional care and inclusion, seen as foundational to community development and maintenance, thus informs the organization of community meetings and how they unfold. In particular, significant attention is devoted to *processes* of discussion, consensus building, and decision-making—that is, how to go about the business of attending to substantive community issues. Form, then, is as important as content.

Quayside Village residents hold community meetings once a month, with the exception of August; there is also an annual general meeting (AGM) each spring.[7] Facilitators for meetings, which require a quorum of representatives from seven of the nineteen units, are determined on an ad hoc and voluntary basis.[8] A call for agenda items goes out a few days in advance, and the agenda is then posted on a flip chart outside of the common room and circulated electronically. Agendas include items for discussion and decision-making, along with committee reports, some of which may involve proposals for particular actions (related to, for example, finances, garden projects, or upcoming social events). Meetings take place in the common room, with members seated in chairs arranged in a horseshoe fashion around the flip chart and a large-screen monitor that can be used for showing slides.

There are two approaches to structuring meetings that are designed to produce fair, mutually respectful engagement. First, meetings are bracketed by check-in and check-out. During the check-in that begins each meeting, attendees take turns reporting on something happening in their life and how they feel about it; then, at the check-out that ends meetings, each participant says a few words about how they experienced the meeting.[19] Below is a typical exchange from check-in, which can take up to fifteen minutes, depending on the number of people present:

CAROL: I was stuck in our elevator. Thursday evening. I came home from a meeting and I pushed the button, and nothing happened. So I rang the bell, and I talked to somebody, and they said, "Oh yeah, okay," and I thought, well how's the person gonna get in? To fix it? Oh, and then I called a couple more times, and they responded. You have to be a psychologist to deal with people trapped in an elevator! But I was fine, you know, the good thing, there's a chair, thank you Brian [Brian had put a chair in the elevator some years previously].

DONYA: We should put some books in there.

CAROL: I had my bag, with meeting minutes. I didn't have any tea, but that was okay. And then the technician came, opened the door, and I said, "Ah," he also [said], "Are you okay?" I said, "Yeah, I'm fine." I'm kind of a bit claustrophobic, there's nobody around.

DON: Did the lights stay on?

CAROL: Oh thank god, yes.

DONYA: How long were you in there?

CAROL: I don't know, twenty minutes maybe?

Others followed with reports on their health, pets, work, visitors, and so on. Check-in, then, is not about the community business that will be the focus of the rest of the meeting but about personal lives and relationships. The assumption here is that if people are aware of each other's lives and concerns, they are then better able to work together as a group to build consensus and make decisions that meet the needs of both the community and its individual members. Check-out provides an additional opportunity to reflect on the process of working together. Check-in and check-out help to build the interpersonal foundations on which community is built, serving to remind residents that Quayside Village is composed of diverse individuals and that each person's feelings, experiences, and perspectives are worthy of attention and respect.

Occasionally, there can be a type of check-in in the middle of a meeting focused on a particular event or process. Several months after spearheading a reorganization of the recycling room, for instance, Donya asked for a quick round of comments on how the changes were working:

> DONYA: I just wanna hear some feedback about how the recycling room is working for everybody
>
> CAROLLYNE [facilitator]: Peter.
>
> PETER: Everything is very good. Two suggestions. One, we did have a larger space associated with things we don't know what to do with. And I know we sort of piled them in, and we might need some clarity about where that space goes. And the second thing is, sometimes there's a bit of a mismatch between the size of our buckets and the amount of recycling that goes in [them], and I think that the prime example of that might be the used clothing one. Those are the only two [suggestions], but brilliant how it's working, much cleaner, blah-blah-blah, it's all very good, thank you, for all that.
>
> CAROL: It's a joy to go in there. What's missing is some more people to sign up to take things, and that will be a pizza and participation meeting that we talked about. We can discuss it at the next community meeting, perhaps?
>
> CAROLLYNE: Sure. Yeah, let's have that be a do-or-die sign-up moment.

Once the meeting begins, discussion follows the sequence set out on the agenda (with changes as needed) and is managed by means of color-coded cards—the second structure for organizing meetings (see table 2.1).[10] In addition to regulating whose turn it is to talk, the cards provide clues about the nature of the contributions people want to make: whether they're asking a question, providing information, voicing an opinion, or objecting to something.

This kind of structured system for discussion and decision-making is common to cohousing communities. In choosing their particular approaches, communities draw on a wide range of literatures providing practical suggestions for how to effectively communicate, build consensus, and resolve conflict. These include guidebooks,[11] articles in the Foundation for Intentional Community's flagship publication, *Communities* (including special issues, for example, "Decision-Making in Community" and "Conflict and Connection"[12]), and resources posted on cohousing websites, such as the Canadian Cohousing Network, the Cohousing Association of America, and LiveWell Cohousing.

Table 2.1. Color-coded meeting discussion and decision-making cards. Table courtesy of Kathy McGrenera.

Cards	Discussion Use	Decision Use
GREEN	Green displayed to make a comment, give an opinion, or ask a question.	Green held up to agree/assent to a proposal.
YELLOW	Yellow displayed to clarify or ask for clarification only (no comment or opinion to be given). *In the speakers' list yellow takes priority over green.*	Yellow held up to stand aside if you disagree with the proposal, but will not stand in its way.
BLUE	Blue displayed to indicate a problem with the process or a need for a break. *May be raised at any time during discussion and in the speaker's list takes priority over green or yellow.*	Blue used for discussion only.
RED	Red used for decision only.	*Red held up to indicate standing in the way of a community decision. A rare and extreme form of dissent, taken only if a resident believes that a basic principle or value of the group is being violated by a proposal.*

At Quayside Village, the green card, signaling comments or opinions, is typically used to provide information and make suggestions, underscoring the value of *welcoming new ideas for the community to consider*. One evening, during an informal discussion about how decision-making unfolds at Quayside Village, Carol, Kathy, and Elizabeth, all long-term residents, illustrated the value of welcoming new ideas in an exchange about two cases that exemplified how "two minds are better than one." The discussion itself illustrates how community is collaboratively produced.

CAROL: I was thinking of our dishwasher in the common house, and, did we have another one? We did, but it was not working well, and we gotta replace it. So we had this discussion, "Well why don't we keep it? And get it fixed and buy and new one and have two dishwashers?"
  CATHERINE: Have two.
  CAROL: [I would have] *never* thought that by myself.
  CATHERINE: Right, right, so it's kind of putting heads together.
  CAROL: The decision, yeah.

CATHERINE: People come up with different ideas.
CAROL: Yeah, yeah.
CATHERINE: That must be fun, right, like you have a problem and people come up with different ideas.
KATHY: It's fun, it's fun when you solve something that's contentious, like in the watering system, that was a contentious thing.
CAROL: Oh yeah.
CATHERINE: Or for the irrigation.
CAROL: The irrigation.
KATHY: The irrigation system.
CATHERINE: I was here for that meeting, or one of the meetings.
KATHY: Yeah, that was a tough thing, but in the end a solution came.
ELIZABETH: And it works.
KATHY: That was pretty good, and better than what was originally proposed.[13]
CAROL: Yeah.
ELIZABETH: Yeah, that's a great benefit.
CAROL: That's a great example.
ELIZABETH: [If] you have enough minds looking at it [in] different ways, then you come up with something better . . .
CAROL: Better.
ELIZABETH: . . . than one person could have thought of, you know, pretty cool, yeah.

Most notable with regard to both processes of decision-making and the need to remain attuned to foundational community values are the blue and red cards, which, when deployed, prompt all those present to step back and consider how specific agenda items fit into the framework of the community and its values as a whole. At the same time, these cards also make space for individual emotional expression; someone can feel that their perspective, their contributions to community life, or their experience and expertise are not being sufficiently recognized, and they can use the blue card to indicate this. The point here is that decisions—about, for instance, how to organize the recycle room, water the gardens, or decorate the common room over the holidays—are not simply mechanical, cut-and-dried, or based on neutral, value-free "facts." Rather, they are informed to a large degree by particular ideas about the environment, about efficiency and workloads, or about diversity. It is not surprising, then, that people will have strong, and sometimes opposing, views about particular options. Here the confluence of process and substance reveals itself: they are not, in practice, distinct, but, rather, part and parcel of each other. Process is also substance.

The blue and red cards, in particular, speak to the principle that *differences make our community and our collective decisions stronger*, and to the value of *having the courage to raise difficult issues*. The blue card also marks, to a certain extent, a culturally specific approach to emotional expression that may be dubbed the hydraulic theory of emotion. Developed in eighteenth-century Europe, and based on concepts of *flow*, this theory holds that psychological health depends on expressing emotions rather than repressing them.[14] In this framework, pent-up emotion is considered bad for the individual and the community alike, since it might lead to "explosions" or simmering resentments that are counterproductive in the long run. If, on the contrary, people are given space to air their feelings instead of keeping them bottled up, so the theory goes, then everyone will know what is happening and there will be no under-the-table dynamics, allowing for the development of healthy relationships and decision-making processes that take everyone's views into account. This will, in turn, increase the likelihood that joint decisions will be upheld by everyone. However, although the color-coded card system provides ample space for personal emotional expression, use of the red card to block decisions is intended only for those situations when a community, rather than a strictly personal, value is being violated.

These structured processes for the doing of community—check-in/check-out and the use of color-coded cards to regulate discussion—work to balance and intertwine individual and community needs. As they engage with each other by means of these practices, residents coproduce a social milieu that simultaneously recognizes individuals' orientations and desires; capitalizes on what they can contribute in the way of skills, knowledge, and insight; and underscores the importance of building community *together*. Peter's and Juhli's reflections on the twentieth-anniversary values update expressed this well. Peter, in his sixties, had been living at Quayside Village for over seven years, while Juhli, in her thirties, was one of Quayside's newest members.

> PETER: A few meetings ago, I think we started a meeting with Kathy reiterating some parts of how we approach these meetings, and I think, particularly [with regard to] disagreements, that the value is that we all sort of *kumbaya*. The value is that, but the reality is that we have [issues] around this place where people differ, and sometimes differ dramatically, and I thought that the introduction that we had a couple of meetings ago normalized disagreement, so that it wasn't weird, it was just normal. And [it normalized] that, as an outcome of the discussions, sometimes you don't get your own way in these things, and that's okay, too. It makes it safe to disagree and also [reminds] us that in the deference to

community that sometimes your own individual sort of agenda might be frustrated. And I just felt that [those ideas] just normalized things, and still embrace the overriding sense that we're in this together, to figure stuff out, and that mitigates whatever disappointments there might be in terms of individual decisions that are not reached that you happen to favor. And everybody felt sort of safe to talk about stuff that maybe confronts a different point of view than your own. So, that was a kind of a neat thing that happened, and I don't know if it might become more of the protocol around here, that we understand those things and get reminded of them all the time.

JUHLI: There's a parallel I wanna point out, between what we're trying to do here in the community and the goal of singing in harmony. And that is, that your individual voice in a harmonious ensemble, there, each voice makes a personal sacrifice of a little bit, in order to blend in. Because if every voice was at its absolute fullest, then there would not be—there's clashing. So everyone sacrifices a little bit of their own individual character, so that the ensemble can be one harmonious thing.

Building community together thus requires that individual members orient themselves outward, toward others and toward the whole, in a spirit of collaboration. The emphasis on safe spaces and listening to all voices, which focuses on meeting the needs of individuals, thus simultaneously encourages residents to hear *others'* voices and to align themselves to what is best for all concerned—even if, as Peter and Juhli point out, it may entail some personal sacrifice.

Significantly, these structured practices for interaction also have an influence on the kinds of people those raised in Quayside Village become, as Elise indicates in her narrative in chapter 1. She made a similar point during an informal group discussion one afternoon, noting that her and Jana's participation in community meetings as they were growing up

> made us more confident, especially talking with adults or just talking with anybody. We were both in [high school] student council, and I don't know if that's just a personal thing too, like the way we grew up, but mainly, also growing up with very political people around you too, we were around them discussing politics and discussing all these issues when we were young, and that was just normal, and they would ask our opinions on stuff, and we would just always be included in the discussion no matter what, even if we didn't understand what was going on we'd always be incorporated in.

In other words, participating in discussions focused on tough financial decisions, or on how to deal with conflict, as well as in informal conversations at common meals and other social events, encourages the development of communicative skills and self-confidence. Not only do check-in/check-out and the color-coded cards provide a means for connecting "community" and "individual" and for going about the business of community building and maintenance in a fair, measured, and considerate fashion, they also model an approach to communication and interpersonal engagement that radiates out into life in general.

In addition to these meeting structures, Quayside Villagers have put in place a series of mechanisms for communication that occurs outside of meetings and that facilitate and complement everyday face-to-face encounters. First, residents can leave messages on the whiteboards situated at the entrance to the laundry room, next to the elevator. These range from asking after lost items, announcing a meeting or movie night, and offering to walk dogs to inquiring about interest in bulk purchases. One of Quayside's younger residents, Jazzy, also puts out a monthly newsletter, the *Quayside Quibbler*, documenting residents' activities and community events.[15] Finally, Quayside Village also has a listserv where residents can send out information or queries of all kinds, reflecting both community-relevant and personal interests. These notices are often responded to immediately, as the following incident illustrates:

> One day, Stacy, who was suffering from food poisoning, sent out an email in which she described how she couldn't keep water down or even stand up without vomiting. She asked if someone could come fix her a cup of broth, and gave instructions on where to find the broth base in her fridge. Within minutes, Patrick wrote that he was out but should be home shortly and would stop by to make the broth. A few minutes later, however, Heather wrote to say that she'd already prepared the broth, and that Stacy was resting. Maureen then wrote to say that soda crackers would probably be useful, and within minutes Vera had volunteered to go pick some up.

This kind of exchange is typical: calls for help with dealing with sickness, for rides to the doctor's office or the sea bus, for the name of a good plumber, or for help with moving heavy furniture circulate through the community as often as requests for feedback on or participation in committee initiatives and community events—and they are always responded to quickly. Hardly a day passes without some kind of activity on the listserv, which parallels the frequency of serendipitous face-to-face encounters.

Camaraderie: We value camaraderie for creating and sustaining a positive, healthy community.

Quayside Village's twentieth anniversary value statement lists a number of practices that create camaraderie. Here I focus on three in particular: the division of labor regarding community maintenance, eating together, and kindness. I then turn to a discussion of residents' approaches to common space and property, an element of Quayside's organization that is not explicitly stated as a component of camaraderie but that directly contributes to its production.

Completing tasks and taking on responsibilities necessary for a functioning and thriving community. In a conversation about the common meal system with Haruko, one of the Kankanmori residents who visited Quayside Village in December 2017, Vera underscored the importance of shared contribution: "I believe that all of us are accountable. We don't have any leader per se, we're all owners in this building and responsible for it, and responsible for the work that needs to be done." Significantly, however, this shared responsibility does not manifest itself in a clear, predetermined division of labor or in a set number of labor hours required of each resident, as is the case in many cohousing communities.[16] Instead, the way in which Quaysiders approach managing their community reveals one of its most foundational values: *each-according-to-their-strengths, each-according-to-their-desires.*[17] Although not articulated in its value statement, *each-according-to-their-strengths, each-according-to-their-desires* informs the vast majority of everyday practices of community at Quayside Village.

In addition to its Strata Council, which includes all residents and is organized according to a series of bylaws,[18] Quayside Village has four committees: the *Thriving Committee*, an umbrella committee charged with creating and nurturing an environment in which the community and its members can flourish; the *Maintenance Committee*, responsible for all shared building maintenance; the *Finance Committee*, which attends to any budgetary or legal issues related to the building; and the *Garden Committee*, which oversees the gardens in the front of the building and in the courtyard. In addition, although they are not allotted financial resources, some activities, such as recycling, can occasionally take on an informal committee structure when, for example, a large-scale reorganization effort is underway. Composed of anywhere from three to twelve members, committees report to the community at monthly meetings and seek residents' input and approval for any proposed projects.

The philosophy of *each-according-to-their-strengths, each-according-to-their-desires* is directly reflected in committee participation, which is by invitation rather than obligation.[19] Participation in community-wide activities organized by committees, such as fall or spring garden or parkade cleanups, is also voluntary. The idea here is that committee undertakings will be most fruitful—to the benefit of both individual residents and the community as a whole—if those participating are engaged in work in which they are skilled and that they enjoy.

Given this loose framework, it comes as no surprise that committee participation is uneven: some residents are more active than others, and any one person's participation can wax and wane over time, depending on their interests and on what else is going on in their lives. For example, when Donya arrived at Quayside Village in her early thirties, she was the single mother of a young child, Jazzy. Like Yuki (see narrative in chapter 1), she was told by other residents that she should only participate as much as she wanted and felt able to, and so she did very little during her first three to four years: she attended meetings and listened, but not much else. Gradually, as Jazzy grew and Donya remarried and became financially secure, she found the time and energy to participate more actively, eventually initiating a major reorganization of the recycling room and getting involved in a number of Thriving Committee initiatives.

This invitation-rather-than-obligation approach can occasionally engender resentment against those who are not seen to be contributing enough to community life. Some members can disappear off the radar for months at a time, and over the years of research I was privy to more than a few gripes about people who were perceived to not be doing their fair share. During a discussion of the benefits and challenges of living in cohousing, for instance, Elizabeth noted that

> there's a few people that do not come to meetings at all, and I don't really know what their reasoning is for that. I always feel I'm getting the message [that] "we just don't want to come," and they must have a reason for that, but I'm not sure of what it would be.

Later, however, Elizabeth speculated that perhaps those who didn't attend trusted those who did to make the right decisions. Thus, despite ongoing concerns about participation—the Thriving Committee occasionally initiates activities designed to increase residents' levels of involvement—complaints and resentments tend to be relatively short-lived and contextualized, as Elizabeth's reflections indicate. This makes sense, given the self-selected nature of the people who live at Quayside Village, all of whom moved in because they wanted to be part of a self-governing community. In addition, inscribed in the *each-according-to-their-strengths, each-according-to-their-desires* approach is a long view that recognizes that someone who disappears for months can reemerge to become actively engaged in a project for an equal number of months. Appreciation of this—however difficult it may be at times, and however frustrating it may be that some people will simply never be as engaged as others—is part and parcel of mutual care, of acknowledging and accepting that each person has their own strengths and weaknesses and their own life issues and events to contend with. The appropriate response to this, as Carol noted, was "not to shame people and not to antagonize people, but [to ask], 'What is it that you can contribute? These are the things that need to be done. And it's in your own best interest to do them because we want to maintain the building.'" A founding member, Carol felt strongly that hard and fast rules violated the spirit of cohousing.

The force of *each-according-to-their-strengths, each-according-to-their-desires* is revealed by the fact that most things that need to get done do in fact get done. Of course, projects can, on occasion, be delayed. As Carol once pointed out, "Everything needs a champion. If there isn't a person there, it doesn't happen. [But] *it will next year."* The strength of *each-according-to-their-strengths, each-according-to-their-desires* is also revealed in the many contributions residents undertake of their own initiative, simply because they *want* to—perhaps because they are not obliged to contribute but are free to do so on their own time and in accordance with their skills and inclinations. Marylee, for instance, is the resident photographer; she regularly sends out emails with images of individual residents going about their everyday lives, Quayside events, and local wildlife. She is, in a sense, the community's visual archivist. Her work is complemented by Stacy, who has kept meticulous written records of meeting minutes and copies of a range of media reports over the years. To give another example, Carol, who doesn't like to cook and never participates in preparing the Monday common meals, can often be seen on Tuesday mornings wiping down the counters and sweeping the floors in the common kitchen. And if someone notices a load of Quayside Village laundry in the dryer (the dish towels and cloth napkins used for common meals or special events), they will likely fold it and put it away. And so on.

A *functioning and thriving community* is also characterized by a rich and varied social life that encourages comembership. Some of this social connection is produced as an artifact of doing necessary community maintenance tasks together, but some of it is produced simply for the sake of connection. Thus the Thriving Committee, and residents more generally, initiate a range of social activities: Thanksgiving, Christmas, and New Year's parties, game nights, bridge, and fundraisers for refugees or for communities suffering the devastating effects of forest fires. Many of these events are relatively unorganized. As Carol explained to the Kankanmori visitors: "And we say, 'Oh yeah, there's going to be a potluck at 6:30,' and when you come in it's maybe crackers and cheese, and, 'Oh, maybe nobody's going to show up,' and then everybody shows up, there's all kinds of food, everything's perfect, and that's the way it works!"[20]

On a more ad hoc basis, residents will use the listserv to invite others to go see a movie, visit an art gallery, attend a performance (especially one in which one or more of Quayside's resident artists is featured), participate in a political demonstration, go snowshoeing, etc. Occasionally residents will come home to find that someone has mysteriously left small gifts on their doorsteps. Finally, listening, providing emotional support, and just being around to socialize with are recognized as key markers of camaraderie and are highly valued.

The point here is that while the committee structure provides a foundation for community living, it by no means encapsulates all the activities that go into building and maintaining the good life at Quayside Village. Official organizational structures are the skeleton—absolutely essential for holding up the body—but not the flesh. It is the residents themselves who collaboratively realize the potential of the community and shape it in particular ways, by either joining a committee or contributing other skills, practical or otherwise, or both. The *each-according-to-their-strengths, each-according-to-their-desires* approach, despite the occasional hiccups produced by uneven participation, thus provides the conditions of possibility for a community marked by self-motivated volunteerism and the creation of a social space in which individual residents can build on and express their unique talents, maintaining their autonomy and agency while simultaneously creating and enjoying ongoing connections with others.

Cooking and eating together. Everyone I spoke with saw common meals as a significant component of life at Quayside Village, providing the opportunity to catch up with neighbors while enjoying a delicious and inexpensive meal.[21] As Linda once told me, shopping, cooking, and eating together enriches the cohousing experience, and, in Vera's view, "a number one key thing for helping resolve conflict is the fact that we all eat together" (see section on "Disagreement and Conflict" below). Common meals are usually held once a week, on Mondays. In the summer, they take the form of potlucks in the courtyard, to which people sometimes bring a dish to share and sometimes bring just their own meal to eat while enjoying the company of others. As with committee participation, common meals at Quayside Village are voluntary: residents cook and join in eating the meals only when they want to. Typically attended by at least ten people, the meals are lively affairs, and adults often stay to visit long after they have finished their meals, while children go off to play together.

Although the values statement specifies that building camaraderie entails both cooking and eating together, common meals are more often than not prepared by one person alone. Whoever that person is begins by writing out the menu on the common meal form, which is then displayed on a table in the lounge; in some cases the cook also posts an announcement to the listserv. Those who wish to participate sign up on the common meal form next to their unit number, indicating how many people will be attending.

Once cooks know the number of attendees, they purchase the necessary ingredients and go about preparing the meal. In addition to endeavoring to keep costs below five dollars per person and to incorporate leftovers from previous common meals, effort is made to accommodate food preferences by, for example, making milder versions of dishes for those who don't like spicy food. Special consideration is given to allergies by cooking some foods in private apartments rather than in the main kitchen or by making separate dishes that don't include allergens. Once prepared, cooks lay the food out on the kitchen island, with labels to indicate particular ingredients or spice levels if necessary, and then ring the dinner bell in the courtyard to announce the beginning of the meal. Those attending arrive at their leisure, serve themselves, and arrange themselves at one of the two large oval tables in the dining area. If someone is unable to attend but still wants the meal, the cook will put a plate aside for them.

Cooks are not responsible for cleanup. Instead, everyone loads their own dishes into the dishwashers, and many will also help put away leftovers (stored either in the fridge, for anyone to help themselves to, or in the freezer, for use in future common meals), wash pots and pans, and so on. Yet others will take care of the laundry and put away clean dishes and laundry the following day. The accounting is also handled by a volunteer, who once a month circulates an Excel spreadsheet indicating how much each person owes. These notices often include reminders of the importance of reimbursing cooks in a timely manner and of contributing to cleanup and laundry. Occasionally, a second notice is required.

The following vignette describes a typical common meal:

A Common Meal
On my first visit to Quayside Village, I volunteered to help Stacy, the resident anthropologist who had introduced me to the community, prepare a common meal. We decided on a menu of baked salmon, rice, salad, and, for dessert, almond meringues. Stacy took care of circulating the menu, and I took care of the shopping. Keeping in mind that costs were ideally kept to five dollars per person, and that salmon was fairly expensive, Stacy sent me with her portable shopping cart to visit various markets along Lonsdale Avenue in search of the best deals. (I later learned that common meal cooks often purchase ingredients in multiple shops, depending on which have the best prices on which items.)

I began, at around 4:00, by making the meringues. Stacy then joined me at 5:00 and we prepared the salmon (olive oil, lemon, salt, pepper, and a few spices), cut up vegetables for the salad, made a salad dressing (olive oil, balsamic vinegar), and put on the rice. At one point, we ran out of common room olive oil, so Stacy sent me to her apartment to fetch some (the door was unlocked). All through the preparation we chatted about our shared teaching interests and about our children's lives. At one point Stacy took a phone call from one of her graduate students, after which we discussed the trials and joys of supervision.

I rang the dinner bell in the courtyard at 6:00, and shortly afterward residents started to arrive. There were twelve people in all. No one brought their five dollars with them. People sat in small groups, so there were multiple conversations unfolding simultaneously. People reported on events in their lives, chatted about politics, and so on. Cleanup started around 7:00, with many residents sitting back down to continue chatting after loading dishes in the dishwasher. Three residents helped with the pots and pans and composting, one of whom also put in a load of laundry. Everything was wrapped up by 9:00. I don't remember to whom I gave the grocery receipts, but we did come in under the five-dollar threshold, and I was reimbursed before the end of my trip.

Special common meals are held on holidays, such as Thanksgiving and Christmas, and are also often part and parcel of other social events, such as movie nights and birthday parties.[22] In the latter cases, the meals often take the form of a potluck. Sometimes there are impromptu meals, announced at the last minute and attended by only a handful of residents.

The only complaint I heard about common meals is that they don't happen frequently enough. Nevertheless, although Quayside Village has gone through phases during which common meals were held more frequently, and while residents periodically contemplate expanding current practices—say, to twice a week rather than once—during the course of the research for this book residents' busy personal schedules meant that one regularly scheduled meal together, supplemented by ad hoc events, provided the most workable model.

Kindness. An ethos of consideration for and generosity toward others permeates everyday life at Quayside Village. Two occurrences serve to illustrate how this plays out. One year, Kathy got in a bicycle accident and broke her pelvis. She was unable to walk up stairs (she lives in a two-story townhouse), and so she was installed in the guest room for some time, during which other residents took turns bringing her meals, doing her laundry, and helping with any other physical requirements that needed looking after. The following year, Elizabeth broke her hip. Although she was able to stay in her own place, she was unable to look after her dog, and so others took turns taking Midge on her morning and evening walks; they also brought Elizabeth groceries, coffee, and whatever else she asked for. On other sudden-crisis occasions I witnessed—when the dogs were attacked by raccoons, or when the water pipes burst in someone's apartment—residents immediately dropped whatever they were doing, seemingly appearing out of nowhere, to offer their assistance. On a more routine basis (since, happily, major crises are relatively infrequent), residents call on others to look after their pets or plants when they're out of town, or drive them to doctor's appointments or to the sea bus as needed. Linda's depositing of a resident's favorite vegetable on their doorstep, and the periodic small gifts left in mailboxes or on door handles, are the icing on the cake. This does not mean that all residents feel that all their needs are always attended to—Quayside Village is not a therapeutic community in any traditional sense, and residents are not always aware of and do not always have the time to look after other's needs. But these practices do point to an environment that encourages members to orient to and provide caring support for each other whenever possible.

On an abstract level—since the issue has yet to emerge in any practical sense—this framework of a caring environment has informed conversations about "aging in place." Although they are not equipped to look after someone with major physical or mental needs, residents have proven themselves more than willing to prepare meals, walk dogs, and provide transportation to medical appointments. This willingness, when coupled with professional home-care services, could allow older residents to stay at Quayside Village longer than might otherwise be possible.

As the above descriptions indicate, camaraderie, a keystone of the Quayside Village community, is established informally as well as formally: in the same way that the form and substance of meetings spill into each other, so organized and spontaneous forms of sociality merge in everyday practice. Once again, stated values and the structures devised to reflect them provide the foundation on which, in this case, camaraderie emerges and unfolds via the everyday actions of residents.

Common Space and Common Property

Slightly more than 12 percent of Quayside Village comprises intimate public space. As described in chapter 1, this includes the common kitchen and dining area, laundry room, guest room and bathroom, office (currently occupied by the midwife, Vera), lounge (with couches and a faux fireplace), a third floor deck (with enough space to hang laundry, or, in the evening, have guests over for a meal), and the dome room, also located on the third floor and available for yoga and meditation, practicing music, or small group meetings.[23]

When not being used for meetings or common meals, the main common room is available to all to inhabit as they see fit.[24] Residents sometimes use the space for activities that their units are too small to accommodate, such as large cooking or sewing projects, or movie nights. When these activities are in process, others come and go as needed (to access the guest room or bathroom, for instance), although they try to avoid interrupting, if, for example, a movie is playing. The common room can also be reserved for private use, such as a private dinner or dance party, yoga classes, midwifery training, or voice workshops. In these cases, residents book their events on a calendar provided for that purpose and also announce the booking via email and on the whiteboards so that other residents know to avoid going into the common space at those times.

Despite the common room's central location, however, ad hoc use is relatively infrequent, certainly compared to the pattern at Kankanmori (see chapter 3). On a daily basis, through traffic tends to dominate the common room—for example, walking through to put clean towels and napkins away or to access the compost bins out back. Residents rarely "hang out" in the common room to read, work on their computers, or visit with other residents or friends. Other common spaces, such as the lounge or, in summer, the courtyard and third floor deck, are much more likely to be used in this manner.

There is a range of common property at Quayside Village, all of which is managed informally. The kitchen, for example, has a large collection of dishes and cookware, and residents freely appropriate wine glasses, large casserole dishes, or food processors for use in their apartments, returning the items at their convenience. When someone needs to use an item but finds it missing, they will send out an email or post a message on one of the whiteboards requesting its return. Although there have been occasional attempts to institute sign-up sheets for borrowing kitchen items, this has never been successful for long, and occasionally borrowed items are absent for extended periods of time or, on occasion, disappear altogether.[25] The common kitchen also has a stock of basic cooking ingredients, such as spices and oil, along with coffee and tea for meetings. If someone cooking a common meal runs out of a particular ingredient—say, flour or olive oil—they might provide it from their own kitchen or borrow it from someone else's, and vice versa: if someone is cooking at home and runs out of a particular spice, they might borrow some from the common kitchen, although it is understood that no one should make excessive use of designated common room ingredients.

Quayside's guest room, containing one queen bed, is located just off the common room and shares the common room bathroom with other residents, visitors, and Vera's clients. Use of the guest room is by donation (recommended at ten dollars per night) and is managed by means of a sign-up calendar on the door. There is no specified time limit to the use of the guest room, although if someone has a guest who would like to occupy the room for more than two weeks, they need to check with their coresidents to make sure that others are not inconvenienced. Those hosting guests are responsible for cleaning the room and for washing sheets and towels once their guests have left. Sometimes friends of friends of a Quayside resident will use the room, on which occasions there is no direct relationship between a guest and a Quayside resident.[26] Other times, when the room is not in use by guests, residents will appropriate it for other purposes, such as ongoing sewing or art projects that can't be left in the common room.

The laundry room and children's play area are located on the opposite side of the common room from the guest room. A community freezer and sauna divide the space in two, with the play area, consisting of a couch, library, and some toys and craft supplies, at one end and the laundry facilities at the other. The laundry space holds two washers and two dryers, an ironing board and iron, a number of large drying racks, and shelving on which residents store their detergent (with their unit numbers clearly marked). Early on, Quaysiders paid to use the washers and dryers, but eventually it was decided that this was too much trouble, and residents now use the machines free of charge. The assumption is that "it all comes out in the laundry"—that things even out in the long run.

If a wash cycle has been completed and someone wants to use the machine, they empty its contents into a laundry basket and leave it; the owner of the clothes will eventually show up. Similarly with the dryers. There are often multiple baskets distributed throughout the room, especially on weekends. Sometimes these are placed right below and in front of a washing machine in use to indicate that the basket's owner wants to use the machine next; however, if they're not present when the cycle has been completed and someone else comes along, they'll claim the machine for themselves. The drying racks, which are often full of clothes, are not considered "private," that is, for the exclusive use of only one resident at a time. Instead, people put their clothes wherever there is space. Occasionally, when someone runs out of detergent, they will use someone else's, leaving them a note offering to reciprocate or mentioning it the next time they encounter each other. Residents use their own detergent when running laundry from common meals.

Quayside's office, which stores its archival material and a few other items, including board and other games, is located off the lounge. Not used actively by residents in general, the office is occupied by Vera's midwifery practice, with the understanding that residents can have access to it if they need to retrieve anything during the times when she is not receiving clients.[27]

There is no common Wi-Fi at Quayside. Those desiring access to the internet in the common room can use the Wi-Fi from Vera's office. A number of residents have their own routers in their apartments, while others have access to the Wi-Fi of those who are willing to share.

As the idea of common property implies, all of Quayside's common property belongs to and is managed by everyone. Although common space is not to be used for storing a resident's personal property (and some conflicts around this issue have indeed occurred), some donations of personal items have been accepted over the years (for example, Mihaela's canning equipment and Connie's portable sauna). When residents feel that it's time to update certain items (a worn-out chair in the lounge, an old kitchen mixer, or guest room linen) or add new items (drying racks for the laundry), they can make a pitch at a Community Chest party. Money from the Community Chest Fund, which includes donations from the guest room and Vera's use of the office for her midwifery practice, is earmarked for both special social events and material items that will enhance community life, as described below:

A Community Chest Party

Shortly before a Community Chest Party, Linda sent out a notice to the community:

As recently agreed, we're moving forward with our Community Chest Party this month. We have $3,000 in the pot for our July 18th Happy Hour Community Chest Party. That's $160 spending money per QV family.

To sponsor a project, please prepare a poster and explanation in advance of the party. These should go up this week, with a hard deadline of Monday, July 15. The sooner the better, so that others can see what's up for bidding on.

There's no fixed dollar limit for a project, but if spending over $1,000, you'd be more likely to succeed in the Large Project funds process, which we plan to manifest later in the year.

When putting up your proposal in the common area, include:

- Community values that will be met by your project
- Communicate *your* passion and enthusiasm
- Explains why or how you and others would use it
- Has clear costing—a little research on prices + tax to set upper range of cost
- Anticipate questions people will have
- Have a plan for your project (i.e. if it will need ongoing stewardship, how could that be handled? If there are specific decisions about features or

model, or placement, how will consultations be organized?); if relevant, there is a proposed plan for long-term management or upkeep.
- Be able to execute the proposal in a six-month window of spending

The party was held in the evening in the courtyard, and residents perused the proposals, awarding their spending money to the projects of their choice. Marylee, the resident photographer, documented the event and later posted photos to the listserv. Funded items included the following (along with the name of the proposer):

- two large elegant planters and plants for the common house lounge (Elizabeth)
- shop vac for easy handling of big jobs (Don)
- Vitamix for common house kitchen (Linda)
- drying racks (Stacy)
- ceiling fan for guest room (Connie)
- side table to go alongside reading chair and lamp in lounge (Stacy)
- community book-trading box for outdoors (Marylee)
- step stool for accessing upper shelves in common rooms (Stacy)

Making decisions about the use of Community Chest funds collaboratively, and in a party-like atmosphere, invites everyone to participate in monitoring, taking care of, and updating common property.

In general, Quayside's approach to managing common space and property reflects its emphasis on camaraderie: on kindness (care and consideration for others), sharing responsibility, and simple, easy organization. It accomplishes this by means of two of its other key values: trust and communication. Residents *trust* each other to return borrowed items and to be considerate in the use of laundry facilities and the guest room. This trust is perhaps most evident in the handling of keys: the storage closet next to the common bathroom contains a safe in which copies of all unit keys are contained, and all residents know the combination to the safe. It goes without saying that no one would contemplate entering someone else's unit without their permission (for example, when pet sitting). *Communication*, which, according to the value statement, includes *assuming others have good intentions and they are doing the best they can*—with the implication that this applies to all communication, not just that in meetings—is also pivotal to the care and management of common space and property. It might just be the case that a self-managed system based on trust not only "relies on people to be motivated to help," as Linda put it with regard to committee participation, but also engenders it.

Disagreement and Conflict

Quayside Village's emphasis on attending to and fostering the well-being of residents' diverse individualities lays the groundwork for and invites individual expression, which in turn provides the conditions of possibility for open disagreement and sometimes outright conflict. A number of the components listed under the values of *trust, communication,* and *camaraderie* embody recognition of the dilemmas that such invitations might generate and are designed to serve either as preventatives or as means to address conflicts that do emerge: *listening with an open mind, recognizing the diversity of communication needs and styles, supporting each other in working through challenging communication issues,* and *safely working through disagreements knowing that differences make our community and our collective decisions stronger.* These statements all reflect a desire to work through differences and disagreements collaboratively. Significantly, they also embody a perspective that sees disagreement as a potentially productive generator of ideas.

Conflict can emerge in a number of ways. Sometimes residents collaborating on a particular project, such as designing garden space, will disagree on how to proceed. In these cases, they might sit down together and talk it through, or, as I observed several times, they might ask a third person to mediate. On other occasions, when, for example, a resident is violating a particular community value or bylaw, a small contingent of two or three might approach the person in question to discuss it quietly and privately in an effort to avoid a more public, and thus potentially more fraught, discussion at a community meeting. Conflict can also emerge in email if someone posts something inflammatory—"drops a bomb"—when, as Kathy phrased it, "they don't have that reflex to be careful, to be thinking about the receivers." In these cases, another resident will often intervene. All it takes, Kathy said, is "one diplomatic response for everybody to go, 'Oh, yeah, we don't want to go down this rabbit hole.' It just takes one person with a clear head to just set the bar, and then people stop, usually."

The issues around which conflict tends to emerge include, first of all, finance. Here there can be a tension between minimalists, who exemplify a save-it-for-a-rainy-day position, and those who argue that spending earlier rather than later, and on high-quality interventions, will save money and headaches in the long run and also improve the general quality of life. Financial tensions can overlap with another area of potential tension, that concerning aesthetics. Should we be a minimalist community in terms of beauty and comfort, or should we enjoy the best that we can afford—again, as a means to enhance community life? These are the kinds of issues around which personality differences emerge and are sorted. And, finally, there are ongoing issues related to the tension between self-interest and community interest. For example, community interest requires that residents collapse their cardboard boxes before putting them into the recycling bin, that they compost regularly, and that they remove their laundry from the laundry room in a timely manner. The exigencies of everyday life, however, may mean that people take shortcuts or skip steps.

One issue that generated tension during the course of the research for this book serves to illustrate how Quayside Villagers formally approach these kinds of trouble. The matter in question concerned the timing and structure of decision-making; in particular, how project proposals were communicated, how long they would be open for discussion, and the kinds of opportunities residents would have to provide input before decisions were finalized. The topic came up at a Thriving Committee meeting when it emerged that several residents felt that they had not been given adequate time to contemplate and then contribute to a decision about proposed changes in the common room. Concerns about feedback mechanisms and the timing of decision-making were, of course, not new; as Carollyne had pointed out in a community meeting several months prior to the Thriving Committee meeting in question, "There are different accelerators, you know? You have different gas pedals on the floor, and some people really are not comfortable deciding right away, and others are like, 'What's taking us so long?'" But, on this occasion, those participating in the meeting took the opportunity to develop an explicit policy. The following excerpt from their discussion illustrates how community members worked to balance the need for flexibility with a desire to get things done:

> KATHY: But with anything we see, like a change to the laundry room, how it's organized or whatever, and if you're not part of it, those things are gonna happen, and maybe just acknowledging that we're not all gonna be totally comfortable with decisions that are made, but we can celebrate that things are moving ahead. Yeah. You all have the opportunity to be involved in decision-making, and if you are too busy in life, which many of us are, to participate in every single decision that gets made, then, I don't know.
>
> CONNIE: I think you're right, and I think it's a bit of a reeducation. I think it's reeducating the community to get used to a little bit faster pace and a new system of doing things. We're not gonna back down or get bogged down again and get back to discussing things for a year before anything happens. Once we start the process, it is gonna happen, so if you wanna get involved, get involved early, get on the committee, and then you have a chance to participate. If not, things are gonna happen without you. And I think getting people used to the fact that that's the

way it's gonna work, so that they know what's coming, it's a reeducation process at the moment, I think.

CAROL: And I think there's not only one way to be involved. If you can't come to the meeting, as long as you know who's on the committee you can talk to the person who's the focus person for that committee about your concerns, and have that recognized.

CONNIE: Yeah, maybe we should make that point more clearly.

CAROL: Yeah, and are there other ways? It could be email, you know, you could email them, speak with people. It's just a small community, and you know who everybody is and what they do, so it shouldn't be difficult.

CONNIE: Yeah, there's no reason to feel left out.

DONYA: What if we add a protocol that says, if you're gonna have a committee that's gonna discuss some change, write an email saying, this is when the committee's happening, come and talk about it, and if you can't, come and talk to me.

MULTIPLE: Yeah, yeah.

CONNIE: Or this is who's on the committee, speak to somebody on the committee.

MULTIPLE: Yeah.

DONYA: So that there's that extra layer of, you know, communication and invitation to be heard.

The result of this discussion was the following policy statement, which Donya read out at the community meeting held that evening:[128]

> When a decision-making task group is formed, inform the community who is on the committee and when they are meeting. If someone is not able to attend, and has input, speak to a member of the committee who can communicate it to the group. Once a decision has been made and communicated to the community, it will not be changed.

After reading the statement, Donya underscored its message:

> So, we wanna make sure that people have an opportunity to have early input, and be part of the discussion, and then once the committee makes its decision, that there's no last-minute "But I didn't get my voice heard" kind of business. So better communication, early input by anybody who cares. Sound good?

Those involved in discussing and drafting this policy decided to both improve channels of communication regarding proposed projects and put mechanisms in place to ensure that projects could still unfold in a timely fashion. They were not open to "discussing things for a year before anything happens," as Connie put it, but instead designed more active consultation processes. These could extend the time frame of decision-making, requiring patience on the part of those who preferred to make immediate decisions, but at the same time they would place limits on how long projects would be open to discussion, requiring those who, as Carollyne put it, "are not comfortable deciding right away" to try to accelerate their own thinking processes. Although this approach to decision-making was intended to give everyone an opportunity to have input, a year later some residents, who had not attended either the Thriving Committee meeting or the community meeting that followed, still felt that it wasn't adequate. They told me that they first heard of this approach only when reading the draft of this passage of the book, and so, from their perspective, the discussion about decision-making, let alone actual decision-making, was insufficiently inclusive. Timely and clear communication, then, are ongoing issues at Quayside Village, as is the case in all cohousing communities.[29]

Sometimes disagreements are not so easily resolved, and things can get "stuck," as Kathy explained during a discussion group on the benefits and challenges of living in cohousing:

> Some things, you can work through it, and there's an evident kind of path ahead, and even though it's conflictual it's moving, and it's not stuck, it kind of is moving and shifting and people are working it through. But some of them just get *stuck* and there [is] no clear path forward or somebody isn't willing to shift. So it sits there and kind of pops up periodically.

Some residents used temporary avoidance as a way of dealing with things that were "stuck" and that no one wanted to address directly because they might escalate conflict or cause people to dig in their heels. Although relatively rare, there were also occasions when residents physically removed themselves from a situation (leaving a meeting, for instance)—a kind of calling "time out"—or withdrew from community activities for a period of time. Other times residents just avoided particular residents for a while, as Donya described:

> I think the most challenging thing for me is when there's conflict, 'cuz I don't like that and it takes practice and consciousness and courage for me to deal with that stuff. I mean it's easier to just hide in your own house, not ever meet any of your neighbors, but then you don't know any of your neighbors. Earlier in the spring there was a fairly significant conflict that sort of just ebbed away, it never really got dealt with. And so, for a while there, it was like emotional eggshells, walking around, I totally avoided people, I mean if I saw certain people coming I'd be like, "Oh I'm just going to do this later, until, you

know, until things cooled off." There are maybe ways we could deal with that better but it's also really challenging.

Occasionally, then, meeting structures, informal mediations, and other forms of intervention were unable to "deal with that." In these cases, as Donya's comments indicate, selective avoidance until things simmer down may become the only option—although delaying direct discussion might sometimes produce less of an ebbing away of conflict than an underground simmering of resentment. When this occurs, two additional informal mechanisms for dealing with tension could come in handy. The first, mentioned earlier, was eating together, which Vera noted was key: "I think that eating together, you get to hear about people's lives. And so when it then comes to talking about, you know, something that's a little bit more difficult, it's easier [because you know each other]." The idea here is that doing things together, such as sharing common meals, creates opportunities for mutual understandings that work to either preclude the development of conflict in the first place, provide the grounds for quick resolution, or work to resolve tension indirectly. Here, simple proximity serves as both prophylactic and antidote. The second strategy, less to do with community organization itself than with the communicative skills that the organization ideally engenders, is patience, as illustrated in an exchange between Vera and Marylee:

> VERA: I think one of the different things about dealing with a conflict in a community is that I think we've also learned to give people space, and, yeah, "wait and see" is very often the best medicine, you know?
> MARYLEE: The old sleep-on-it kind of thing is very, very true, like with loads of things. Until fairly recently in life I don't think I did that. And the other one is I say to myself, "Marylee, you're going to be with these people 'til the day you die," and so that kind of has shaped how [I] think about things and interact with people.

In the same way that practical manifestations of community values are contingent on residents' specific engagements with them in particular contexts—which means that they are always unfolding and subject to shifts over time—so disagreement and conflict emerge under specific circumstances and in light of particular individual orientations. Although Quaysiders have put in place a number of ways of dealing with disagreement and conflict, both structured and ad hoc, there is no formula, and there are no guarantees that all disagreements that arise can be dealt with in ways that meet everyone's needs and desires. Nonetheless, however difficult they may be, and however much some residents may avoid them, Quayside Villagers accept disagreement and conflict as inevitable parts of community life. On the one hand, this recognition reflects the idea that emotions need to be expressed rather than suppressed (as per the hydraulic theory of emotion, mentioned above), which in turn underscores Quayside residents' orientation to the individual needs and well-being of its members. But there is also an awareness that disagreement and conflict have the potential to generate new ideas and innovative solutions, and, perhaps, once resolved, stronger bonds: *Differences make our community and our collective decisions stronger.* The exchange on the common kitchen dishwasher and the irrigation system referred to earlier illustrates this idea: two minds are better than one, whether putting heads together to solve a problem or butting heads in the face of competing views, as long as everyone recognizes, as Peter put it, "that we're in this together."

Community Engagement: As individuals and groups we value participation in the wider community to build a better world.

According to Linda, Quayside Village "educates other people just by existing." As noted in the introduction, urban cohousing communities are not oriented exclusively inward, and they do not fully reject the societies within which they are embedded. Rather, they interact with, build on, and work to improve existing social and environmental conditions. In being integrated with rather than segregated from society, they serve to model emergent alternative approaches to living that outsiders—including policy-makers, the media, and members of the public at large—can easily access.[30]

Quaysiders maintain close connections with several other cohousing communities, attend cohousing conferences, and host meetings about cohousing in their common room—all of which serve to support the global spread of intentional community models that I outlined in the introduction. In addition, reporters and researchers, who also disseminate information about cohousing, are always welcome. Quayside residents are also available to give tours to community members interested in cohousing, and there are several events each year that are open to the community at large, such as Art in the Garden, a two-day citywide celebration showcasing local musicians and visual artists as well as gardens.[31] Vera's midwifery practice, Kathy's daycare, and Heather's prenatal classes have similarly served to expand Quayside's presence in North Vancouver. Finally, activities to benefit the wider community, such as donation drives for Big Brothers/Big Sisters and fundraisers for various causes, are a regular feature of life at Quayside Village.

A number of Quayside residents are active in local politics. This extends beyond participating in demonstrations and political initiatives, around, for example, environmental causes or antiracism, to include active efforts to educate local politicians about cohousing so that they can better support it as a possible framework for living, campaigning on behalf of those seeking City Council or mayoral positions, holding fundraisers at Quayside Village for political candidates, and even, in one case, actually running for office.

Quaysiders also foster a number of smaller-scale, perhaps more intimate, connections with members of the wider community. Several times a year, for example, Carol hosts dinners at Quayside for staff and volunteers of the North Shore Women's Centre, a drop-in resource center that provides a range of programs, including basic computer training, single-mother support groups, and empowerment camps for girls. She has been involved in the Centre for years. And Mihaela, a dancer for over twenty years, offers both meditative and celebratory dances in the common room so that people can experience community in "a joyful, connecting, healing way." Many of the events she organizes are intended to mark the seasons of the year, thus "opening up the connections beyond the 'human community' to the earth and gardens." Residents involved in gardening also see it as a way of making connections: people walking down the street will often stop to ask questions or share tips on gardening, and chitchat can sometimes morph into discussions about cohousing when the passersby wonder "what kind of place this is," as Linda put it. Quayside Village even has two "honorary" members: Brian and Randy, who live an hour's drive away, regularly attend common meals and movie nights (sometimes preparing a meal for everyone to share) and are a fixture at Monday night bridge games.

Two additional small examples illustrate the flavor of what these connections look like. One year, Vera had a client whose finances and living arrangements made it difficult for her to do laundry, so Vera asked the community if that client could use the laundry at Quayside Village, for free, for a short period of time. The answer was a resounding and unanimous yes. On another occasion, one of Vera's clients wanted a home birth but lived outside the city, so the birth happened instead in Kathy's place. The couple and their child periodically visit to reminisce with Kathy and her daughter Elise.

Conclusions: The Good Life at Quayside Village

In a world in which increasingly busy lives mean that socializing is often planned rather than spontaneous, Quayside residents value the immediate and serendipitous nature of their community, as the following exchange between Donya and Connie illustrates:

Donya: I never phone someone and say, do you want to have coffee? Never, never, never. I'll book like *weeks* ahead with a friend to go have lunch, or you know whatever, of course it's possible, but then you know these people are right here!

Connie: But I think there are also those spontaneous contacts that happen that I think to a large extent fill the need that you might otherwise fill by calling a friend and going for coffee. Because I mean I'm out and watering my flowers out front, and somebody's out walking the dog or, like, I chat with you over the fence, or Marylee or somebody's out weeding or something, and there are those little short conversations that go on that make you feel connected, without having to sit down and actually have coffee and arrange that kind of thing. And I think there's also the knowledge that if you need somebody you can walk out your door [and] there is someone around.

Earlier in the same conversation, Donya, Carol, Kathy, and Elizabeth discussed spontaneous meetings in the laundry room, which in their view, given its small size, is conducive to a certain kind of intimacy:

Donya: From my experience of being in there and doing my thing and having someone come in, it's a chance to have a slightly more intimate conversation, 'cause it's a small area, there's probably only two of you in there, you're doing laundry. Maybe there's a bit of gossip that happens?
Catherine: Is there gossip that happens in this community?
Carol: Gossip goes with laundry.
Donya: Just a little.
Catherine: Gossip does go with laundry.
Elizabeth: It's all about doing your laundry in public.
Catherine: Yeah, that's right, airing your dirty sheets.
Kathy: I have conversations in there with people I don't have conversations with very much. I think of seeing Mark in there, or Don in there, or, and because you're there for a little bit, you gotta, you know, take something out and then put it in and, you know, find your soap powder, and you can have a little brief interaction. Or with Carol, Carol spends a lot of time in there 'cause she organizes the laundry room, so when she's in there, you know, she's in there for a while, and then she usually folds the common laundry and she organizes, so I usually, if I see Carol in there, I'll hang out with her.

Permeable boundaries between public and private space also increase possibilities for face-to-face encounters. Although not everyone can walk into anyone else's unit at will, a number of residents leave their doors wide open during the summer months, providing not only fresh air but also opportunities for residents to wave and say hello and possibly have a quick chat as they pass by. In addition, several residents leave their doors unlocked most of the time, whether they're at home or not. Kathy is well known for this, and other residents or visitors have been known to pop in to use her bathroom, as she recounted one day in a conversation about space:

> One time I came into my house and someone was in the bathroom. I yelled, "Elise [her daughter], are you home?" "No, it's Stephanie" [Elise's friend]. "Stephanie?" [I asked], and she goes "Yeah, I was walking home from the bus and I really had to use the bathroom."

The fluidity of boundaries between intimate public space and individual apartments mirrors, in some ways, the relationship between residents' personal lives and the business that gets done at community meetings. In the latter instance, space for personal emotional expression is structured in, while in the former it happens on an ad hoc basis. It is certainly not the case that residents are compelled to leave their units open and available to all at all times, just as they are not forced to reveal everything about their inner emotional lives during check-in at community meetings. On the contrary, in keeping with the ethos of Quayside Village, such things are voluntary, unevenly distributed through the community, and changeable over time. What this does mean is that the public and the private are not separated in any strict or rigid fashion. Each can spill over into the other. Happenstance, then, and the approach to space that provides possibilities for it to occur are foundational to community life, serving as antidotes to previously fragmented and sometimes isolating lives. As Marylee reflected:

> [Quayside Village] quite literally saved my life. Because there's no doubt in my mind I would've committed suicide, because when I went through a very long business reversal and was just panic-stricken for years, really, if I had come back to my [previous] wonderful place, alone at night—you know, I mean I've got lots of friends and all that, but alone at night, with all that I was going through, and for all those years, I mean I simply would have not been able to make it. I simply would've killed myself. And so here has literally saved my life.
>
> You can close the door, and be on your own, as long as and however you want, and there are people around. When I'm working here [in the lounge] late at night and somebody passes through on their way from work or back, for me psychologically that's fine, there's people around in that sense. And so it suits my personality. So here I am.

The comfort provided by proximity—just knowing that others are around, as Marylee put it, or that there's always someone around if you need help, as Connie noted—is also highly valued by parents. As Phil, in his early forties and a resident for three years at the time, expressed it:

> [Jazzy] leaves the house, and she'll come back hours later. Maybe she's up meeting with Carol, maybe she's up with Jade, maybe she's up at Natassja's, or maybe they're down here. Totally independent, but in an interesting way, this building's kinda like a shield from the real world. The way that it's just built kind of keeps [the children] locked in, and safe, right, from what's happening out there, and we trust that the people here will look out for them, right away. So we feel very safe.

Finally, two residents' summations of life at Quayside Village (the first of which opened chapter 1) say it all:

> When I kind of took stock a year or two after [moving in], I looked at things and I thought to myself, well if I had sat down and written down all the things I would like the situation to be in, and all the things I might like in a place to live, if I had sat down and written that, it wouldn't have been nearly as good as this is! And that's true, I mean, I absolutely, I'm getting goosebumps, I absolutely believe that. I could not dream this up. You know? So I'll be eternally grateful. (Elizabeth)

> The idea of what it means to live in this type of experience, I would say it's not because it works, which it does, it's because we celebrate life, we create life with each other, there's a larger force at work here. A sense of, you know, meals together, and you know, Peter's dog dies and the whole community rallies around him, and Marylee does her solo show at the Fringe Fest, and everybody goes, and Juhli had the concert at Ambleside, and we ran into you guys there, and half the building was down at her concert! And that to me is cohousing. You know, yeah, we get the garbage out together, and yeah, we get the recycling done together, but something bigger is happening here. (Phil)

All of the reasons for moving into and remaining in cohousing for the long run come out in these statements and exchanges. In keeping with the findings of scholars investigating the relationship between cohousing and well-being, as outlined in the introduction,[32] Marylee, Phil, and Elizabeth voice the sense of comfort and fulfillment that comes from connections with others—even in the face of the struggles, and occasional conflicts, that accompany living in a small, tight-knit community. For Quayside residents, cohousing is predictable in the sense of guaranteed proximity, safety, and opportunities for mutual enjoyment, care, and autonomy. But it is also open, creative, and serendipitous, as residents go about the daily business of living together. Maureen, a long-term cohouser, put it best: "It's an experiment. No matter when you come in [to cohousing] it's an experiment, like, 'how is this gonna go?'"

Notes

1. See *Life at Quayside Village*, "Donya and Jazzy Discuss Cohousing," 1:25, and Elise's speech at "The 20th Anniversary Party," 16:55.
2. See *Life at Quayside Village*, "Jazzy's Tour," 0:51.
3. See *Life at Quayside Village*, "Recycling," 7:25. See also *Exchange at Quayside Village*, "Haruko and Carl See the Recycling Room," 2:25.
4. See *Life at Quayside Village*, "Composting," 9:05. See also *Exchange at Quayside Village*, "Brian Teaches the Visitors about Composting," 2:45.
5. See *Life at Quayside Village*, "Gardening," 5:37. See also *Exchange at Quayside Village*, "Haruko Explores Quayside Village," 0:07.
6. See *Life at Quayside Village*, "Beautification," 6:39, and "Carol Enjoying Her Balcony," 2:00.
7. See *Life at Quayside Village*, "Community Meeting," 3:29.
8. Toward the end of the research for this book, Quayside Village began trialing a facilitation team of three (see chapter 4).
9. See *Exchange at Quayside Village*, "Carl and Haruko Attend a Thriving Meeting," 5:21.
10. See *Exchange at Quayside Village*, "Carl Learns about Meeting Cards," 6:17.
11. E.g., Durrett and McCamant, *Creating Cohousing*; Fromm, *Collaborative Communities*.
12. "Conflict and Connection," special issue, *Communities* 104 (1999); "Decision-Making in Community," special issue, *Communities* 109 (2000).
13. It's worth mentioning that not everyone in the community felt that the solution to the watering issue was the best approach.
14. Rachel Hewitt, "Do 'Animal Fluids Move by Hydraulick Laws'? The Politics of the Hydraulic Theory of Emotion," *Lancet Psychiatry* 5, no. 1 (2018); Robert C. Solomon, *True to Our Feelings: What Our Emotions Are Really Telling Us* (New York: Oxford University Press, 2007).
15. See *Life at Quayside Village*, "Jazzy's Newsletter," 1:14.
16. Sargisson, "Second-Wave Cohousing."
17. This is Donya's phrasing, which she expressed during the exchange visit to Kankanmori.
18. As already noted, *strata* refers to a legislated provincial framework for organizing and regulating shared properties, such as condominiums, townhouses, and, in this case, cohousing. Typically, Strata Councils are composed of a small subset of a building's residents. Quayside Village bylaws address the range of issues (e.g., building maintenance, meeting requirements, consensus building and conflict resolution, and rules about pets and smoking) typical of strata properties.
19. Once on a committee, residents are encouraged to remain for at least a year, in the interest of stability and continuity.
20. See *Exchange at Quayside Village*, "Kankanmori Visitors Attend a Community Meeting," 6:30.
21. See *Life at Quayside Village*, "Working in the Common Kitchen," 2:15, and "Common Meals," 4:22.
22. See *Life at Quayside Village*, "Birthday Celebrations," 14:26, "Vera's Birthday," 15:12, "Preparing for the 20th Anniversary Party," 16:00, and "The 20th An-

niversary Party," 16:10. See also *Exchange at Quayside Village*, "Anna's Birthday Party," 10:31.
◗ 23. See *Life at Quayside Village*, "Community Yoga," 9:59.
◗ 24. See *Life at Quayside Village*, "The Perfect Storm Singers," 12:53.
25. When I bought a GoPro and audio recorder for Quaysiders to use for the research project, some residents told me that I needed to think carefully about where to locate the equipment and how to handle sign-out procedures so that equipment didn't disappear. The decision was made to leave the equipment in a cabinet—clearly labeled and accompanied by a sign-out sheet—in Kathy's unit that anyone could access at any time, since her door is usually unlocked. The sign-out sheet was rarely used, and the camera did occasionally disappear, but never for long.
26. Given this practice, someone from Quayside Village once asked me if they could have access to the guest room at Kankanmori during a trip to Tokyo. They understood when I told them that this was unlikely, since Kankanmori's guest room is for the specific use of residents' friends and relatives, but the request indicates something of the informality of procedures at Quayside.
◗ 27. See *Life at Quayside Village*, "Vera's Midwifery Practice," 12:31.
◗ 28. See *Life at Quayside Village*, "Decision Making," 3:40.
29. Christian, *Creating a Life Together*; Durrett and McCamant, *Creating Cohousing*; Fromm, *Collaborative Communities*; McCamant and Durrett, *Cohousing*.
30. Meltzer, "Cohousing Sustainability"; Schehr, *Dynamic Utopia*.
◗ 31. See *Life at Quayside Village*, "Art in the Garden," 13:33.
32. Grinde et al., "Quality of Life"; PBS, "Cohousing Communities"; Sargisson, *Fool's Gold*; Williams, "Predicting an American Future."

3 KANKANMORI

Collective housing is about sharing a part of daily time or space with the other residents while freedoms as an individual are assured. There is a wide range of shared spaces and they are managed and run by residents.
— Kankanmori Collective House Inc.[1]

It's more fun to live with more people.
— Eleven-year-old Kankanmori resident

ONCE, AT THE END OF a long hot summer in Tokyo, and shortly before leaving to return to Canada, I came down with a bad cold. When I appeared in the common room one morning looking particularly poorly, Yoshie, who was working on preparing a common meal, immediately put her cooking aside to take me to the doctor; and later that afternoon, she and Emiko decided that I should move from my apartment to the guest room, where they thought I would be more comfortable, since it had air conditioning. News of my illness spread fast, and the next day Junko and Hideki prepared a special lunch for me and Yoshie. We ate the meal, which was presented *teishoku* style—soup, grilled fish, rice, and vegetables—in the common room. The following afternoon, while waiting to board my flight at Narita airport, I wrote a thank-you email to Hideki and Junko. When I arrived home, Hideki's reply, courteously written in English given my limited Japanese language skills, was waiting:

> About the lunch I cooked when you were sick. I'm feeling that was the collective-house-ness. For example, we live at the normal apartment. And you live at the next room of mine. I say "Are you OK?" You say "I feel sick." Maybe, I don't say, "Shall I cook the lunch for you?" If I say so, you will say "No, no. I'm OK. Thank you." In the collective-house, we are closer than "neighbors."

Yoshie's, Junko's, and Hideki's responses to my illness were not simply a reflection of my status as an outside visitor: over the course of my stays at Kankanmori I regularly observed similar expressions of mutual concern and support among residents. When I first met Junko several years before the special lunch and about six months after she had joined Kankanmori with her husband and infant daughter, she told me that it wasn't until she had actually moved in that she came to understand just how close relationships in collective housing could be. This closeness was particularly evident to her during common meals, when residents routinely looked after others' children, bringing them food, feeding them, and playing with them.[12] She explained to me that residents of Kankanmori were "not friends, and not family, but something different, something new." The orientation of Kankanmori members to each other's needs, then, was not based on ties of kinship, nor did it reflect the extension of a kinship idiom to encompass the entire community. Instead, it reflected the deliberate, intentional development of a way of life that would accommodate the dispersal of extended families characteristic of Japan's contemporary economic and social landscape while allowing, at the same time, for individual expression and independence. As such, Kankanmori represents an innovative approach to living that works to realize complementary ideologies of mutuality, conviviality, and autonomy in a changed—and ever-changing—environment.

How Values Unfold: A Conversation between Philosophy and Practice

As at Quayside Village, Kankanmori's creators worked closely together to articulate a set of values—a "charter," as Emiko called it—to guide formal organizational structures and everyday life alike. This charter consists of three core intentions, accompanied by a set of aspirational organizing principles.

Core intentions:
- To share space and time with others
- To have independent and private space as well as communal space
- To spend time together in common activities

Organizing principles:
- Everyone needs to cherish their own independent life as well as sharing
- Everyone from single people to large families can enjoy Kankanmori
- Living at Kankanmori needs to be both practical and ecological
- Life needs to be open to the outside world
- There needs to be a focus on communication and diversity: we need to grow and learn from each other

Several additional statements of philosophy, noted on Kankanmori's web page,[3] complement and extend this charter; for instance:

- Our principles are self-management and self-operation
- Everyone is equal no matter how old one is or what kind of career one has
- We believe our lives are enriched by developing relationships with our neighbors
- The basis of collective housing is common meals

In chapter 2, I described how, at Quayside Village, some values, such as environmental stewardship, lend themselves to practical planning and implementation, while others, such as diversity of family form, do not often make it onto meeting agendas but instead are expressed informally. Values, in other words, circulate among community members along two tracks, the one official and the other informal—"in the air," as it were. Sometimes these tracks overlap, and sometimes, when the ideals in question do not lend themselves to concrete intervention, they do not. While values are also expressed among Kankanmori residents in both formal and informal ways, Kankanmori's members nevertheless work together to translate *all* of their principles into concrete practices.

Multigenerationalism, a value Kankanmori shares with Quayside Village, provides a case in point. Multigenerationalism is absolutely central to Kankanmori's vision of the good life: as Junko's observations of how residents attend to children at common meals indicates, Kankanmori's children are both a group responsibility and a collective joy. Kankanmori's older and single residents enjoy the energy that young children bring, while parents value the safe play spaces and the companionship—of adults as well as of other children—provided by the community. It is extremely rare for children to be excluded from any activity, including official meetings, and there are also events designed specifically for them, such as the "children's meeting" and arts and crafts activities.[4] Parents are, in the last instance, responsible for their own offspring, but others pitch in on a regular basis: if a child is crying, most adults in the vicinity will turn to see if they can do something to help; and similarly, when a child is acting up, any adult can intervene to tell the child to calm down and behave. The principle of multigenerationalism—the idea that *everyone from single people to large families can enjoy Kankanmori*—is so important to Kankanmori residents that at one point, when they experienced what they considered a "shortage" of children after some residents had to move out for their jobs or to look after elderly parents, they decided to lower the rental rate for households with children. The difference was nominal (five thousand yen/month; about fifty dollars), but it sent the signal that Kankanmori does not just allow children but actively seeks them out. The value of multigenerationalism includes other age groups as well: in 2017, Kankanmori residents felt that they had too few residents in their twenties, and so the five-thousand-yen monthly discount was extended to potential residents in that demographic as well. Multigenerationalism, then, is not just an ideal but a practice.

In contrast to Quayside Village, then, Kankanmori's age composition, like its other aspirational values, *does* lend itself to practical planning and intervention. The higher rates of turnover resulting from its rental-based organization no doubt increase opportunities for this kind of social engineering; however, as I hope to make clear throughout this chapter, Kankanmori's practices also reflect an approach to planning that is in general more deliberate and systematic than that of Quayside Village. In what follows, I explore the thoroughgoing ways in which Kankanmori's values are taken up in its organizational structures and translated into everyday life. I take as my starting point the idea that *everyone is equal no matter how old one is or what kind of career one has*, which, coupled with the principles of *self-management and self-operation*, lies at the foundation of the good life at Kankanmori.

"Everyone Is Equal"

Everyone is equal means that all residents have an equal right to have independent space and time, to be who they are (the value of diversity), and to enjoy life at Kankanmori. Other than the financial background check by the real estate company to ensure that prospective residents can meet their rental obligations, there are no community rules restricting the professional, philosophical, spiritual, geographic, or political orientations or backgrounds of those who join the Kankanmori community.

Everyone is equal also means that there should be an equitable division of the labor involved in maintaining community life. Here, equality is about *fairness*, and fairness translates into *sameness*, into each resident contributing in equal measure. Accordingly, each adult is required to sit on two committees, participate in preparing one common meal per month, contribute to bimonthly cleaning, and, in the summer months, take six turns watering the vegetable garden. This structure for the distribution of tasks is designed to ensure that no one is doing either too much or too little, thereby precluding the development of the resentments that, it is assumed, would accompany unequal workloads. The ideology of *equality* → *fairness* → *sameness* is also woven through Kankanmori's approaches to rules regarding finances and decision-making. Overall, it produces a set of procedures that in many ways mirrors the management style of Japanese neighborhood associations (*jichikai*), semicompulsory organizations that oversee everything from local festivals to nighttime rounds monitoring neighborhood safety.[5] This framework is familiar to residents, and many consider it essential to the production and maintenance of collective well-being.

Committees

Kankanmori has twenty-four committees, divided into nineteen groups and five subgroups (see table 3.1). The sheer number and specification of mutually exclusive territories of activity reflects a comprehensive and carefully considered detailing of the full range of areas that need to be tended to in order to produce a smooth-running community. Although each adult is required to sit on two of the nineteen main committees, the realities of everyday life nevertheless engender a "conversation" between the fixedness of committee obligations and the flexibility required to accommodate both individual residents' proclivities and their unique and changing life circumstances. The former is addressed by members' freedom to select which committees to join. Although incoming residents may be invited to join a committee that is experiencing a shortage of members, residents nevertheless choose, before each year's annual general meeting (AGM), which committees they would like to sit on for the following year. The sheer number of possibilities means that they are likely to find at least one committee that piques their interest, and the ability to change committees over the years provides opportunities to experience different forms of engagement in community maintenance over time. As Shoko, a relatively new resident in her fifties when she made this statement, explained:

> There are [twenty-four] committees, which I see as divided between two types. The first type people want to do because of interest or professional experience or whatever. Gardening is one of these. But committees like Cleaning or Laundry or Guest Room, they're different. I'm not interested in cleaning actually. So there are two basic types of committee: genuine "tasks" and others that are more like group hobbies. My approach is to join one committee that interests me and another that's more like, "Fine, Cleaning it is." That's how I think about it. I was interested in Gardening too, but doing PR and Gardening would be a bit "hobby-hobby." I mean, I don't think of PR as a hobby, but I held off because it didn't feel quite right.

What comes across in Shoko's statement is a deliberate effort to balance her personal interests with the recognition that there are some tasks that simply need to be done—that is, with a sense of obligation to the community and a commitment to fairness. This inclination to balance personal proclivities with community interest was echoed by Etsuko, also in her fifties, and at the time a resident for two years:

TABLE 3.1. Kankanmori committees and subgroups. Table courtesy of Kankanmori Collective House, Inc.

No.	Group	Description of Duties
1	Members	Managing email lists of Kankanmori's residents as well as its supporting members, and accepting new supporting members
2	Orientation	Holding open houses, orientations, and informational sessions for prospective residents as well as interested researchers and developers, and the promotion of such events
3	Public Relations	Media relations, DVD sales
4	Research Relations	Helping researchers study on Kankanmori
5	Neighborhood Association	Participating in and assisting with meetings of the neighborhood association
6	Handbook	Amending the handbook, providing information to new residents
7	Common Meal	Managing common meals, keeping the kitchen supplied, and taking care of kitchen equipment
8	Cleaning	Allocating cleaning spots, managing supplies
9	IT	Setting up the IT environment
10	Mori-ken Tickets	Selling Mori-ken tickets, the residential currency
11	Laundry	Managing and cleaning appliances in the Laundry Room and collecting Mori-ken tickets
12	Gardening	Taking care of vegetables in the garden and plants on the Common Terrace
13	Guest Room	Managing and running the Guest Room
14	Energy/Ecology/Recycling	Taking care of recycling errands, making reports on recycling, sorting out collected recyclables
15	Event	Organizing annual parties, welcome and farewell parties, and seasonal events
16	Fire Prevention Management	Delegating the responsibility for locking up common areas with residents according to a schedule, accompanying the fire department on fire drills and checking smoke alarms
17	Document	Logging event data, blogging, and creating the residential newsletter *Morinokaze Dayori*
18	Equipment/Interior	Managing equipment and interior design in the communal spaces
19	Treasurer	Managing the treasury of Kankanmori
No.	Subgroup	Description of Duties
20	Little 'uns Parent	Keeping in touch through a mailing list
21	Wood Shop	Managing the Wood Shop
22	Library	Managing communal books on the second and third floors
23	Group Purchase	Managing group purchases at the Co-op
24	Pet	Setting rules for pets

Last year I did Guest Room and Orientation, and when it was time to decide on this year's committees in June, I applied for PR. Because PR is what I do for a living. But I got some advice then from someone who's since left: you can't do PR unless you really know the place. You also have to respond to inquiries in a fairly timely fashion no matter when they arrive, and I thought that might be a problem. I was also told that joining a committee with as many members as possible lets new arrivals make connections with more people. So I went for Orientation and Guest Room. Guest Room only had two members, but my room is very close by, and it didn't seem too challenging. This year I stayed in Orientation. My job keeps me busy, so I decided a committee with more members might be better.

In addition to awarding residents the freedom to choose which committees to sit on, Kankanmori's structure of participation also has built-in exceptions: pregnant women and mothers with newborns are given a one-year maternity leave, new residents have a month or two to situate themselves and contemplate which committees they might be most interested in joining, and residents with a medical certificate are excused from any duties for the duration of their illness. (These exceptions apply to the bimonthly cleaning and summer garden watering as well; see below.) There is, in addition, a certain amount of situational fluidity. During a discussion group one day, for instance, Carl, who had been living at Kankanmori with his wife and their two daughters for over seven years, voiced the concern that some residents might have left Kankanmori because they could not meet its committee obligations due to personal circumstances that they were not comfortable sharing with the community at large (see section on "Public/Private" below). Rather than making their personal hardships public and asking for relief from committee obligations, he conjectured, they chose to simply move elsewhere. Shoko responded with a set of reflections on the nature of life and the purpose of living in community:

> Can I say something? Not knowing what lies in store is just a fact of life. It's the same for everyone, in equal measure, whether they live in Kankanmori or not. You might have an accident, or get sick. Something could happen to me tomorrow. It makes me so sad that anyone would think "I have to leave Kankanmori now." Helping each other at times like that is exactly what I think a community is for. It doesn't bother me at all if someone can't take on certain duties for a while. Even if it's just because they're busy at work, because, in a sense, that's the same thing. My own work is busy, and not being able to be as involved as I'd like makes me want to quit my job sometimes.

Recognition that "not knowing what lies in store is just a fact of life" could, then, open up some room to maneuver.

Nevertheless, despite the freedom to select committees, the structured exceptions to the obligation to participate, and the informal recognition of the exigencies of life, flexibility remains constrained by the philosophical connection between fairness and sameness. When I asked if there was ever a problem with people refusing to contribute, Emiko, a long-term resident highly active in Kankanmori life, said that "that's never become a problem, even if someone has felt that way." The requirements are clear, so not participating (outside of formal exceptions) is not really possible, either conceptually or in practice. What *is* possible, according to Yoshie, is selectively choosing to sit on less active committees:

> There are some committees that don't take up any time, that you only have to be involved with twice a year or so. And there are some people who only do committees like that and never join ones where you have to discuss things in a group and work together, like Common Meals or Orientation. We feel that too, but you can't just decide, "This committee is busy so it's valuable, this one is only active twice a year so it has no value." It's left up to the people involved. But you do notice that some people always choose that kind of committee and never join one where you work as a group. We feel that too, but we don't say it aloud.

Even the two-committee rule, then, does not guarantee the fair distribution of work: certain committees undertake more tasks than others, and some residents might strategically choose to join committees that they know will take up less of their time and energy, leading to resentments ("we feel that too"), however unstated they may remain ("we don't say it aloud"). *Fairness = sameness*, then, can lead to ever more minute calibrations regarding the division of labor.

Resentments, however, expressed or not, can be contextualized, as Junko, living at Kankanmori for over three years at the time, explained:

> It's okay to just do what you can, whether you're good at it or not, because everyone's in a committee, and the minimum workload for each committee is set. You might be busy, not busy, have health problems, but in the end everyone wants you to do your part. If you don't, they'll remind you, and if you just can't they'll bring someone else in to help, but the expectation is that you will do committee work. That's possible for some people, impossible for others, and the workload for each committee isn't equal to begin with so there's a degree of unfairness. Sometimes you think, "I'm working so hard and they aren't doing anything," but that doesn't last forever. You're working on a committee you chose, you're doing what you can, and I think if you carried that feeling of unfairness with you, you couldn't live here. It does come to you, but in a sort of resigned way. Not a negative type of resignation, just

sort of putting it aside, like, "Oh, well, one day." That's just me, but I think a lot of us are like that.

That everyone does the best they can, contributing some kind of minimum, thus maintains a general sense of equality, even if workloads are not precisely the same. And just knowing that you are "doing what you can" on a committee that you chose is what is most important. Again, Junko, at an afternoon tea discussing the differences between Kankanmori and Quayside Village:

> Compared to what we heard about QV just now, Kankanmori's committees have more detailed rules, and there are other specific obligations, like common meal duty once a month, cleanup every two months, locking up. But I wonder if that isn't what preserves the sense of fairness. It seemed to me that the greater freedom at QV might also make the things that are unfair worse. The question is whether you do think of it as unfair—and if you mind that unfairness. Or whether there's something that regulates that.

What regulates perceptions of unfairness at Quayside Village, as I described in chapter 2, is a loose sense of contribution that includes but is not limited to committee participation, along with a long-term view, facilitated by an owner-based organization, in which the waxing and waning of participation is seen to even out over time. At Kankanmori, in contrast, fairness is regulated via the rules about participation that apply equally to all, with exceptions specified in advance and structured into the system, along with, as Junko notes, pressure from one's committee comembers: "Everyone wants you to do your part—if you don't, they'll remind you." These twinned approaches are not foolproof, as Yoshie's comments on strategic decisions about which committees to join based on workload indicate, but they go a long way, in this context, to preserving "the sense of fairness" to which Junko refers.

Still, exceptions, especially those related to illness—and, increasingly, to aging—present a problem. As Yoshie pointed out:

> The other thing is that we're starting to see cases at Kankanmori where people are getting older and unable to work. If it's just one person, that's okay, but if we have three or four older people who can't do anything, I'm not sure if this community can survive. We have to start thinking about this. The time has come.

Efforts to recruit members in their twenties, referred to earlier, thus make sense. On the other hand, as Shoko hints below, retirees may have more time to devote to community maintenance; and, in any case, hopefully in the end things will balance out:

Ultimately, with this large a group living together, some people will be sick sometimes, [and] some will be busy. On the other hand, sometimes people will have more of their own time they can use for the community. It depends on life stage and timing. There are a lot of facets, so every case is different. And community is about how you absorb all these different things and find a balance. The "weak ties" in a community. People with all sorts of things going on gather together and find a balance between what each person can and can't do. So, rather than looking at it as a problem, I think it's better to ask how to deal with it, facet by facet. Ideally, you'll be able to cover everything properly.

I have organized the discussion above in a deliberately meandering way, in order to capture Kankanmori residents' vacillation between the desire for absolute uniformity in the distribution of tasks, on the one hand, and recognition that the vicissitudes of life require some form of accommodation, on the other. This back-and-forthness is not equally weighted, however: there are exceptions to the rules, both formal and informal, that serve to insert flexibility into the system, but in the last instance it is the structure of obligatory contributions, reflecting a primary orientation to equality as sameness, that dominates. I explore residents' engagements with this philosophy more generally below, but first I outline three additional structures of equality at Kankanmori.

General Cleaning and Gardening

Although a professional cleaner comes in once a week to clean all the common floors, there are other parts of Kankanmori that require regular cleaning, such as the windows in common areas, the office, the common room patio, and so on. Accordingly, the Cleaning Committee assigns tasks on a bimonthly basis to each adult resident. At the beginning of each two-month period, a form listing the jobs by unit number is pinned to the community bulletin board, on which residents note the date when they have completed their assignments. The tasks tend to be small in order to avoid excessive burden (for instance, I was once assigned two glass doors to clean). In addition, during the summer months, the vegetable and flower gardens require regular tending. A community work party organizes and plants flower gardens,[16] while members of the Gardening Committee take responsibility for planting and weeding the vegetable garden.[17] The job of watering the vegetable garden, however, is shared by everyone in the community. At the beginning of the summer a large calendar is taped to the wall next to the common room entrance, and residents select six dates to do the watering. Members of the Gardening Committee then take turns checking, after 9:00 A.M. each day, that the watering has been done. If it looks as if the garden has not been watered, the team member does the watering themselves, and a general reminder to remember watering days is sent out to everyone. Even if it is well known who has forgotten to do their watering, care is taken to avoid singling anyone out. The fruits of everyone's labor are then incorporated into common meals or placed in bowls in the common room for residents to take for their personal use.

Financial Fairness: Mori-ken

In addition to the equal allocation of tasks, fairness is also accomplished by means of an equitable distribution of costs, ensuring that everyone pays their share—again, no more and no less. This approach reflects Kankanmori's philosophy of independence as well as its ideology of equality; as Emiko explained to me during my first visit to Kankanmori, residents do not share material goods, and so everyone is "totally independent" in that sense. Thus, just as each resident is responsible for their own rent and utilities, so they are responsible for their own expenses associated with doing laundry and eating common meals.

In order to maintain both equality and independence, Kankanmori has devised its own currency—*mori-ken*—which is used for laundry, common meals, and the guest room. *Mori-ken* come in denominations of one hundred, four hundred, and five hundred yen. Members of the *Mori-ken* Committee will often set up shop in the common room after common meals so that people can easily purchase them. Residents fill out and sign a form on which they indicate how many *mori-ken* they wish to purchase and in what denominations; money and *mori-ken* exchange hands, and a record of all sales is kept. When residents use their *mori-ken*, they write their name, date, and apartment number on the back and place the currency either in the box provided (in the case of common meals) or in the slot for their unit in the laundry room. In the case of the guest room, *mori-ken* are handed over to one of the Guest Room Committee members, along with the relevant form.

In addition to using *mori-ken* for common meals, laundry, and the guest room, residents pay a community membership fee of between seven and eleven thousand yen, depending on the number of adults in the household, to cover common electricity and other basic maintenance costs. Residents also pay a monthly fee for access to the common room Wi-Fi.

Finally, it is worth noting that, in contrast to this individualization of expenses, Kankanmori residents serve as guarantors for each other's rent. This represents a form of pooled risk: if someone was ever unable to pay their rent, the remaining households would split the cost among themselves. Although this has never happened, it does mark dedication to the idea of community while at the same time encouraging individuals to meet their financial obligations so as not to burden others.

Meetings and Decision-Making

In addition to the AGM in June, community meetings are held monthly, with the exception of August.[18] Since meetings are generally well attended, there has never been a need to establish a quorum requirement. Agendas are written onto a specially designed form, a hard copy of which is distributed to each attendee. Listed next to each agenda item is the name of the person who will be speaking to the topic and how much time they have been allotted (usually between one and ten minutes). Tables are arranged in a square around the perimeter of the common room, with the person chairing the meeting and the minute taker sitting at one end. The roles of chair and minute taker rotate among residents.

In some ways community meetings are quite formal and businesslike, with a firm focus on what needs to happen to keep the community running smoothly. The agenda is followed carefully, and there is no official space for the display of strong personal emotion or conflict. Although residents can occasionally get upset at meetings, this is a rare occurrence, and I never witnessed overt conflict. Rather, I was told, if a conflict about a committee issue could not be resolved at the meeting, the committee in question would host a workshop to discuss the issue further and then bring the topic back to the community during a subsequent monthly meeting. The committee could present the community with either a united opinion on the issue or two or three options that could then be discussed by everyone. The point was for committee members to take the issue as far as they could in their meetings/workshops and to avoid lengthy community meetings.

Community meetings are far from rigid, however. Residents sometimes raise their hands to be called on by the chair, but on other occasions they simply interject when there is a pause in the discussion. Jokes are common. And despite the formal arrangement of space, there is a looseness about comings and goings: children wander in and out freely, and adults come and go as they wish, in order to get sweaters, something to drink, or, more often, attend to their daughters and sons. In 2016, Kankanmori hired a babysitter for their AGM for the first time, and some of the mothers told me that they appreciated being able to focus on the meeting without interruption.

Kankanmori's philosophy of equality is inscribed in its decision-making processes. There is no formal voting system at Kankanmori; instead, discussions will continue until everyone is in agreement. In explaining to me how this works, Emiko recounted the story of a woman who proposed that the Common Meal Committee purchase a cheaper rice for common meals. Kankanmori had been purchasing a slightly more expensive rice from a co-op, the Seikatsu Club Seikyo, for some years, since it is cultivated with fewer agricultural chemicals than the rice available in grocery stores. Instead of taking a vote, discussions continued until the woman was convinced that using the more expensive co-op rice was worth it. On another occasion, when participating in a meeting during which the menu for the yearly anniversary party was being discussed, I found myself feeling puzzled by how long the meeting was taking (almost two hours!) until I realized that the menu would not be finalized until everyone was happy with it.

If agreement on a particular proposal cannot be reached, it will either be rejected or put aside to be revisited at a later date. As noted above, discussions of committee issues are supposed to occur during the committee meetings held prior to monthly community meetings. Haruko explained: "If we start discussing in a monthly meeting, it's going to take up too much time, so let's first talk within the group or the committee, or have a series of workshops beforehand, and then bring it to the table, and then we can shorten the time." During these discussions or workshops—and sometimes there will be multiple such events in preparation for a monthly community meeting—"everybody has to be heard," Carl noted; "everyone has to agree in these workshops more or less and then we have an official acclamation at the end." The approach to decision-making in these meetings is the same as that practiced in the monthly community meetings: everybody has a voice, and discussions continue until a consensus is reached.

Kankanmori's approach to decision-making thus clearly reflects its *everybody is equal* philosophy. Within the parameters of this philosophy, whatever processes of deliberation are followed have to ensure that everyone can voice their opinion. Any process that does not allow for all voices to be heard will produce unevenness. These deliberations, however, do not have the same valence as at Quayside Village: there is no blue card to express a feeling of being excluded or claim that proper process is not being followed, or a red card to veto something on the grounds that it violates community values. Although there may be strong emotions behind it, what is expressed in deliberations at Kankanmori remains focused on practical, substantive considerations—about what to plant, when and where to plant it, or about guest room procedures, common meal accounting, and so on. Residents of course recognize that the practice of deliberating until everyone has been heard and the group has come to a shared agreement does not necessarily mean that no one will feel pressured, or that some residents do not have greater power to sway things in a particular direction. But it does manifest a strongly held aspiration to create a community of peers.

How Equality and Procedure Grow Community

Given Kankanmori's fine-tuned calibrations and rigid set of committee obligations, it comes as no surprise that residents sometimes feel overburdened. Once, for instance, when I told someone that I thought their Christmas party was fabulous—amazing decorations, food, musical performances, and even an appearance by Santa—their response was, "Yes, and that's why we're all so tired!" Such grumblings about too many duties and time-consuming processes, however, were usually accompanied by recognition of the benefits of working together: not only a well-functioning community but also strong connections with others—the foundation of well-being. During a discussion group one day, for instance, Mariko, an academic in her thirties who originally came to Kankanmori for a tour with some of her students, explained that it was only after she had moved in, five years previously, that she was able to experience how community is built:

> What I experienced was—I understood for myself how this lifestyle grows a community. Without thinking about it, as you serve on committees and play your part in daily life, bonds gradually form with others. That's how the system, or way of life works. I mean, I knew that before, but I felt it for myself, if you like.

Furthermore, as Shoko put it, something originally considered a burden can be recast as a positive challenge:

> Challenges aren't always bad. Trying something new is always a kind of challenge, but everyone looks at it differently. Is it an unpleasant obligation, or part of living a rich and colorful life? It's all in how you look at it. I'm basically the sort of person who tries to take things positively.

On another occasion, Haruko told me that while the monthly preparation of a common meal can take the better part of a day, it means that on ten or more occasions a month residents can come home from a long day at work and not have to cook, encountering instead a delicious common meal for a mere four or five hundred yen. Chores, she added, echoing Mariko's comments, are a good way to get to know your neighbors.

Others also pointed to the community-building aspects of order and procedure. Aya, who had moved into Kankanmori only a few months before she joined one of the project's discussion groups, had lived in collective housing before. When she needed to move to be closer to her workplace, she searched for another collective housing community, not only because such communities offer particular kinds of facilities (such as large common kitchens) but also because they provide precisely the kind of organization and order that she felt was at the very foundation of community:

> So I looked at all kinds of places, and at a collective house—it's the same here—it's not just the facilities aspect. They're also rather systematic about how they run the common meals you share and so on. There are regular meetings and committees to share work—it's all fully decided, and it made me think that I could settle down here, so I chose the option that offered not simply shared facilities but also a community.

In Aya's view, it was precisely the systematic and regularized aspects of Kankanmori's organization that make it a community. Ruriko, a young architecture student working in a lab associated with the late Ikuko Koyabe, similarly valued order:

> Sharehouses are full of people about my age who get together to live like hippies. That was really unappealing. But here, there are children and families—I thought it looked orderly. Thinking about it in the long term, it sounded appealing.

If the initial planning of a collective housing community—the multiple workshops during which founding members systematically attend to the details of organizing everything from the parameters of the built environment to what kind of miso to use at common meals—provides the social connections that serve to create community, the routines involved in collaborating to fulfill common tasks solidify the connections that serve to maintain it. As noted on their website, Kankanmori members *believe our lives are enriched by developing relations with our neighbors*. Working together on committees and to prepare common meals is precisely how such relationships develop. It is also how residents can *grow and learn from each other*—another key organizing principle of the community. *Everyone is equal*, then, and its culturally specific translation into sameness—into each resident contributing in equal measure—is the very bedrock of community, creating, in turn, the social ties that enliven everyday life and that produce well-being for the community as a whole as well as for each of its members.

"To Have Independent and Private Space as well as Communal Space"

Public/Private: "Everyone Needs to Cherish Their Own Independent Life as well as Sharing"

In contrast to Quayside Village, there are clear boundaries between the public and the private at Kankanmori. Yumiko, one of the older and more long-term residents, explained to me that people who live in collective housing need to be "strong individualists and know what [they're] doing," in order to be "a part of the community but not invaded by it." Others, referring to the challenges of balancing their private lives with their participation in community affairs, said that they were grateful to have their own private apartments to retreat to when needed.

During my first visit to Kankanmori, I conducted a series of life-history interviews. The vast majority of these took place in the common room. Emiko, who instead invited me to her apartment for our conversation, took the opportunity to explain to me that residents usually visited with each other in common spaces rather than in their apartments, a pattern that Yoshie, Haruko, and Carl also mentioned in their interviews. Emiko gave as her example her relationship with Yoshie: although they had both lived at Kankanmori for years and were close friends, they had never been inside each other's apartments. A few years later, I was staying at Kankanmori when Naoko, a Kankanmori resident for four years, was preparing to move to Kyushu. She invited a number of us up to her apartment to see if anyone would like any of the things she was not taking with her. None of the people I went with had seen the inside of Naoko's place before. There were exceptions, of course—Yumiko was completely comfortable with having visitors in her place—but the general pattern is that apartments are considered private. This boundary applies to children as well, despite their occasional violation of it. Hideki, for instance, recounted an occasion shortly after he and his family moved in when some of the older children arrived at his place and simply let themselves in. They also left on their own, without being told; but, still, he found this surprising and confusing, since it was not what he had expected.

During a discussion over afternoon tea focused on how people balance their lives in the community with their jobs, extended family relationships, and so on, referred to above, it became clear that privacy was about more than space. Mariko revealed that she had recently developed an allergy that prevented her from preparing common meals or serving on the Common Meal Committee. "To be honest," she said, "I'm wondering if it might be better just to leave if I can't serve. It's a family discussion, with my partner. It'll depend on my condition, but that is something I think about." Carl responded to Mariko's revelation by talking about his own struggles with depression. He wondered if, given the tendency of people to keep personal issues to themselves, Kankanmori might have lost some members that it didn't need to lose, and he made a plea for more sharing and mutual care and support. Shoko made a similar point later in the discussion:

> I've only been here five months, but I feel like we could be more open to deeper conversations. It's true that we aren't living together as, you know, a tight-knit group of friends. It's more of a loose organization or solidarity, so

there may be some private things that we don't reveal to that extent. Yoshie mentioned this too, but I'm in charge of Public Relations, and I think that, if we want to be more public about this system called a collective house and convey its appeal to people, it would be better to write stories or articles about the people who live here, describe our hobbies, show our faces, and post it all to Facebook. Start from the hobbies. I started writing one for myself, since it was my idea, and Yoshie's feedback was, "Well, we've never really talked about our private lives this much before." I was like, "Huh? You lived together but didn't even talk about your hobbies?" For a moment I wondered if perhaps I was breaking some taboo.[9]

Yoshie's response to Shoko was revealing:

She only has just over a year (of time here).[10] She's an active person. Most of what she writes I already know, like what sort of person Keiichi is. She's surprised, but I already know. What sort of music Junko likes—I know that from Facebook, but in just one year she's learned the things it took me ten years to find out.

On another occasion, Hiromi (in her forties and a resident for seven years at the time), Yoshie, and Carl were discussing how some romantic relationships had formed at Kankanmori without anyone being aware. There was some speculation about where one romance in particular might have blossomed:

YOSHIE: So Carl said, maybe it was the laundry room, but in fact it was when they were cooking the common meal and so on that the man made the first move. We didn't know anything about it. A year later, they said "We're getting married."
CARL: Keep it secret. They went underground.
HIROMI: Suddenly there was a notice saying that the two of them were leaving.

Shoko provided a cultural explanation for this kind of occurrence:

The cultural differences are huge between Japan and Canada. I lived in the United States for about nine years, and I've been in Japan too, and comparing the two cultures, people interact in completely different ways. So even living in a shared community means different interactions in different countries. What surprised me when I came here was hearing that people don't talk about their private lives much. I was like, "Huh? Then what does everyone talk about at common meals?" That's basically how Japan is, but I was surprised that people who would specifically choose to live in a collective house still wouldn't talk about their private lives. I knew that Japanese people were like that, but I thought that people who chose to come here might interact more openly. I think it was when I'd just come here that I invited everyone to come see my room. Apparently that was a very unusual thing to do. People were shocked.

Privacy, then, is marked not just by space but also by the limits of what people reveal of themselves to others. I received two responses to my questions about this. The first, and most common, was that people avoid sharing their troubles or asking for help for fear of imposing on others. This could extend to the kinds of things that Shoko was referring to, such as the sharing of hobbies: people did not want to draw attention to themselves or impose their views about what was interesting or not. As the above excerpt indicates, Shoko attributed this to culture: Japanese people, she said, tend in general to share less about their private lives. A second response was that keeping one's opinions to oneself—especially strong political opinions, regarding, for instance, nuclear power, a controversial topic post-Fukushima—allows residents to live together peacefully, since it precludes heated debate and conflict. Such practices also fit with the cultural tendencies outlined by Shoko, perhaps underscoring even further a desire for a harmony that is produced by avoiding imposing one's opinions on others. Scholars of Japanese culture, who underscore the high social value placed on both modesty and the avoidance of conflict, would agree with Shoko's assessment.[11]

Despite the problems associated with fixed demarcations between the public and private aspects of residents' lives—diminished community support potentially leading to a loss of members, as Carl pointed out—the desire to avoid burdening others, coupled with the aversion to open conflict, help to protect individual privacy and independence, both of which are highly valued by Kankanmori residents. Natsuko underscores this priority in her personal narrative in chapter 1, in which she expresses surprise and concern at how quickly information about her son's injury and her husband's new job circulated throughout the community. While her story clearly indicates that the boundaries between public and private information are not as rigid as Carl and Shoko may claim, it does point to the primacy of place that privacy and independence have in residents' imaginations.

Common Space/Common Property

The common room is the center of collective life at Kankanmori. The adjacent hallway, where official announcements and forms are posted, is also a key informal gathering place, as residents stop to check out the latest happenings and to chat; but the common room is the hub where all aspects of collective life, both formal and informal, meet in one way or another.

The common room at Kankanmori is used much more frequently than the common room at Quayside Village. Although it is usually empty in the morning after people have left for work or school, later in the day it is more often than not occupied. As I noted in chapter 1, founding members' decision to design the built environment to include ample shared space reflected a desire to encourage residents to extend their personal space beyond the confines of their individual apartments. In other words, intimate public space was seen as a mechanism for building and maintaining community. This mechanism has by and large been successful. On any given afternoon, the common room will be occupied by residents reading the newspaper or working on their computers, small groups gathered for a committee meeting or an impromptu afternoon tea, and children playing or doing homework. In the evening, a mother and daughter might bake cookies together while others just sit around and chat, adults play with children, children run in and out while playing with each other, and so on. Even when doing things on their own, then, Kankanmori residents are doing them *together*, in the company of others. Residents also often use the common room to host friends or relatives for dinner, since it provides plenty of space to spread out; also, impromptu parties of latecomers from work—often a weekly occurrence—can easily last until 1:00 or 2:00 in the morning.

Common property, such as dishes, pots and pans, and major kitchen equipment, remains in the common room. Although residents occasionally take dishes to their apartments when they arrive home late for a common meal or when they want to eat the common meal in the privacy of their own apartment, they always return them promptly.[12] If someone wants to make use of some of the larger cooking equipment, they will do so on site, and common cleaning equipment also remains on site. In marked contrast to Quayside Village, disappearing common property has rarely been a problem at Kankanmori.

There is a clear set of procedures for use of the guest room, which is reserved for friends and relatives of residents, at a cost of twelve hundred yen per night. Use of the guest room is limited to one week; if a resident would like to host someone for longer, the request is brought to a community meeting for approval. The sign-up sheet for the guest room is posted on the common bulletin board. There is, in addition, another chart posted on the closet door in the guest room, on which the host writes their name and the dates of occupancy and checks a number of boxes indicating which sheets and blankets have been used. After the guests have left, the host notes when the room and downstairs bathroom have been cleaned, when the linen has been washed and put back in place, and when the *mori-ken* have been paid; the latter are stapled to another form pinned to the bulletin board downstairs for someone from the Guest Room Committee to collect and process. Once, before the chart in the guest room was put into use, I borrowed a futon while waiting for a rental futon to be delivered. In the spirit of proper documentation, Emiko, my host in this instance, took a photo of the futon and sent it to someone from the Guest Room Committee.

A similar set of detailed procedures regulates the laundry room, which has four washing machines and one dryer. One load of laundry and thirty minutes of dryer use cost one hundred *mori-ken* each. People write their name, apartment number, and date on the back of the *mori-ken* and place them in the slot for their unit on a burlap hanger on the wall. In addition, they write their name, date, and number of loads of laundry and dryer runs on a chart on the wall and place their wooden name plate on top of the washer or dryer when it is in use. Individuals keep their own detergent in their rooms, but they can use the Kankanmori detergent and name plate when washing the towels, aprons, and head coverings used at common meals. Sometimes, if someone notices that a load of laundry has been sitting in the machine for a while, they might call to remind the relevant person (thus the requirement to place name plates on the machines). I never saw baskets of laundry—dirty, wet, or cleaned and dry—sitting in the laundry room. Similarly, the iron and ironing board are always neatly put away after each use.

"Living at Kankanmori Needs to Be Both Practical and Ecological"

Earlier, I mentioned that Kankanmori purchases the rice for common meals from the Seikatsu Club Seikyo Co-op. The rice is part of a subscription box, received weekly since 2003, that also includes basic seasonings, oil, and detergents. In addition, a number of Kankanmori residents purchase their eggs and milk in bulk from the co-op. Buying in bulk, particularly from a co-op dedicated to supplying food produced more sustainably than that available in grocery stores, helps to reduce Kankanmori's environmental footprint and awards residents the economic benefits of pooling.

The Common Terrace garden, where residents produce organically grown vegetables and herbs that can be used in common meals or consumed by individual residents, provides another mechanism for realizing a practical and ecological lifestyle.[13] The terrace originally had a composting system, consisting of three boxes through which organic waste was moved sequentially in order to be transformed into compost for the vegetable and flower gardens. As at Quayside Village, this labor-intensive system was the project of a single Kankanmori resident. When she moved out of the community, another resident took it up, but eventually she moved out as well, and the project was not adopted by the community as a whole, since residents were occupied with other tasks; some also felt that the composting boxes took up too much space. The boxes were then removed and replaced by a smaller, open pile for compost, reserved exclusively for the waste from common meals. Since then, residents have placed their compostables in the "burnables" garbage bag picked up by the city on a weekly basis. Cardboard, glass, metal, and plastic can be deposited in the recycle shed shared with the upstairs retirement community; these recyclables are also picked up on a weekly basis.

On the terrace that surrounds the common room there is a bottle for collecting rainwater that is used to support a small tank of goldfish. Emiko referred to this practice, along with others related to gardening, as the *biotope*, which entails using various mechanisms, albeit often artificial, to revive the natural environment in order to support plant and animal life. The point, she said, is to "restore the environment where creatures can live so that we can see and enjoy the sound of water or the creatures that gather there." This is a small-scale intervention, but, like the flower garden on the common room terrace—into which residents put an enormous amount of effort—it is one that sets the tone, and that creates connections, however modest, with the natural world in a densely urban setting.

Despite the desire to live in environmentally sustainable ways, in some residents' view the possibilities for sustainable practices are constrained by space limitations. Indeed, Kankanmori's two terraces together make up about one-fifth of the gardening and composting space available at Quayside Village. Similarly, the recycle shed at Kankanmori serves a twelve-story building, while the recycle room at Quayside Village, which is of similar dimensions, serves only a four-story building. Nor does Tokyo's recycling infrastructure match that of Vancouver's. Nevertheless, although the opportunities at Kankanmori are more restricted than those at Quayside Village, residents work within available parameters to create as environmentally and economically sustainable a community as possible. Moreover, some residents, Carl in particular, challenge the idea of limited space and have expressed an interest in resurrecting the more elaborate composting system; and so the conversation continues.[14]

"To Spend Time Together in Common Activities I"

Common Meals

During an afternoon discussion on the future of Kankanmori, Yoshie asserted that common meals are at the core of collective housing:

One very specific thing is the fact that we share common meals. In Sweden,[15] common meals were a rationalization of housework, but here, on the contrary, they're a very important space for communication. I do want common meals to continue forever as the core of the collective house.

In contrast to Quayside Village, where common meals are held only once a week and always on the same day, common meals are a frequent occurrence at Kankanmori; they take place up to three times a week and can be held on any day, depending on cooks' schedules. This frequency reflects the requirement that each adult resident contribute to preparing a common meal once a month. But it also reflects the idea, as Yoshie expressed, that the common meal is, perhaps, *the* defining feature of Kankanmori's approach to collective housing—the "core," as she put it, or the "basis," as noted on Kankanmori's web page.[16] Eating together, then, is as important as working together on committees; both are essential to creating bonds of mutual support and pleasure.

The preparation of common meals is itself a collective activity. In contrast to the often lone cook at Quayside Village, common meals at Kankanmori are usually prepared by three cooks, although on occasion there may be as few as two or as many as four. The cooks begin by filling out a form indicating the menu, date, price (four or five hundred yen, depending on the ingredients), and the deadline for signing up, which they then post to the common bulletin board. Those who wish to attend check the box next to their name on the form and indicate how many people from their household will attend. There are separate columns for listing children, whose meals cost less (one hundred yen for those twelve and under, and two hundred yen for those aged thirteen to eighteen), and for noting if someone will not be attending but would like a portion to be saved for them; names of outside guests are listed at the bottom of the form. At least three people must sign up for the meal to proceed. Ideally, common meals occur in the evenings, but if someone's work schedule precludes this, they can choose to prepare a breakfast or brunch on the weekend.

Once they know how many people will take part, the cooks follow a specific formula for costing: for a 400-yen meal, 80 yen per person is deducted for gas and electricity, while for a 500-yen meal, 110 yen will be deducted. The cost of rice—60 yen per cup, where each person is allotted 0.6 cups—is also deducted. The remainder, minus 8 percent sales tax, is what the cooks can spend at the grocery store.[17]

In planning and preparing meals, effort is made to accommodate children by, for example, not making food too spicy or by making separate dishes, one more spicy and one less so. Cooks also endeavor to accommodate individual tastes. Katsuji, for instance, hates cilantro, so either dishes are made without it or a separate serving is made for him. Once the meal has been prepared, cooks typically plate the food themselves, with different serving sizes for children and adults, although rice, and miso soup when included, are always freely available. On occasion, the food is set out in large pots for people to serve themselves. In these cases, a sample plate is displayed, so that everyone can see what the meal, and basic portion size, should look like. Dessert is always divided up in advance.

In addition to purchasing ingredients and preparing the meal, cooks are responsible for cleaning up afterward. This includes not only cleaning the kitchen but also running the laundry for towels and aprons, hanging it up, and folding and storing it the following day. Cooks also look after the accounting, which involves checking to see that everyone has paid, submitting the receipts for groceries, and making sure that the costs of groceries and the attendees' payments add up. Any leftover food is either given away or divided into portions and sold. Once the accounting has been completed, *mori-ken* and receipts from the grocery store are stapled to the common meal form and placed in a binder stored in the pantry, although if someone has not yet paid, the form is tacked to the main bulletin board as a reminder. Cooks are later reimbursed for expenses by someone on the Common Meal Committee.

Immediate cleanup is the one aspect of the common meal that is not regulated by clear procedures. Instead, cleanup happens spontaneously, and everything somehow gets done. Everyone takes their own dishes (and those of their children) to the sink and prepares them to be put into the dish sanitizer, and many help with drying dishes and putting them away. Cooks, however, remain responsible in the last instance.

Although common meals have a standard start time of 6:00 P.M., there can sometimes be delays, and so once the meal is fully prepared, one of the cooks uses the intercom system to individually call each person who signed up to let them know that it is ready. People arrive at their convenience, put their *mori-ken* in a box placed on the counter for that purpose, and then enjoy the meal, sitting with whomever they like.

From purchasing food to finishing cleanup and accounting, it is not uncommon for cooks to put in five or more hours of effort. It is, then, no small enterprise, as my notes from a common meal I helped to prepare indicate:

A Common Breakfast
Akari, a working mother of two in her early forties, is usually unable to prepare common meals during the week, so we decided to make a Saturday breakfast. The menu included mini hotdogs with homemade rolls, cabbage, soup, and a gelatin dessert. Akari, her husband, and I began our preparations

at 9:00 P.M. the night before, after Akari had picked up all the ingredients. We made a consommé (carrots, onion, and consommé powder), chopped and sautéed the cabbage, made the "jelly" (grapefruit pieces suspended in gelatin), and prepared the bread dough. We finished shortly after 10:00. We were back in the kitchen again at 5:30 the next morning to bake the rolls, make tea, wash the tables, set out the dishes, and cut the jelly into equal pieces. (Akari explained that it is very important that the pieces be equal. This is always the case with the desserts—so much so that some Kankanmori residents will use a scale to measure out portions.) Naoko, although not part of our common meal "team," made some coffee. Residents began arriving at 8:00 A.M.; there were eighteen of us altogether. Afterward was the cleanup: selling and giving away leftovers, washing the dishes, checking off on the *mori-ken*, and doing the laundry. Akari had to leave for work around 9:00. Her husband and I finished at around 10:00, when we hung up the laundry.

Although guided by a strict set of procedures, common meals are not just a duty; nor are they simply a "rationalization of housework," as Yoshie indicated was the case in Swedish collective communities. On the contrary, they tend to be joyous, energetic events. Cooks enjoy easy banter among themselves while preparing the food, and the meals themselves are marked by animated conversation and much laughter. Parents tend to their children, often with the help of others. If a household would like to eat alone, as a family, they might set up a separate smaller table. Often before the meal begins, but almost always afterward, children play freely, running in and out of the common room and, in the common room, circulating through the living room and play areas as well as through the dining room. Having arrived for an evening meal at 6:00, diners can still be engaged with each other at 8:30, long after they have finished eating and cleaning up. Sometimes common meals morph into after-parties (*nijikai*, or "second party") that can continue for several hours, occasionally lasting into the wee hours of the morning. When this happens, residents bring food or drink to share and settle in for lengthy visits.[18]

Special Events

There is a yearly round of special events at Kankanmori arranged and coordinated by members of the Events Committee. These include, among others, the annual anniversary party, the Autumn Festival, Halloween, Christmas, and the annual mochi-making event.[19]

Preparing for social events at Kankanmori is itself a creative social activity, as illustrated in the following excerpt from my field notes:[20]

Anniversary Party Preparations

Last night I helped to decorate for today's anniversary party. I worked with Mayumi, Emiko, and Junko. They started by giving me some green cloth to put on the walls, but my arrangement was sloppy by their standards (as Emiko joked, "Japanese are very precise"), so they gave me balloons to blow up instead. We started at 8:00, and were still going strong at 11:00.

At first I was a little surprised by how much time everything was taking. Hanging the green cloth on the walls took at least half an hour, even though this is done each year and I could imagine doing it in about five minutes. Then a decision had to be made about where to put a piece of shorter green cloth—in the common room itself or over the entrance to the common room. We decided to put it over the entrance. It took over an hour! There was a great deal of discussion (and no small amount of laughter) about how to hang it, and how to handle the mechanics of different designs. It seemed to me that everything was being invented anew, even though Mayumi had photos from last year as a guide. We tried what seemed like a million ways of hanging it; Mayumi even brought out an expanding shower rod from her place as an option. I found myself growing impatient. But then it clicked: maybe this was about process? Maybe it was about hanging out together—*to spend time with each other in common activities*—more than about getting something done efficiently? And maybe it was also about equality: no one would dominate, but everyone would have their say, and we would proceed only when everyone was in agreement. Once these thoughts occurred to me, my impatience vanished and I found myself having fun. In the end, we hung the cloth, in a straight line, over the entrance door to the common room.

We then piled on the couch the forty or so balloons we blew up for Hiroshi to hang from the ceiling when he got home from work. Keiichi arrived back from his job at around 10:00 or so and joined a number of us in putting labels on Kankanmori's homemade beer. More people came into the kitchen to cook. It was clearly going to be a late night.

When we were done with the cloth, balloons, and bottle labels, Mayumi went to the corner store to get some drinks (mostly beer and shochu, a distilled beverage), while Emiko distributed some treats to eat. A break before moving on to the next thing.

The Events Committee also organizes potlucks for special occasions, such as, for example, when residents are moving in or out of Kankanmori:

A Farewell Potluck

One family of four and two single people were leaving Kankanmori. One of the latter, Naoko, had lived at Kankanmori for four years; the others for somewhat less. Thirty-two people—a large chunk of the community—attended, each of whom had indicated on a sheet posted on the bulletin board what they would contribute to the meal. The dishes were spread out on the counters that circle the kitchen, each with a tag providing a description of the dish and the name of the person who had prepared it. Once everyone had a drink in hand—champagne, beer, wine, tea, or juice—Hiroshi, a member of the Events Committee, started to announce the names of attendees. When their name was called, each person explained what their dish was. Everyone then served themselves and sat down to eat. The tables were arranged in a large square, as for a community meeting, with the guests of honor seated at one end. Partway through the meal, Hiroshi announced that it was speech time, and each person who was leaving Kankanmori stood up and spoke for a few minutes. Each speech was met with applause. After the departing residents finished their speeches, lively conversation resumed. Eventually, Hiroshi announced that the event was officially over, and people got up to help clean. Some left portions of their meals on the table while they went to help, and then returned to finish eating. Others collected leftovers to take home. Many people lingered for hours, chatting with those who arrived late from work, either in the common room or in the hallway just outside of the common room. Akari brought out her children's pet hamster for the other children to look at. Animals are not permitted in the common room, so we stood in the hallway. One child was afraid, but the others were enchanted.

While the majority of Kankanmori's committees are oriented to the physical and financial aspects of community maintenance, the existence of an Events Committee, and the kinds of work that its members undertake, indicates that social life at Kankanmori—reflecting the value of *spending time together on common activities* and the belief that *our lives are enriched by developing relationships with our neighbors*—is as amenable to practical operationalizations and orchestration as its other values. Community, then, is collaboratively produced in a deliberate, overtly planned way.

"To Spend Time Together in Common Activities II"

Yuki, a Quayside Village resident who grew up in Japan but had been living in Canada for over twenty years, twice visited with me at Kankanmori when she was in the country visiting her parents. When I gave her a tour and outlined guest and laundry room rules, she commented that they were "typically Japanese"—that is, procedural. Yuki's assessment is certainly correct when it comes to anything categorized as "Kankanmori business," for instance, accounting, the distribution of tasks, and the organization of the laundry and guest rooms. In these cases, patterns observed by anthropologists and cultural psychologists provide some insight. Most notable here is the emphasis on relational harmony and an associated desire to avoid conflict, both of which I mentioned above in my discussion of public/private boundaries.[21] As Holthus and Manzenreiter put it, "In Japan, adapting to social norms is commonly appreciated as something that guarantees social harmony, which is valued over conflict. Japanese perceive interdependency of individuals as an important element of understanding the self within society."[22] Clancy further points to a distinction between *honne* ("real feeling") and *tatemae* ("socially accepted principle"), noting that neither is more "authentic" than the other but, rather, that the distinction is one of situational appropriateness.[23] In the context of activities considered part of "Kankanmori business," then, it would make sense that *tatemae* would predominate. The running of the community is in this sense collaboratively depersonalized: the focus is not on individual personalities but on institutionalized processes that lie outside of any one person's whims or desires. This serves to reduce the possibility of arguments about people monopolizing the guest room, leaving their clothes lying around the laundry room, or not doing anything to contribute to the running of the community, since such behaviors are unlikely to occur in the first place. Writing about Kyōdō No Mori (Forest of Kyodo), a collective housing community in Tokyo, Graham Meltzer highlights two organizational principles that apply at Kankanmori as well: "No one person or household should be singled out for criticism or censure. Personal issues should not be brought to meetings."[24]

Having spent time in both Kankanmori and Quayside Village, I would venture that the depersonalization of certain aspects of community life at Kankanmori does indeed translate into fewer interpersonal conflicts, or at least fewer overtly expressed ones. In distinguishing in practice between official business and the rest of living together day-to-day, the work involved in maintaining community structures and processes does not spill over into interpersonal relations; and likewise, interpersonal relations do not spill over into the practical business of running Kankanmori. This mitigation of potential conflict by means of depersonalization is built into Kankanmori's formal organization, in particular into the uniform distribution of tasks, the clear demarcation between personal and community finances, and the decision-making processes that, at least officially, give equivalent power to each voice. As Junko stated when comparing Kankanmori's framework of obligation versus Quayside Village's focus on invitation and volunteerism, "It seemed to me that the greater freedom at QV might also make the things that are unfair worse." Here, a sense of unfairness is seen as a potential generator of conflict, similar to the introduction of controversial topics of discussion at common meals. The ideology of *equality* → *fairness* → *same-*

ness, then, and the depersonalization of community procedures that it involves, is a powerful prophylactic against the emergence of disagreement and strife. In this context, it is not surprising that, in contrast to Quayside Village, Kankanmori does not have a robust tool kit for addressing disputes. Instead, effort is placed into avoiding their appearance in the first place.

There is a downside, of course, to this depersonalization, especially when coupled with the relatively rigid boundary between what is considered to be the private versus the public. As already discussed, residents may keep their troubles to themselves in ways that undermine the viability of the community, since interdependence—marked by picking up the slack for someone who is overworked, for instance—may accordingly be reduced. This is an issue of balance, and, as I describe in more detail in chapter 4, it became a central topic of discussion during the exchanges between Kankanmori and Quayside Village.

The official organization of tasks and obligations, however, is only one aspect of life at Kankanmori, and attending solely to regulations regarding residents' contributions to the community, which clearly give primacy of place to the good of the community rather than to individual practical or emotional needs, would give the false impression that relationships among residents are excessively formalized and characterized by rigid proceduralism. While proceduralism is indeed central to Kankanmori, it captures only half of the picture. The other half looks very different. Kankanmori residents are acutely attuned to each other's needs, and they care for each other in myriad practical ways. For example, when anyone brings a special treat—say, watermelon—to an event, someone will always set aside portions (complete with name tags) for those who aren't present at the time. *Omiyage* (souvenir) practices provide another instance: when residents go away on business trips or holidays, they usually bring back a food treat for the community, which is placed in the common room with a note indicating where and who it is from. The examples are endless: Keiichi receives a box of persimmons each year that he always places in the common room so that others may benefit from his mother's generosity; Katsuji collects Anna from school when Haruko and Carl are busy with work; parents post announcements of their children's birthdays on the bulletin board, on which other residents write congratulatory notes; and it is not uncommon for residents to leave small gifts (usually of food) on each other's door handles. This general taking-care-of-each-other is constant.[25]

There is, in addition, a great deal of informal and spontaneous socializing at Kankanmori that occurs outside of the numerous official activities organized by the Events Committee and in addition to the regular common meals. As already noted, it is not unusual, as the day winds down, for several residents to have an impromptu gathering for afternoon tea, and post–

common meal parties are a regular occurrence. Small groups of residents will also go out to dinner, sometimes visiting a karaoke bar afterward, and then return to Kankanmori to share dessert in the common room. Some residents attend political events together or take short holiday trips out of town. Such ad hoc, informal social gatherings occur more frequently than the events organized by the Events Committee, and they are more commonplace than at Quayside Village. Together, these practices of mutual care and spontaneous socializing reflect the informal rather than orchestrated realization of Kankanmori's core intention *to spend time together in common activities* and of the value that *our lives are enriched by developing relationships with our neighbors.*

One unofficial event that has taken on the character of tradition but that remains outside of the orbit of the Events Committee is Cocktail Night. Kayo, who lived at Kankanmori in 2004–5, met her husband David, a British academic, while pursuing her PhD in the United Kingdom. They spent some time at Kankanmori together, and even held their wedding ceremony there. They eventually moved to Canada for David's job, but they returned to Kankanmori for ten months in 2013 with their son, Francis, while David was on sabbatical. It was during this stay that David initiated what became known as Cocktail Night. The event is now held every year when the family returns to Kankanmori for its annual monthlong visit. As David explained to me in an email, the idea emerged quite organically from the informal post–common meal get-togethers:

> During one of those afterhours drinks and snacks in the common room, I was quite interested in making cocktails, more in theory than in practice, so I said I would give it a go. For some reason everyone treated me as the expert on the subject, and somehow I just play the role that people expect. I think that's how a lot of roles are acquired and develop in Kankan Mori. For the first [Cocktail Night] we just asked around for contributions of ingredients from residents who wanted to come (so we got a rather strange array of things, and too much whisky!), and we then went out and bought a core selection of bitters and so on. Everyone dressed up as if this really was a proper Tokyo cocktail bar, and we arranged the common space and changed the lighting so it almost had the right look. It was very successful, and we've done it again every year since.

While David takes care of the cocktails—listed on a specially prepared menu, along with a price list—Emiko and Yoshie prepare gourmet dishes, such as borscht, plates of specialty cheeses and meats, and condiments. Regular florescent lights are replaced with dimmer lights, and soft music plays in the background. The event often lasts until 2:00 or 3:00 in the morning.

At Quayside Village, attending to individuals' needs and interpersonal relationships provides the grounds of possibility for community building and maintenance. At Kankanmori, the relationship seems to operate in the reverse: its official organization and clear division of labor, nested in the frame of *everybody is equal*, provides the foundation for rich interpersonal relations. In her research with elderly attendees at a community salon in Osaka, Iza Kavedžija found that it was a balance between intimacy and dependence, on the one hand, and autonomy and freedom, on the other, that, in the view of those she worked with, provided the grounds of possibility for the good life.[26] More specifically, she writes, "it was precisely by maintaining a degree of independence that warm, intimate relationships were thought to be preserved."[27] This parallels, perhaps, the situation at Kankanmori: an externalized, depersonalized system for running community affairs is precisely what clears the grounds for warm and intimate relations, where a night out at a sushi bar and karaoke will not be sullied by the kinds of tensions related to committee participation, common meal preparation, or use of the laundry room that could emerge were there no clear procedures in place. Similarly, the planning and organization that goes into common meals and official social events—procedural as it may be—is precisely what lays the groundwork for the often boisterous camaraderie that inevitably ensues.

"Life Needs to Be Open to the Outside World"

Reflecting on Kankanmori's early years, Ikuko Koyabe wrote that "each person who lives here has a diverse network of contacts with the outside world, both for work and play, so I hope to create, by working together, an open and airy community where there is always a breeze from the outside, rather than having all of our lives fulfilled within the building."[28] Initially, this openness was meant to extend to those living in the retirement community upstairs. This relationship, however, did not materialize: many of the retirees felt that Kankanmori's children were too noisy, and the public baths on the twelfth floor, originally meant to be available to everyone in the building, were eventually allotted for exclusive use of the retirees. There is some informal interaction with a few of the retirees, who occasionally come down to attend social events at Kankanmori, but this is limited.

Kankanmori's other attempts to create linkages with the wider society have been more successful. Most notable here are its efforts to serve as a model for those who might be interested in collective living. Although founding members drew inspiration from the Swedish approach to collective housing, the design of Kankanmori was uniquely Japanese, as Yoshie explained during a conversation about Kankanmori's future:

After two years of thinking and thinking, we made a collective house in Japan. So, the idea of a "collective house" is really a Japanese collective house. Not just here, but after that Seiseki was founded, Sugamo was founded, Ōizumi, and they're all collective houses. Their principles are the same. So people may live in them and many things may change, but those principles are those of the collective house as born in Japan.

In the view of its residents, then, Kankanmori can serve as a blueprint for collective housing that is specifically suited to the Japanese context. In their 2014 self-published book on their community—itself an embodiment of the effort to spread the word about collective housing—Yoshie wrote that

> the low birth rate is a big issue in Japan but you don't see that problem in Kankanmori. I think that parents living here know that they are not alone when raising their children. Collective housing gives some solutions for raising children, addressing the low birth rate, and ensuring that elderly people are cared for and do not die alone.[29]

In order to promote their approach, Kankanmori established two committees—Public Relations and Research Relations—which serve to publicize Kankanmori's organizational design and to assist those who want to learn more about, and perhaps even develop, collective housing. Members of the Public Relations Committee deal with the media, while those on the Research Relations Committee vet research proposals, which are submitted on a specially designed form that includes questions about focus, method, timing, and, in particular, dissemination.

Given this openness, as well as its uniqueness in the Japanese context, Kankanmori is frequently visited by researchers and journalists, and it has been the subject of numerous international as well as national TV documentaries, news clips, and newspaper reports—significantly more than is the case with Quayside Village. In addition to the work of the Public Relations and Research Committees, the Orientation Committee, as already noted, holds regular sessions for anyone interested in learning about Kankanmori, including not only prospective residents but also journalists and researchers who may then go on to conduct more detailed investigations.

More locally and intimately, Kankanmori hosts a number of events to which residents of the surrounding neighborhoods are invited, including Café Kankanmori, the Autumn Festival, and, more recently, open common meals, to which ten residents of the neighborhood are invited. These events sometimes have the effect of recruiting new members to the community. Ko, for instance, retired and in his mid-seventies, had installed his mother in the upstairs retirement community a decade earlier; he learned about Kankanmori in part from attending the Autumn Festival:

Ten years ago, I put my mother in the care facility on the fifth floor, so I was here all the time, looking in from the outside. Also, at the Autumn Festival and so on, I had the chance to see what kind of people lived here and what they were doing, bit by bit. That continued for seven years. I moved in a year and a half ago.

Other events at Kankanmori, such as its yearly anniversary parties and the occasional formal presentation by researchers, are widely attended.[30]

In addition to inviting the public in, Kankanmori residents also go out into the world to build connections with others. This takes a variety of forms, ranging from participating in local protest events to traveling to different cities and giving presentations on collective housing and/or interviewing people who have been active in a range of housing initiatives. While the latter serves to spread the word about collective housing and provides a means for learning more about other possible approaches and practices, the former works to create connections with various sectors of society, engaging people and institutions that are interested in such issues as environmental sustainability, nuclear energy, and electoral politics—even as these are not often discussed *within* the community—thus tying Kankanmori to larger processes of social development and change.

Stability and Change

Just as there is a dynamic relationship between the equal distribution of tasks and efforts to accommodate the exigencies of individual residents' lives, and between the rule-bound nature of Kankanmori business and the rich looseness of its unofficial social life, so there is a productive tension at Kankanmori between stability and change. Stability and continuity are provided by Kankanmori's clear criteria for participation in community life and its explicit sets of procedures for collective endeavors—for common meals, use of the laundry and guest rooms, cleaning, watering the vegetable garden, and so on. Stability and continuity are also enhanced by the presence of long-term residents, such as Yoshie, Emiko, and Katsuji, all of whom had lived at Kankanmori for over a decade at the time of this study, and each with deep, detailed institutional memories.

Change, however, is also an integral feature of life at Kankanmori. Its rental-based organization means that turnover among residents is higher than in owner-based communities such as Quayside Village. Given this, there is perhaps less danger of stagnation at Kankanmori than risk of upheaval. Thus Yoshie noted that there have been times in Kankanmori's life when "there was so much moving in and out that we were sort of searching for stability." Levels of turnover are not the same each year, however, and constant upheaval is not a regular feature of life at Kankanmori. And yet, when residents who have played a key role in the community leave, there may be gaps that are not easily filled—whether they be technological, as in the mechanics of particular processes; philosophical, as in the ideas underlying particular practices; or both. When a resident with expertise in IT issues moves out, for instance, there is no guarantee that someone with similar expertise will move in. Composting provides another case in point. As I described earlier, at one point in time Kankanmori had an elaborate composting system that rivaled that of Quayside Village. However, when the residents who looked after it moved out, neither the technical knowledge nor its underlying philosophy were effectively transmitted to others in the community and the system collapsed. (The story does not end there, of course, as conversations about composting continue; see above.)

At the same time, turnover in residents creates possibilities for the introduction of fresh ideas. When Shoko moved in, for instance, she took an interest in expanding the presence of Kankanmori in society at large. She joined the Public Relations Committee and infused new life into Kankanmori's Facebook page, in the process working to enhance residents' knowledge of each other's hobbies and interests. Longer-term residents also sometimes propose new activities, which can be energizing, as Emiko observes:

> But when something new is proposed—like last year, for example, we haven't done it yet, but Carl said, "Hey, let's redesign the whole Common Terrace," and we had three workshops with amazing attendance, right? So, maybe that energy flares up when someone proposes an interesting idea.

Residents' movements from one committee to another can similarly inject new energy into the community. In the long run, then, ongoing change and adaptation are considered by some to be at the heart of successful collective community. As Haruko put it:

> I have no concrete ideas, but as the people living here change, I imagine their needs, the things they need to do, the things they want to do will change too. One thing I can say is that it seems to me that continuing to transform in that way is how Kankanmori will continue to exist as a collective house.

There is thus a balance between stability and change that reflects the turnover in residents, as well as the reality that collectivity is an ongoing, collaborative process of creation that unfolds via everyday negotiations and practices. Long-term residents with institutional memories and clearly outlined sets of regulations and procedures provide a foundation—a kind of playing field—on which changing circumstances, the exigencies of everyday life, and residents' unique personalities unfold and express themselves.

One set of changing circumstances that Kankanmori residents will have to address in the not-too-distant future concerns aging. As noted earlier, the community takes intergenerationalism seriously, so much so that it occasionally lowers rental rates for members of those demographic groups that it wants more of, in order to balance out the number of older and younger residents. However, this process for recruiting people from desired demographics to maintain generational stability does not fully address the problems that will emerge as the already present residents grow older and are less able to contribute. Recall Yoshie's observation that

> we're starting to see cases at Kankanmori where people are getting older and unable to work. If it's just one person, that's okay, but if we have three or four older people who can't do anything, I'm not sure if this community can survive. We have to start thinking about this.

So far, there have not been any cases at Kankanmori of older residents becoming significantly disabled, either physically or mentally; thus, while Yoshie asserts the need to "start thinking about this," the necessity to do anything specific has yet to occur. Perhaps as older residents become feeble to the extent that other residents are unable to look after them properly, they will move upstairs to the retirement community or reintegrate themselves into their extended families. In any case, aging will at some point become a challenge to Kankanmori's efforts to balance out stability and change.

Conclusions: The Good Life at Kankanmori

Over the course of my time at Kankanmori I was periodically asked to give presentations on the project and its progress. Responding to one of my talks focused on collective housing as an alternative, nonindividualistic model for producing happiness and the good life, Yumiko asserted that people did not move to Kankanmori in order to pursue personal happiness. Instead, she said, people moved in to find connection and to live in community. On another occasion, she told me that people who live in collective housing need to be "strong individualists and know what you're doing" in order to be "a part of the community but not invaded by it." Together, these two points summarize Kankanmori's concept of the good life: it is about a togetherness that nurtures, rather than swallows, the individual.

Yumiko's insights mirror those of Iza Kavedžija, who claims that Japanese conceptualizations of happiness and well-being are about balancing sets of oppositions.[31] She writes that, in the Japanese context, sociality, intimacy, and interdependence, on the one hand, and freedom, independence, and autonomy, on the other, are considered equally essential.[32] Kankanmori provides precisely such a balance between interdependence and independence. Nevertheless, in their discussions about life in collective housing, Kankanmori residents, although pointing to independence, tended to focus most on interdependence. It is worth noting in this regard that Japanese terms referring to happiness include not only *ikigai*, "what makes life worth living," but also *shiawase*, "bringing things together," and *tsunagari*, which can be translated as "link."[33] Ruriko, the architecture student referred to earlier, expressed the ideas of bringing together and linkage well:

> I work at a [university] research center working on collective houses, and I borrowed a book from the lead professor there by Koyabe-sensei, who was heavily involved in building Kankanmori. Of course I'm still studying, but what the book said was that the decisive difference between a collective house and housing for the elderly was that the main point of the former is participation. Things aren't just provided, you don't just get fed, you have to participate—that's the appeal. Being excused from that isn't something to envy or resent. Everyone who lives here does so because they want to participate.

This bringing together, or participation, as Ruriko puts it, has direct benefits for those who engage in it. Hiroshi, for instance, a systems engineer in his mid-forties, had been living at Kankanmori for just over three years when we met. He told me that "living together is better" than living in isolated houses or apartments, and then went on to explain how his perspective on life changed after he moved into the community. Before, he said, all he did was "work, work, work." Now, in contrast, he looked at himself "more objectively," reflecting carefully on how he wants to live his life. The exposure to different ways of thinking and living that he encountered as he came to participate more in Kankanmori activities led him to the conclusion that work was not the only important thing in the world, and he started remembering how much he used to care about little things, like the color and design of curtains, for instance. These little things can make life better, he said. As Ikuko Koyabe once explained to me, while collective communities need to start at the level of the individual—since they are, after all, composed of individuals—and although the production of individual well-being is clearly an important goal of collective housing, personal goals are only ever accomplished via engagement with community, that is, by learning how to live with difference and how to communicate. Living at Kankanmori—collaborating with diverse others, on a daily basis, in the project of building and maintaining community—served to broaden Hiroshi's perspective, allowing him to create a more balanced, fulfilling life in the company of others.

During my first visit to Kankanmori, in 2014, I spent some time chatting with Katsuji, a long-term Kankanmori resident then in his early eighties. He told me that humans cannot live by themselves. He referred to the Chinese character for the person (人), which visually depicts connection with others. If you're just by yourself, he said, and value only the individual, you're not human anymore. Collective housing, he claimed, thus both reflects and enhances a basic characteristic of humanity. Referring to *nagaya*, a style of one-story, longhouse living formerly prevalent in Japan, he told me that he would like to see a "mutual dependency spirit" rejuvenated. This is Kankanmori's project: to endeavor to collaboratively establish a community of balanced interdependence and independence based on something other than shared blood or ties of geography or profession. As Junko put it, "We are not friends and not family, but something different, something new."

Notes

1. Kankanmori Collective House Inc., website, 2020, retrieved 17 June 2020 from http://www.collectivehouse.co.jp.
2. See *Life at Kankanmori*, "Common Meals," 5:23.
3. Kankanmori Collective House Inc., website.
4. See *Life at Kankanmori*, "Children's Meeting," 4:07, and "Children's Painting Project," 8:04. See also *Exchange at Kankanmori*, "Children's Afternoon Tea," 3:22.
5. Robert J. Pekkanen, Yutaka Tsujinaka, and Hidehiro Yamamoto, *Neighborhood Associations and Local Governance in Japan* (New York: Routledge, 2014); Sugimoto, *Introduction to Japanese Society*.
6. See *Life at Kankanmori*, "Gardening," 6:13, and "The Flower Garden," 7:12.
7. See *Life at Kankanmori*, "The Vegetable Garden," 7:32.
8. See *Life at Kankanmori*, "Community Meeting," 3:27.
9. Interestingly, Kankanmori residents were quite open about their personal lives in the discussion groups and life history interviews conducted for this project. This reflects, perhaps, residents' stereotypes of what formal group discussions or interviews are all about. The project might have also provided the space for the kind of interpersonal revealing that generally does not occur at Kankanmori.
10. Neither Shoko nor Yoshie address the discrepancy between their accounts of how long Shoko had been living at Kankanmori (one year versus five months).
11. Patricia M. Clancy, "The Acquisition of Communicative Style in Japanese," in *Making Sense of Language: Readings in Culture and Communication*, 3rd ed., ed. Susan D. Blum (New York: Oxford University Press, 2017); Barbara Holthus and Wolfram Manzenreiter, "Conclusion: Happiness as a Balancing Act Between Agency and Social Structure," in *Happiness and the Good Life in Japan*, ed. Wolf-

ram Manzenreiter and Barbara Holthus (New York: Routledge, 2017); Gordon Mathews, "Happiness and the Pursuit of a Life Worth Living: An Anthropological Approach," in *Happiness and Public Policy: Theory, Case Studies and Implications*, ed. Yew-Kwang Ng and Lok Sang Ho (New York: Palgrave Macmillan, 2006); Uchida, Ogihara, and Fukushima, "Cultural Construal of Wellbeing."

12. When I arrived at Kankanmori for an extended stay in 2016, I needed to borrow a few kitchen items: one knife, one fork, a set of chopsticks, one glass, and one coffee cup. Given the length of my visit, I was asked to list the items on a piece of paper, sign and date it, and post it on the community bulletin board.
13. See *Life at Kankanmori*, "The Vegetable Garden," 7:32.
14. See *Exchange at Quayside Village*, "Brian Teaches the Visitors about Composting," 2:45.
15. Recall that a number of founding members, among them Yoshie, visited collective housing communities in Sweden during the development phase of Kankanmori.
16. See *Life at Kankanmori*, "Common Meals," 4:42. See also *Exchange at Kankanmori*, "Having a Traditional Japanese Meal," 7:42.
17. See *Exchange at Kankanmori*, "Common Meal Accounting," 5:33.
18. See *Exchange at Kankanmori*, "After Dinner Drinking Party," 5:56.
19. See *Life at Kankanmori*, "Mochi Making," 8:57, "Celebrating Christmas," 11:35, "15th Anniversary Presentation," 14:08, and "15th Anniversary Party," 14:28.
20. See *Life at Kankanmori*, "Decorating for the Christmas Party," 10:38.
21. Clancy, "Acquisition of Communicative Style"; Holthus and Manzenreiter, "Conclusion"; Mathews, "Happiness and the Pursuit"; Uchida, Ogihara, and Fukushima, "Cultural Construal of Wellbeing."
22. Holthus and Manzenreiter, "Conclusion," 243.
23. Clancy, "Acquisition of Communicative Style," 108.
24. Meltzer, *Sustainable Community*, 109; see also Graham Meltzer, "'Urban Biotope'—Japanese Style," *Communities* 129 (2005).
25. I encountered such care firsthand during my various stays. The first time I stayed in an apartment at Kankanmori, the only furniture I rented was a futon and a refrigerator, and I took to eating all my meals in the common room. One day, Yoshie and Emiko showed up at my door with a small table and chairs, so that I would have the option of eating breakfast and lunch in my apartment if I so chose. Emiko and Yoshie were also concerned about my diet, since I have celiac disease. Emiko regularly brought me things to eat—gluten-free pasta, wheat-free curry mixes, crackers, etc.—and, on more than one occasion, Yoshie baked special rice-flour buns for me.
26. Kavedžija, "Good Life."
27. Ibid., 94.
28. Kankanmori Residents, *Collective House*, 132.
29. Ibid., 3.
30. See *Life at Kankanmori*, "Student Presentation," 10:22, and "15th Anniversary Presentation," 14:08.
31. Kavedžija, "Good Life."
32. Ibid.; see also Uchida and Kitayama, "Happiness and Unhappiness"; Uchida and Ogihara, "Interpersonal Construal of Happiness"; Uchida, Ogihara, and Fukushima, "Cultural Construal of Wellbeing."
33. Manzenreiter and Holthus, "Introduction," 11.

4 THE EXCHANGES

Wow, I learned how seriously laissez-faire Quayside Village is. We're really way over on the other end of the continuum from Kankanmori.
—Donya

They don't set rules yet still make it work out.
—Haruko

COHOUSING IS A CREATIVE PROCESS. It is never a static, finished product but, rather, an ongoing experiment, as Maureen from Quayside Village put it, that unfolds in the course of daily living. In addition to the conversation between philosophy and practice that marks everyday life in cohousing communities—or as part of it—cohousers often participate in networks for the exchange of ideas about intentional community in order to gain insight into pitfalls and hazards, learn about possible solutions to common problems, and discover new, creative ways of building and maintaining community. Such networks, composed of national and international organizations and academic centers, along with the publications and conferences they support, serve as circuits for the global travel of cohousing as a model of the good life.

Members of cohousing communities also occasionally visit other communities to get a direct sense of how things are done elsewhere. This kind of active, embodied experience complements the more passive learning that happens when residents consume information from websites and publications. As I noted in chapter 1, during Kankanmori's planning phase, a number of its creators visited collective housing communities in Sweden to explore approaches they might consider in designing their own community.[1] Although founding members of Quayside Village were unable to visit the Danish cohousing communities that served as their template, they were exposed to the Danish model via the work of Kathryn McCamant and Charles Durrett,[2] and they also benefited from the experiences of members of other cohousing communities closer to home, most notably those of WindSong, in Langley, BC. In addition, two of Quayside's creators, Linda and Brian, had previously lived in an intentional community themselves, and they brought their knowledge and insights with them to the planning table.

When I first began visiting Kankanmori and Quayside Village, residents of both communities immediately expressed an interest in learning about the other. How did they operate? What were their priorities? What kinds of challenges did they encounter, and how did they address them? Reflecting on this, I decided to incorporate a reciprocal exchange between the two communities into the design of the research for this book. Such an exchange would, first of all, meet the ethical imperative of reciprocity—of the need to give something in return for the time and energy residents contributed to the work. It would also enhance the collaborative aspects of the project insofar as it would transfer ownership of the research process, at least in part, to members of Kankanmori and Quayside Village themselves. Just as providing each community with a GoPro enabled residents to visually document life in their communities from *their* perspective, so the exchange would position participants as co-researchers rather than as research subjects.

In general, cohousers' visits to other communities tend to be short-lived: a day or two, or maybe just an afternoon at each community visited—a pattern mirrored by academics and other researchers. While no doubt beneficial, especially during the planning stages of a new community when founding members might want to canvass as many approaches as possible, I reasoned that, at this stage in the life of their communities, residents of Quayside Village and Kankanmori might find longer, sustained visits at one site even more useful. So, in consultation with both communities, I set up ten-day exchanges—long enough, I felt, for participants to get a solid sense of the rhythms of daily life in the other community and for members of the host community to learn from the visitors, but not so long as to be burdensome.

Finally, given that Quayside Village and Kankanmori are situated in markedly different societies, I saw the exchange visits as an opportunity to trace how ideas and practices of cohousing travel and are translated. How would exchange participants experience cohousing in another culture? What would capture their attention? How would they understand and evaluate the approaches of the other community? Would they encounter ideas or methods that their home communities might like to experiment with? Would they become more critical of taken-for-granted aspects of how things are done at home? Or would they reassert the appropriateness of their own practices? In other words, how would the process of visiting another community work to place what their home community takes for granted—as normal, natural, or inevitable—into relief? My goal was to encourage reflexivity, a heightened awareness of and reflection on one's own philosophy and practice that has the potential to prompt new thinking, validate existing practices, or both. At the community meeting that took place while Carl and Haruko were visiting Quayside Village, and after Connie, Juhli, and Donya had returned from Tokyo, Connie underscored the importance of precisely this kind of reflection:

> It's been so interesting having this exchange, I really am so appreciative of [it], because we have learned so much, not only in seeing how another community operates but also in having to explain the way we operate to another community. It requires us to examine why we do things, and compare how we do things with another community, and see if we're really doing things the best way. So this has been just so interesting, and informative, and useful. And I think it will get to be more so as time goes on and we digest all of this.

Juhli concurred: "It's just been a good time for processing and learning and examining as well, as Connie said, about the who, what, when, where, and whys of Quayside, and our processes. So it's an interesting time."

This methodological framework articulates with an approach to studying happiness and well-being that moves away from measuring people's happiness according to survey questionnaires that elicit "inevitably artificial and simplified answers"[3]—and that are often designed by cultural outsiders[4]—in favor of orienting to "how people are happy, and how people think about and pursue happiness."[5] Here, what exchange participants and their hosts attended to would serve as pointers to how they are happy, to how they envision well-being, and to how they go about the business of producing the good life.

In keeping with this collaborative framework, I invited each community to determine for itself who to send on the exchange. Not surprisingly, the process of choosing exchange participants was different in the two sites. At Kankanmori, the study group for the project decided to send a family of four to Quayside Village: Haruko and Carl, a couple in their forties who had lived at Kankanmori for seven years, and their two young daughters—Anna, who turned seven while at Quayside Village, and four-year-old Lisa. Members of the study group, of which Haruko and Carl were members, felt that it would be most useful to send people from a younger generation on the exchange as opposed to founding or long-term members, since, as they explained to me, it was the younger generation that would be responsible for carrying Kankanmori into the future. In addition, both Haruko and Carl were fluent in English, which would make communication much easier. Finally, Anna and Lisa, whose participation in the exchange embodied Kankanmori's strong desire to maintain its intergenerational character, could potentially provide insight into children's experiences of growing up in cohousing.[6]

For its part, the Quayside community decided that the best way to proceed would be to hold a community meeting during which those who were interested in going on the exchange could explain why they wanted to participate and what they hoped to learn. Three women put their names forward, and all three were chosen: Donya, Juhli, and Connie. Their ages spanned from thirty-four (Juhli) to seventy (Connie), and their years living in Quayside Village ranged from two (Connie) to eight (Donya). None of the women spoke Japanese, but we felt that we could rely on those Kankanmori residents who speak English (of which there are a number, in contrast to Quayside Village, which has only one Japanese speaker, Yuki), on the interpreter I would be hiring for portions of the exchange, and on the general goodwill (and gestures) with which people find ways to communicate across language barriers.

Below are the biographical sketches that each visitor wrote to introduce themselves to their host community (Haruko wrote the bios for Anna and Lisa, and members of the Kankanmori study group generously translated the Quayside Village bios into Japanese). These were circulated among residents of both communities well in advance of the exchanges.

From Quayside Village

Connie will be seventy on 25 September. She grew up in the central part of Canada, near Toronto, and most of her family still lives there, but she moved to Vancouver forty-eight years ago and can't imagine living anywhere else, though she loves to travel. She has three children and three grandchildren. Connie worked for thirty-three years as a flight attendant, mostly with Canadian Pacific and Air Canada. She flew many times to Japan when she was working (mostly Tokyo/Narita but also Nagoya and Osaka) and found the culture, architecture, and landscape very interesting and beautiful. She is excited to return and see it from a different point of view. Connie's hobbies are quilting and sewing, travel, reading (fiction, biography, history, politics), volunteering for environmental causes, and her grandchildren. She moved to Quayside Village two years ago because she knows how important it is to be connected to a community that cares for and supports its members. Both the giving and receiving are important. She is looking forward to experiencing the community of Kankanmori and seeing some of the beautiful textiles that Japan makes.

Donya, forty, has been living at Quayside for eight years with her daughter, Jazzy. She and her husband, Phil, were married three years ago in the first wedding at Quayside (and of course, he moved in too). She is a voice teacher and singer and studies Somatic Experiencing, a nervous system–based modality for healing trauma. Donya cooks common meals once a month or so, serves on the Thriving Committee, and is a mediocre gardener but always happy to dig holes or move dirt. Earlier this year Donya spearheaded an effort to clean up and reorganize the recycling room—no small task for a community that is very close to a "zero waste" lifestyle. Her daughter Jazzy, eleven, is working with a group of other young people to reinvent the "kids' room" at Quayside Village into a more teen-friendly hangout. Donya is very happy to be visiting Japan and is in particular looking forward to spending time at Kankanmori and learning about how living in community works there. She has visited quite a few countries and is fascinated with culture, people, and relationship. She likes to play games and get into good conversations.

Juhli is a thirty-four-year-old musician who keeps an active performing schedule with various jazz and event bands. She performs locally and internationally, including trips to New Orleans in 2014 and China in 2015. Additionally, Juhli works as a teacher/conductor and balances a number of private piano/voice students with her role as the director of an adult community jazz choir. As an avid cyclist, she often commutes by bicycle and loves to go bike touring; highlights include a six-week-long European tour, and more recently a trip down the coast of British Columbia from Haida Gwaii. She moved into Quayside Village in 2013 to be closer to her mother, who also lives at Quayside Village. She has always admired Japanese culture and was very excited to hear about the exchange opportunity with Kankanmori. As a travel lover, she has often found it a far better experience when she has been able to spend time with locals. She is looking forward to getting a close look at how Kankanmori cohousing functions, as she has been exposed to many local cohousing communities within the greater Vancouver area. Juhli grew up in WindSong Cohousing, was involved in the early stages of Vancouver Cohousing's development, and has lived in Quayside for three years; additionally, both of her aunts are involved in two other cohousing communities in the area. She is looking forward to getting to know the people at Kankanmori and is very grateful for this cultural exchange opportunity.

From Kankanmori

Haruko is a forty-four-year old working mother originally from the west of Japan (Otsu, next to Kyoto) who has lived at Kankanmori for seven years. She moved to Kankanmori when she was pregnant with her first daughter, Anna. During her seven years at Kankanmori, she had Anna and Lisa, both born and raised at this cohousing place. Haruko has been in the television industry for nearly two decades, working as a translator in the beginning and now as a fixer and producer for foreign productions filming in Japan. Her recent interest, though, has shifted to nutrition and health as her physical strength has reduced with aging. Haruko grew up in a relatively big family of six and lived in a well-connected neighborhood until the age of twenty, when she left for the United States to study in college. So it may be natural for her to find herself fitting in at Kankanmori, although she decided to move out of a student dorm after a semester because she was tired of the food at the cafeteria. She has never been to Vancouver or Canada and is thus excited to explore the city. Even though she heard it rains a lot in this season [December], she is looking forward to walking around to see and talk to the people in Quayside Village and Vancouver.

Carl is a forty-four-year-old urban planner who teaches at Tokyo's Waseda University (School of International Liberal Studies) in the areas of urban studies and transition design. Carl grew up in a small village in rural Germany, near the border of Luxembourg, Belgium, and the Netherlands. There he learned about the bright as well as the more serious sides of community. For seventeen years Carl has lived in Japan, but he never grew fond of karaoke. In his research and practice he is interested in citizen-generated community development, urban commons, and social resilience. He is also the cofounder of various nonprofits that assisted local communities in northeast Japan after the 2011 Great East Japan Earthquake. Carl's hobbies include hiking and town walking, movies, and crafts. Haruko and Carl moved to Kankanmori in the summer of 2010.

Anna is going to turn seven while she is in Quayside Village. She was in her mother's tummy when she moved to Kankanmori. She was the only child at Kankanmori at the time she was born because other families with children had moved out. She has been attending a private school taught in English since April. She takes care of her little sister Lisa very well, though they fight a lot too. She is shy in the beginning but loves to dance and sing.

Lisa, four years old, is the youngest of the family. She loves to interact with other kids whenever she has a chance. On a train or at a cafe, she turns around and starts to giggle if she spots other children. She is good at expressing her emotions while her sister Anna needs to be encouraged to do so. She is called a little monkey in the family because she climbs everywhere or runs away if you don't watch her. Her recent passion is scrawling on the floor, wall, or table. She just did it on the common table!

The Exchanges

The exchanges were bookended by conversations, some formal and others informal, between those who participated directly and the other residents of their communities. Pre-exchange suggestions for what Connie, Juhli, Donya, Haruko, and Carl might explore during their visits focused on the practical aspects of life in the other community, such as how they handled common meals, committee structures, finances, decision-making, and recycling. Following the exchanges, each group of visitors gave presentations in their home communities, outlining what they encountered; this prompted further questioning and discussion.

The exchanges took pace in the fall of 2017. Connie, Juhli, and Donya traveled to Tokyo for 10 days in mid-November, followed by Haruko, Carl, Anna, and Lisa, who spent ten days in Vancouver in early December; I was on site for both visits.[17] The visitors lived in apartments in their host community, attended common meals and a monthly meeting, prepared a common meal themselves, and visited another collective/cohousing community in the area. They also gave presentations on life in their home communities[18] and, toward the end of their visits, participated in facilitated "afternoon tea" discussions with their hosts to collaboratively explore the nature of life in their respective communities.[19] Finally, they took part in a number of planned social events, including karaoke and flower-box building at Kankanmori and, at Quayside Village, a movie night and trips to holiday-related events elsewhere in Vancouver. All of these more structured aspects of the exchanges were complemented by numerous informal interactions among the visitors and their hosts over the course of their stays.

I invited the five adult visitors to keep written track of their observations, conversations, and reactions, and to use GoPros to visually record whatever they found interesting and relevant. At the end of their trips, I asked them to reflect on the following questions: What did you find most familiar? What was most different? What surprised you? What would you find challenging were you to move into Kankanmori/Quayside Village? What did you learn about your home community? And, what practices do you feel would, or would not, translate well in your home community? Finally, one year later I invited them to contemplate the long-term impacts on their communities, if any, of the exchanges.

In various discussions with them before, during, and after their visits, and in reading their writing and viewing their films, it became clear to me that while some of what the visitors focused on had to do with pre-trip brainstorming sessions with residents of their home communities, who prompted them to attend to particular items of interest, other observations and reflections were artifacts of their very personal experiences—what struck them as most interesting, distinct, or curious as they encountered life in their host community firsthand. For instance, Donya, Connie, and Juhli did not arrive at Kankanmori with questions about space or about the place of children in the community, but both topics emerged as central once they were on-site. Similarly, once at Quayside Village, Haruko and Carl became acutely interested in the nuances of informality and the relationship between the public and the private.

As Haruko, Carl, Connie, Juhli, and Donya observed and participated in life in their host communities, I observed them observing and participating. In what follows, then, I take as my orientation their orientations to similarity and difference; to what was attractive or not; to what they found curious, interesting, or shocking; and to how what they encountered might relate to the way things worked in their home communities. Although all five adults took notes and wrote responses to my questions, it is worth noting that two were particularly prolific, and so they are perhaps overrepresented in what follows: Carl, for whom this project closely articulated with his own academic interests; and Donya, who filled a small notebook rather than a few pages with her daily observations and reflections. In addition, since all residents of Kankanmori and Quayside Village were involved with the exchanges in some way or another—as hosts, if not as travelers—I include where possible their observations and reactions as well. I begin with constructions and understandings of similarities and differences between the communities, and then turn to the reflections on their home communities prompted by the exchanges.

Family Resemblances and Disjunctures

What was most familiar about Kankanmori to Juhli, Connie, and Donya was the common meals.[10] This came as no surprise, as Juhli noted:

> I do believe that the "common meal" idea is one of the features of cohousing that sticks out the most. When I describe cohousing, that is certainly something I mention and that is a feature you wouldn't find anywhere other than maybe a senior's home. And even there, the seniors don't usually do the cooking. It is a common belief, especially in my family, that eating brings people together. It can be a way to share, relax, and be human together.

Donya echoed this sentiment: "Everyone eats! Just the normal human act of eating together will make people feel familiar. Although we do it a little differently, perhaps, we all do it." During their time at Kankanmori, the Quayside visitors also participated in building flower boxes for the common room patio.[11] Like common meals, this was easily recognizable as part and parcel of cohousing, as Connie noted in her description of the event: "Sharing activities is important in building relationships and communities."

Haruko and Carl focused on a different set of family resemblances. In addition to attending a community meeting, they participated in a meeting of the Thriving Committee (the umbrella group that focuses on the overall well-being of the Quayside Village community).[12] A significant portion of this meeting was devoted to discussing a new set of curtains in the common room that could be used to separate the kitchen from the eating and meeting space when there were multiple activities occurring simultaneously.

The discussion focused on concerns about the decision-making processes involved in choosing the color of the curtains, which, now that they were up, were considered by some to be oppressively dark. This kind of exchange resonated with Haruko: "Regarding the curtains," she reflected afterward, "things like that really happen at Kankanmori too." Carl, for his part, found some of the other challenges of collective living to be quite familiar—for example, residents' differing rates of participation in community; and he noted, in addition, the similar demographic profiles of the two communities, particularly with regard to residents' occupations and socioeconomic statuses.

These family resemblances comprise the basic building blocks of cohousing—sharing meals and undertaking projects together, like flower box building—as well as typical challenges, such as levels of participation in community life and processes of decision-making. The demographic similarities noted by Carl are also typical, since these types of intentional communities, consisting of purpose-built environments co-designed with architects and consultants, are inevitably class based.[13] What was familiar to the exchange participants, then, were the kinds of shared features that would likely be present regardless of differences in cultural context.

How shared features play out in everyday life, however, is another matter entirely, as my discussions of the conversations between philosophy and practice in chapters 2 and 3 indicate. Indeed, as the exchanges unfolded, recognition of similarities between Quayside Village and Kankanmori simultaneously served to underscore the *differences* between the two communities. The family resemblances thus began and ended with the fact that they existed. And it was the disjunctures between what they found familiar, on the one hand, and how these familiarities were materialized differently in the other community, on the other, that most captured the imaginations of the exchange participants and that took up the most conversational and reflective space.

In Connie, Juhli, and Donya's view, what was unique—and perhaps most challenging—about Kankanmori was its organizational structure. Common meals provided a case in point. As Juhli described it, Kankanmori's system for doing common meals "is quite different from ours: they have their own currency, *mori-ken*, and are much more regimented about who cooks, how often people cook, and budget." Donya compared the details of common meals at Kankanmori and Quayside Village in one of her journal entries:

> At QV anyone who *wants* to cook is welcome to sign up. At KKM, every adult must cook once per month. At QV the budget is $5 per person, more or less, with lots of flexibility as long as the accounting balances out over time. At

KKM, there is a sheet completed at every meal with precise calculations for food purchased, taxes, gas and electricity for cooking, and rice. At QV any leftovers are either frozen for future meals or offered to the community—"leftover chili in the fridge!" At KKM, leftover rice is sold that evening in equal wrapped portions, and other leftovers are sold the same way. I guess those differences came down to the need for precision. Everything [at Kankanmori] is accounted for and in its place.

She went on to list Kankanmori's protocols for cleanup, laundry, and accounting (including different prices for adults and children, and for children, different prices for different age groups), and then concluded: "OMG [oh my god], I totally get why people here feel like it's a 'duty' to make a meal."

Actually preparing a meal, rather than simply observing others doing it, brought all of this home:

A Canadian Common Meal at Kankanmori

Wanting to prepare a "Canadian" meal, Connie, Juhli, and Donya decided to make chili with cornbread and salad, followed by an apple crisp for dessert. They began by filling out the appropriate form and applying the deductions for rice, taxes, etc., so that they could calculate what they would have to spend at the store. I took the women to two grocery stores to get the ingredients—one of which, given the exotic nature (from a Japanese perspective) of some of what they had to buy, was located over an hour away by train, in a neighborhood with a high concentration of North American and European expats. They started preparations at 3:00 P.M. At one point they had to ask Emiko to come downstairs to show them how to use Kankanmori's can opener, which was different from any can opener any of them had ever seen before. They made two versions of the chili, a spicier one for adults and a milder one for the children. They did not plate the chili but instead made up a sample dish of chili, cornbread, and salad so that people serving themselves would know what the meal was supposed to look like. They did, however, in keeping with Kankanmori practice, plate the dessert.

About twenty people attended. It quickly became clear that a few people found the spicier chili to be too hot, and some children even rejected the milder version. But most of the adults enjoyed the spicy chili, and it disappeared quickly, along with the cornbread and apple crisp.

At around 8:00, after finishing the cleanup and putting the laundry in the washer, the three women started going over the accounts, with the assistance of Yoshie and the scotch that they had brought with them as a gift from Quayside Village. They were thrilled to discover that they had actually stayed within budget. They then hung up the laundry, which they folded and put away the following morning.

Including the trips to the grocery stores, one of which was admittedly at a distance from Kankanmori, the entire operation took over ten hours. Although Donya, Connie, and Juhli were too tired by the end of the evening to visit an *onsen* [Japanese bath], as we had planned, they felt that learning firsthand how common meals operated was crucial to their understanding of Kankanmori.[14]

In addition to what they felt was a more rigid approach to common meals, the Quayside visitors were also struck by the more structured nature of monthly meetings at Kankanmori relative to those at Quayside Village:[15]

> The community meeting was really something else. Everyone had a printed copy of the agenda at their seat waiting, and it was very clear what was going to happen; and the nature of the meeting was different, it was like "reports" more than discussion, and even items that were like a "discussion" item, there was very little discussion. It felt like there would be a lot more discussion at Quayside maybe. (Donya)

Clearly, then, while both communities held common meals and monthly meetings, they were organized in markedly different ways and unfolded in an unfamiliar fashion to the visitors. There were thus both parallels and dramatic disjunctures between the two communities.

Just as the more procedural aspects of life at Kankanmori came as a surprise to the Quayside visitors, Carl and Haruko were astonished by the relatively more relaxed ethos of Quayside Village. Carl wrote: "I found the fluidity most striking with which the lines between public and private are constantly crossed at QSV." He referred not only to people "briefly knocking and then walking into others' apartments" but also, and perhaps more notably, to the ways in which the personal and the official mingled at meetings. He was particularly interested in check-in and check-out, during which people made "very personal statements" about what was going on in their lives.[16] Given that "private aspects of residents' lives are not exposed in Kankanmori, nor do residents ever attempt that," he found it "difficult to say something about my private state of mind or feelings during the check-ins and -outs." Although he grew up in Germany, where this kind of sharing is also atypical, he felt that the struggles he experienced would probably be considerably augmented had he been "fully socialized in Japan."[17] Haruko explained further when she and Carl shared their experiences with Kankanmori residents upon their return from Vancouver:

> Ah. Okay, so first someone said "I'm checking in," and I thought, *What's that mean?* Then they said, "Hello, everyone. Today I did such-and-such." Every-

one just gives a short update on their situation. The same thing happened at the Thriving meeting.

The permeability of the private and the public at Quayside Village was also evidenced in the kind of language Quaysiders used, reflecting what Carl saw as "a high awareness for community dynamics." He wrote:

> By calling people in charge of a certain task or issue "champions of that project," a sense of responsibility, authorship, and self-efficacy is created on one hand, and of appreciation of the other residents, on the other. Furthermore, I could sense a high trust in the other residents' commitment to the community. Contributions to and utilization of community services are not carefully measured. Residents seem to understand that in the long run contributions to the community in different kind will be brought into balance. And where this is not the case, residents seem to accept and appreciate the differences among each other and that every person contributes to the well-being of the community in their own different and individual ways. This is very different from Kankanmori, where contributions to and utilization of community services are carefully measured, and elaborate systems safeguard that (in general) everybody has to make the same contributions, but also, cannot do significantly more. Perfect equality in the sense of sameness prevails.

Haruko made similar observations. She was surprised that there aren't "set members for their committees" and that "no one is obligated but many of them seemingly participate/contribute to the community to some extent." She noted this more relaxed ethos of Quayside Village in the presentation she and Carl gave after their return to Kankanmori:

> Everything is casual. Even with us there, there was no sense of "Publicly, we do this, we do that." Our presentation [on Kankanmori] was laid back, too, with only people available at that time attending. At the time I was surprised by what seemed like a lack of interest, but then later I was asked questions by people who hadn't been there. So there's no sense of pressure, no "Something's happening, let's go!" (Haruko)

Haruko's comments reveal that even what was marked as "official" at Quayside Village—an announced meeting—felt informal to her, so much so that she initially, and mistakenly, perceived a lack of interest on the part of Quaysiders. Indeed, the way in which Haruko and Carl's presentation unfolded at Quayside Village was in stark contrast to how the Quayside visitors' presentation played out at Kankanmori. The latter was considerably more formal in tone: it took place in a special meeting room on the first floor of the building rather than in the common room; nonresidents were invited and charged a fee to attend; and I hired a babysitter at the recommendation of Emiko and Yoshie so that it would be an adults-only event. Among the nonresidents was Yasuhiro Endoh, an academic heavily involved in promoting collective housing who traveled from Kyoto to attend. At Quayside Village, in contrast, Haruko and Carl's presentation took place in the common room, no outsiders were involved, and the event was so informal that even Elizabeth's dog attended—something that would be unheard of at Kankanmori.

Just as the Quayside Village women took particular interest in what they saw as a rigid common meal regime at Kankanmori, so Quayside's informal approaches to common meals were of particular interest to the Kankanmori community. This became evident in an exchange among Haruko, Yumiko, and Yoshie during Haruko and Carl's post-exchange presentation. Haruko had just reported that Quayside Village residents pay for common meals monthly, rather than on each occasion. Yumiko then asked for clarification on how the accounting for common meals operates:

YUMIKO: I'm not sure I understand how end-of-month payment works.

HARUKO: For example, say that on a certain day, a family eats three servings of the common meal. Servings are five dollars each, so that's fifteen dollars for that day. At the next common meal, you add the number of servings they eat then, and so on. At the end of the month, it's, "Okay, this month you pay fifty-five dollars."

YUMIKO: In that case, where does the money for the ingredients come from?

HARUKO: That's also basically end-of-month. If it's under a certain amount, maybe around eighty-five dollars, there's no need to show receipts. You just make a verbal report: "About so-and-so dollars." When I cooked it was with Catherine, and she bought the ingredients, but she had to go home a few days later so they decided to pay her back early. I saw them talking about it the next day. The treasurer said, "Oh, this is a few cents short, is that okay?" and Catherine said, "Sure, no problem," and accepted the money. That's hard to imagine at Kankanmori. Because we're very strict about paying, down to the last yen, right?

YOSHIE: What's the budget?

HARUKO: The budget's about five dollars per head. No need to worry about gas or electricity bills.

YOSHIE: So if there were twenty people, it'd be five times twenty.

HARUKO: Right. Although I was told, "You don't have to be too strict, up to six or seven dollars per head is fine, just go ahead and cook."

Later in the presentation, after they had described Quayside's Community Chest fund, AGM, and the handling of reports at monthly meetings,

Haruko and Carl displayed a photo that prompted a return to the topic of meals. In this exchange, Kankanmori residents raised a series of questions that pointed to philosophical as well as practical contrasts between the two communities:

> AKARI: At the top [of the photo] there, it says "Christmas Dinner." Is that like Kankanmori's Christmas Party?
>
> HARUKO: Right, except the event is basically a potluck. Everyone brings a dish. Because it's Christmas people do want to eat turkey, so they use everyone's money to order an organic one. I asked who prepares it and was told, "Residents who are good at cooking." So there is a turkey, but everything else is potluck.
>
> RURIKO: Are there any people who don't celebrate Christmas religiously?
>
> HARUKO: I think people who don't celebrate it could just not attend.
>
> RURIKO: It seems like pretty much everyone is in a religion that celebrates it. Actually, what religion are they there?
>
> HARUKO: I intentionally didn't ask, but unless they're Jewish or something, I think they basically all celebrate Christmas.
>
> RURIKO: Including the meal.
>
> HARUKO: The meal is basically vegetarian with meat and fish [added for those who want it]. It was like, "We have to make these two types."
>
> CARL: Also, there's no obligation on the people who make the common meal. The people who want to cook, do.
>
> HARUKO: There's no once-a-month rule or anything like that, it's just "Let's cook on Monday" and "I guess I'll cook, then." The people who want to make something put up the notice, and people apply.
>
> YOSHIE: What happens if no one wants to cook?
>
> HARUKO: I don't think that ever happens, but you know how we have quite a few things that are decided, like, "You have to do this once a month"? I asked a few people there if the lack of that didn't cause any discontent, but I think all of them said, "No, not at all." They don't see it as something to complain about. Everyone tries to be generous. They say, "We have to live with generosity. That's how we want to live." I heard from a few people that generosity was very important. It's an important part of how they think. If you're not good at cooking, for example, you contribute by gardening or some other way. No one thinks of themselves as wronging the others, or worries what the others think of them. It's okay just to do what you can in the way you can do it. It comes down to whether fairness means everybody doing the same thing, or everybody contributing with the time and skill they have. That felt like a huge difference [between Quayside Village and Kankanmori].

AYA: Do people expect quality work from volunteers? If someone says, "I want to make the meal, I'm good at it so that's what I'll do," do the others say, "I'm sure it'll be delicious"?

HARUKO: No, I don't think so. When I went, Juhli's mother cooked, and it was very tasty. But there were also crackers and cheese, and the bread was sourdough from the store, the thin-sliced kind that fills you up. They also sell bread [in Canada] that doesn't cost too much, so the stuff we bought at the supermarket instead of rice was there too, and it all struck me as very undemanding. On potluck days, too, the food ran out fairly quickly. People don't seem to feel the need to make very much food. Our dishes were empty halfway through, and I thought, *What now?* But everyone just sat around drinking.

Akari, Ruriko, Yoshie, and Aya's questions are focused on levels of formality and informality, and on the degree to which collective activities are organized, planned, or obligatory. These point, in turn, to overarching frameworks for how to go about the business of constructing and maintaining community. As was the case with the Quayside women, differences in the two communities' approaches to eating together served as metonyms, as representative of contrasts between Kankanmori and Quayside Village more generally.

The visitors articulated these contrasts in binary terms. Carl, for instance, focusing on how participation in community affairs was framed differently in the two contexts, wrote:

> Although many similar issues exist in both sociocultural and spatial contexts, they are not necessarily perceived as similarly problematic or framed from the same perspective. Nonparticipation in chores, or common meals, for example, is seen as a missed opportunity for a more intensive and fuller community life at QSV, while at Kankanmori it is seen as potentially disruptive for maintaining the harmony because those who do participate *could* be feeling exploited by the free-ridership of nonparticipants, and therefore elaborate mechanisms are devised to safeguard a minimum participation and minimum participation standards.

Connie and Donya were even more stark in how they portrayed the contrasts:

> *Kankanmori*: many rules and regulations, emphasis on everyone being required to participate equally, and to pay equally. Precise and somewhat complicated accounting. Trying so hard to be fair that it was unfair to some people.

Versus:

Quayside: much more relaxed (which has good and bad elements), requesting rather than requiring participation, rewarding participation with expressions of appreciation and a fun atmosphere while working. (Connie)

If there was a spectrum of organized ←→ free flowing, QV and Kankanmori would be pretty much at either end. Kankanmori is *very* organized with clear expectations laid out in a handbook. QV is like a tribe where knowledge and practices are passed slowly from generation to generation, and things are almost constantly shifting. (Donya)

On the one hand, then, the exchange visitors encountered communities that engaged in familiar kinds of activities and had similarly devised organizational frameworks for how to engage in those activities. On the other hand, they encountered similar activities that were, in their view, undertaken in almost diametrically opposed ways. These differences in approach to making community reflected, in turn, what the visitors saw as alternative philosophies of how to build the good life, themselves based on particular assumptions about human nature and ideas about what constitutes fairness.

Disjunctures in the Disjunctures

There were, however, patterns that seemed to interrupt the binary of Kankanmori-as-formal-and-rigid and Quayside-Village-as-informal-and-relaxed. Most notable here was the place of children in the communities. Given the general sense of order that they felt marked life at Kankanmori, Connie and Juhli were surprised to discover that, in contrast, children seemed more or less free to do as they pleased. Connie put this quite bluntly, writing that one of the most surprising things she encountered at Kankanmori was "the lack of discipline and respect among the children. There didn't seem to be any community standards for behavior." Although her tone is somewhat softer, Juhli made similar observations, noting:

> how they interacted with the children at KKM, or rather, didn't. The kids seemed to run the show when they were awake and playing, with little to no interruption from their parents or any of the other adults. They would literally climb on their parents during meetings, which seemed very challenging to keep focus, not only for the climbee, but also for the people around them witnessing the climbing.

In terms of how children behaved, then, Quayside Village appeared *more* structured to Connie and Juhli than Kankanmori. Indeed, when Quayside Village had young children in residence, babysitters were hired to look after them during meetings, and older children simply went elsewhere. Children also tended to disperse after common meals, leaving the common dining area to the adults:

> It's pretty usual after a common meal if there's some kids at a common meal then when the grown-ups are sitting and chatting after the meal, which tends to happen pretty often, then the kids will go play. As soon as they're done they put their dishes away and they go and hang out together. (Donya)

The issue of children emerged as a topic of discussion during the afternoon tea that occurred toward the end of Haruko and Carl's stay at Quayside Village. Haruko mentioned the difficulties involved in constraining children's behavior at Kankanmori:

> They like to run in the hallways, and they like to, you know, play hide and seek in the hallways with the lights off. And maybe they are getting a bit too wild. And we don't wanna hurt anyone over there [see anyone get hurt], but then we [also] don't wanna say, "You can't do this," because this is, you know, cohousing, and [we are not sure] how much discipline should we have of them.

Kathy then explained the history of how Quaysiders had addressed concerns about children's behavior:

> One of us [some time ago] heard one of the older residents call it "arsenic hour"—they said between 5:00 and 6:00 [in the afternoon]—and so we did this rule as parents: we said if your child is in the courtyard and starts screaming, you have to take them in the house. As the older residents explained, the issue wasn't about being bothered by the noise: "It's that we hear a child upset, and we can't do anything, you know? It's upsetting to hear a child upset." So we would just say, "Well let's take that child inside." We always made rules like that, and we taught the kids not to jump on, you know, the kind of things that would make adults upset, like jumping on the furniture or walking on the furniture. We tried to teach the kids about living with a lot of people and respecting other people.

These differences in how children are incorporated into the community may reflect not only general cultural contrasts in child-rearing practices[18] but also differences in the ages of the children in the two communities. At the time of the exchange, the children at Quayside were for the most part older than those at Kankanmori, some of whom still needed to be in relatively close proximity to their parents. The built environments also differ. At Quayside Village, walls separate the dining room from the kids' room and the lounge. This means that children can be nearby (and making noise), while the adults talk in peace and quiet. In contrast, the main children's play area at Kankanmori is not walled off from the rest of the common room, and so children's noisemaking is not buffered in any way.

The Quayside women's impression of Kankanmori as more structured than Quayside Village was also tempered by their experiences of social events. Donya, in particular, noted that there was much more spontaneous socializing at Kankanmori than at Quayside Village. She also pointed to what she saw as the "greater division" between the more businesslike aspects of life at Kankanmori, on the one hand, and spontaneous social encounters, on the other. After-parties following the common meal provided a key example of this.[19] As noted in chapter 3, these spontaneous gatherings occur after cleanup, when smaller groups of residents settle in the common room with snacks and drinks, often visiting late into the night. Here, official structure is left to the wayside, and people simply enjoy themselves. This being "off-duty" at Kankanmori, as Donya put it, became even more obvious when Kankanmori residents took the Quayside women to a local karaoke bar.[20] As she wrote:

> Work hard, play hard—Japanese balance? Social gatherings at KKM were awesome. Especially fascinating was our night out at karaoke. A bunch of us, including a couple old-timer guys, Yoshie and Emiko, and several younger women, went out to a karaoke bar. We were surprised when a few of the older folks suggested that we stop at the corner store to buy alcohol to smuggle in! They said, "As long as we buy one drink we can bring our own extras" and moseyed into the karaoke bar with grocery bags. What was this rule-breaking?! We were shocked. The evening was a joyful and hilarious exchange, and a great party. *Everyone* sang and was encouraged by much cheering and applause, and we laughed so much. I've only rarely had such fun at QV—the Christmas gift stealing game (fueled by alcohol and festive merriment) comes close. Maybe we just need to drink more at QV??

On another occasion, shortly before the end of the exchange, a number of us gathered for what Emiko dubbed "Saturday Night Fever." Donya wrote: "Everyone drank and ate snacks and joked. There was a *lot* of laughing. I get it now, *that's* when the endorphins flow!"

Donya's perception of an official/unofficial bifurcation at Kankanmori mirrored, in reverse, Carl's observation, noted above, of what he considered to be a much more permeable boundary between the personal and the public at Quayside Village. Interestingly, for the Quayside visitors, the clear distinction between official and informal social life at Kankanmori highlighted a pattern at Quayside Village that they had previously been unaware of, and that they now felt could be improved upon. Connie noted in this regard that at Quayside Village there "seem to be more groups that get together around common interests (e.g., the bridge group); but we don't tend to just hang out in the common house without a reason." Similarly, Donya observed that "there is socializing [at Quayside], but it seems like it happens more when there's an organized activity. There's a movie or here's some games or yoga or a party or a potluck. There needs to be some kind of invitation to socialize rather than hanging out." So, while the boundaries at Quayside Village seemed to be more porous than those at Kankanmori, there also seemed to be less social spontaneity.

Haruko, for her part, was curious about overall levels of social connection at Quayside Village. She was puzzled to discover that, aside from common meals and meetings, Quaysiders did not use the common room very often. This contrasted sharply with the pattern at Kankanmori. She had observed that Quayside residents seemed to visit each other's units quite often, and "so that covers the living collectively part." But, she wrote, "I would like to know how their events go too. Because they go with [the] flow more than us, who plan so much in advance, maybe their participation is lower than us?" Her questions, focused on both planned and spontaneous socializing, pointed to a potential disjuncture between Quayside Village's ethos of relaxed informality, on the one hand, and its possible lower frequency of social engagement, on the other.

In general, the Quayside women were quite surprised by the disjunctures they encountered—the looseness of Kankanmori's unofficial social life in light of its rigid structures of participation and its ethos of order, on the one hand, and what they saw as the children's unruliness, on the other. In comparison, Haruko and Carl saw the disconnections they observed at Quayside Village as minor. Indeed, Haruko's reflections, above, provided the only instance of a potential disjuncture in the general pattern of life at Quayside Village that she and Carl observed. For the most part, the various features of life they encountered at Quayside appeared to them to fit together more or less seamlessly.

Explaining the Differences

In working to make sense of the contrasts between the two communities that they observed, the exchange visitors drew on three overlapping frameworks: culture, space, and renting versus owning.

Culture

In Haruko and Carl's view, culture was key to understanding the differences in how Quayside Village and Kankanmori approached the division of labor, the running of meetings, the parameters of appropriate emotional expression, and the regulation of boundaries between the public and the private. As already noted, Carl suspected that an unequal distribution of tasks would threaten to disrupt life at Kankanmori, since it would give rise to "feeling exploited by the free-ridership of nonparticipants," a potential that Haruko interpreted in explicitly cultural terms:

> *I see there is no set rules* [at Quayside Village as] *most different*. Our duties (cooking common meals once a month, cleaning duties once every two months on average, etc.) are provided to everyone equally, and that equality may be cultural.

Haruko also referred to culture, and to the Japanese educational system in particular, when claiming that Quayside Village's ad hoc approach to running meetings would not be viable at Kankanmori:

> In class you are basically silent until your teacher names you to answer. For younger kids, it doesn't happen much but as you get older, this becomes really typical. Generally we are very passive. Hard to imagine it [open, ad hoc process] would work at Kankanmori.

This frame of not-putting-oneself-forward mirrored Carl's interpretation of the more rigid division between the public and the personal at Kankanmori:

> Much of the repertoire of sophisticated social rituals and habitualized forms of interaction in Japan have developed to keep personal things out of the public sphere and to create a pleasant, but ultimately superficial, social situation. There is a sense that people don't want to burden others with their own personal problems.

Recall, in addition, Carl's observation that his struggles to come up with something personal to say during "check-in" at Quayside Village would have been more pronounced had he been "fully socialized in Japan."[21] The Quayside visitors similarly referred to aspects of the "Japanese personality" when trying to make sense of those practices at Kankanmori that they found puzzling. Donya wondered in particular about "the cultural seed of precision in Japan," as well as about a "work hard, play hard mentality: Japanese balance?"

Quayside Village practices were also occasionally understood in cultural terms. During the official afternoon tea at Kankanmori, for instance, Juhli explained Quayside's approach to voluntary participation in terms of

> an understanding or belief, not only in Quayside but maybe in Canadian culture, [that] if you don't give, you don't receive as much, so I think that is very

prevalent. Being with people that are contributing all the time, we feel compelled to contribute, or, you know, when you're seeing that modeled around you, you don't have to be told, "Hey, you should" contribute.

Most invocations of Canadian culture were, however, indirect, implicit in comments about "Japanese culture" that pointed to, without explicitly stating, something "different" from a Canadian culture that all five of the exchange visitors saw as more "relaxed," even if they did not classify this relaxedness as "cultural." Clearly, Quayside Village's philosophies and practices can be as easily interpreted in cultural terms as any at Kankanmori. The hydraulic theory of emotion, for instance, and the *each-according-to-their-strengths, each-according-to-their-desires* philosophy that informs life at Quayside Village are as culturally specific as the emphasis on harmony, the avoidance of conflict, and the *equality = sameness* ideologies that lie at the foundation of Kankanmori's collective life. And yet, reflecting, perhaps, its global dominance, the West seemed to be the unmarked norm against which Japanese "difference" was placed into relief, with the result that the visitors—Haruko and Carl, as well as Connie, Juhli, and Donya—placed more emphasis on Japanese culture than Canadian.

Space

The built environment and the potential uses to which it was put comprised the second explanatory framework visitors used in reflecting on differences between Quayside Village and Kankanmori. In Carl's view, more thought was put into planning the built environment at Quayside Village than at Kankanmori, particularly with regard to the facilitation of social interaction:

> In order to enter the central courtyard and individual apartments, most residents of QSV have to pass the central entrance hall and the common spaces. This is creating further opportunities for social exchanges. People in these spaces cannot be overlooked without greeting. At Kankanmori, on the other side, the common spaces can be bypassed by those who want to avoid them. Clearly architecture does play an important role here [at QV], as more public parts of the apartments face the public courtyard and thus provide semipublic/private interfaces, while private parts are more protected from view.

Carl also noted that there was more room at Quayside Village than at Kankanmori for "customizing" space—for inserting homelike touches. Donya, however, had an alternative interpretation of the impact of space on sociality: "On the first floor at Kankanmori, for anybody to just come out their door the common house is basically right there, and for almost all of us [at

Quayside Village] you have to go somewhere else than your own place [to get to the common room]." She noted that residents whose units were on the first floor at Quayside Village might naturally find themselves near the common room on a regular basis, but that "you really have to make a decision from any other floor to go there." Thus, while Carl found the architecture of Quayside Village to be more conducive to serendipitous encounters, Donya felt the opposite—that Kankanmori's spatial configurations were more encouraging of spontaneous interactions than Quayside's, contributing to her view, shared by Connie and Juhli, that Kankanmori residents experienced a richer social life than did Quaysiders.

Not long into her stay at Kankanmori, Donya noticed another set of issues related to space. "The different use of space is becoming clearer," she wrote:

> Each apartment is so small, the privacy level is different. Inviting people over might be like inviting someone into the intimacy of your bedroom rather than your living room; the common house *is* your living room here. That makes sense to me. Yoshie also said their spaces are so small, it feels embarrassing. I bet that at Quayside we miss out on these spontaneous opportunities for socializing because our homes are "too big." It would be interesting to study the balance of, or I guess relationship between, size of physical space and feelings of connectedness.

The consensus of the women from Quayside Village, then, was that people at Kankanmori did not spend much time in each other's apartments because they were too small, and that this contributed to the greater frequency of spontaneous socializing in the community and perhaps also to a wider range of social connections. They were surprised to discover that "even those with close friendships have never set foot in each other's homes" (Donya). So, again, while Carl felt that the architecture of Quayside Village enhanced social relations, Donya felt that the larger size of Quayside Village units inhibited spontaneous socializing, while the smaller units at Kankanmori encouraged it. They read space, and its impact on social relations, differently.

Renting versus Owning

Finally, the ownership-based organization of Quayside Village versus the rental-based approach of Kankanmori played a key role in the Quayside women's interpretations of the differences between their communities. In Juhli's view, the owner/renter contrast was "the most different element between KKM and QV." She speculated that owners would likely remain in the community longer than renters, and that they might also tend to be more invested in community processes and relationships: ownership "creates a whole different mindset and commitment to the space and the people you're around," she wrote, adding that "I think people at QV are much more emotionally attached to the space than at KKM." The difference in turnover rates between the two communities is indeed significant, with an average rate of 1.36 units per year at Quayside Village and 4 per year at Kankanmori. (The difference remains significant even when the communities are adjusted for size: if it had as many units as Kankanmori, Quayside Village's average turnover rate would be 2.07, still well below that of Kankanmori.)

In the Quayside women's perspective, the rental-based organization of Kankanmori was connected to its more rigid participation structure: "Kankanmori needs its residents to know, without doubt, what to do to contribute to the community," wrote Donya. This was in contrast to Quayside Village, where new residents can take their time getting settled in. Although neither Haruko nor Carl mentioned the owner/renter contrast, both Yoshie and Emiko had discussed this with me on numerous occasions, indicating that, in their view, it comprised a key dimension of contrast between the two communities, influencing both turnover rates and levels of emotional attachment.

These three explanatory frameworks of course overlap: ideas about personality types and emotional expression are reflected not only in approaches to organizing interpersonal relations but also in orientations to space and, perhaps to a certain extent, in ideas about property ownership. Although they did not holistically connect these frameworks—likely an artifact of the relatively short periods of time they spent in their host communities—the visitors' insights into culture, space, and renting versus owning are testimony to the seriousness with which they explored their host community in relation to the grounds of what works, or could work, to produce the good life at home. Their insights also dovetail with some of my own observations, as described in chapters 2 and 3, further underscoring their talents for acute scrutiny: as experienced cohousers, they had a clear sense of what to look for, and they were quick to notice the unexpected.

Bringing It All Back Home

The exchanges opened up possibilities for residents of Kankanmori and Quayside Village to learn about themselves via their engagements with each other—to reflect on the value, positive or negative, of how they went about the business of building and maintaining their communities. It also gave them an opportunity to encounter alternative practices that could potentially serve to enhance or improve what was already in place. In addition, residents of the two communities worked together, across their differences, to collaboratively reflect on cohousing in general and, by implication, to consider how living collectively contributes to happiness and well-being. In what follows, I explore how Carl and Haruko, on the one hand, and Juhli, Donya, and Connie, on the other, took up these opportunities, focusing in particular on what they felt might—and might not—be good to experiment with in their home communities. Their assessments provide insight into how they viewed both the philosophical overlaps and the points of contrast between Quayside Village and Kankanmori, suggesting, in turn, how they evaluated the potential contributions of various practices to well-being.

From Kankanmori to Quayside Village

Juhli, Connie, and Donya all thought that Quayside Village would benefit from adopting certain elements of Kankanmori's more structured framework. Most notable in this regard were Kankanmori's handbook of procedures and its systematic approach to orienting potential and new residents. In her journal, Connie had written that Kankanmori's orientation "is something we need to emulate. We have been very careless in providing information to newcomers." She reiterated this view in a conversation we had when taking a quick break from preparing a common meal at Kankanmori, noting that it would be useful

> to have it all written down, and you hand them [new residents] a sheet of papers and you don't have to go over and take them around and show them this, and you don't have to wait for them to ask questions to let them know how things work. You've got it all written down and they can read it at their leisure and most of their questions are answered by that orientation handbook.

Even with an orientation tour, she continued, newcomers might forget things, and so an orientation manual would give them something concrete to which they could refer later. Juhli concurred: "An orientation manual would be really helpful. There are unique systems at QV that would be learned faster if there was an official orientation, or a manual to look at, for example, [on] the recycling and the compost systems." Donya had written in her journal that it was common for new residents at Quayside Village "to feel unsure of how to contribute. People here have reported that they want to help the community but don't know what to do. There is no handbook, no written expectations, no one 'policing' who does what." She reiterated this point later over afternoon tea:

It took me easily three years of just paying attention to what was happening before I felt like I had anything to contribute. You know, I was just, like, "Well, I don't know," so you figure it out and I'll just go with the flow, until a later date when I was, like, "Well, actually now I have something that I feel like I can contribute."

The women were also impressed with the frequency of common meals at Kankanmori, and at one time or another all three mentioned that increasing the number of common meals at Quayside Village would enrich community life. Indeed, immediately upon their return from Tokyo, Donya, Juhli, and Juhli's partner Ian made a common brunch, emulating the Kankanmori structures that permitted those who were unable to cook in the evenings to host brunches or lunches on the weekend.

The Quayside visitors' reactions to Kankanmori's structured presentation of itself to newcomers and to the frequency of its common meals did not go unnoticed by Carl and Haruko. Working to make sense not only of Quayside Village but also of how Quaysiders made sense of Kankanmori, Haruko reported upon returning to Kankanmori that the Quayside visitors

> said that Kankanmori was rather structural. Things are decided and you have to do them properly. Actually, the people at QV said that they have too little of that, and seeing Kankanmori made them think they should work on it a bit. Take common meals, for example—Juhli always has work on Monday nights, so she'd been there for several years but never cooked. But when we went there, she heard that Kankanmori has common meals for breakfast and lunch too, which made her think, *I see, that's an option, then*, and hold a common brunch. She said, "This is the first common meal I've run, I realized it was okay after hearing about Kankanmori, and that's why I'm doing it today," which was great to hear. I was happy that she would say that. If people who can't do one thing can participate at another time—well, how the people who live somewhere participate, what their lifestyle is like, that seemed the important thing to me.

At the other end of the spectrum from structure, Donya's claim, when writing about the karaoke evening at Kankanmori, that "I've only rarely had such fun at QV," expresses the women's envy of the spontaneity of social life at Kankanmori. This led to a desire for more frequent and, in particular, more impromptu social activities at Quayside Village, and the women contemplated how they might go about creating the conditions of possibility for that.

On the one hand, then, Connie, Juhli, and Donya were interested in adopting aspects of what they saw as the more systematic approach of Kankanmori, and, on the other hand, they wanted to emulate what they experienced as Kankanmori's looser, more spontaneous—and even more fun—way of socializing. Their experiences, then, incited a desire for more structure in some domains of life at Quayside Village and less in others.

There were other features of life at Kankanmori that the women were less inclined to pursue; namely, the requirement that residents sit on two committees and prepare one common meal a month. Here is what they wrote about this:

> Forcing participation only breeds resentment and is counterproductive when we are trying to build a cohesive community. Encouragement and appreciation work much better. (Connie)

> One thing that I don't think would work at QV is the requirement for every adult to cook once a month. QV has a more laid-back approach to community living and socializing, and I think there would be a lot of pushback and resentment if there was a rule like that. I don't even know who would enforce it or how! (Juhli)

> Overall, the duties required by KKM residents would just not fly at QV. I don't think anyone here wants anyone else to feel burdened. There's also a level of trust that even if we all let it slide a while, things won't fall apart. All's well in the end. (Donya)

The issue of voluntary versus obligatory participation emerged during the afternoon tea held toward the end of Donya, Connie, and Juhli's time in Tokyo.[22] Focusing on Kankanmori's committee structure, Donya asked, "Is there any way of recognizing or honoring people's gifts or abilities or energy levels, so that people can be of service to the community joyfully?" Carl responded:

> CARL: I think something like that doesn't really work very well in Japan because if you elevate one person, that means that that person is in that respect better or did more than the others but then automatically you imply that the others did not, and this is what we don't want to do.
> DONYA: And that's not okay.
> CARL: Everything has to be connected, that's what this whole bureaucracy is doing, trying to put everyone, or keep everyone at one level, so you cannot have this kind of distinction because it would create friction that we don't want to have, that we cannot have, that we cannot have or accept somehow in Japan.

Later in the same conversation, Carl circled back to ask:

> CARL: Is there no case whatsoever where you feel that there's one person or a couple of persons who are just not contributing enough and

where you feel personally also angry or something—"move your butt" or something like that? How would you deal with such a situation, or is there no need to deal with it because we are all connected?

CONNIE: *Kumbaya.*

DONYA: Well, so, there are people that don't contribute, and they're also the least connected.

Toward the end of the conversation, Connie summed up what she saw as the key differences between Kankanmori's and Quayside's approach to participation:

You can't always make everything completely equal because that's not always fair. There are different needs and different capacities and those things we feel need to be respected. So it's not always a question of making sure everyone is equal, we don't expect that.

What emerges in this exchange are the different, even diametrically opposed, philosophical frameworks within which Kankanmori's and Quayside Village's practices of community participation unfold. In her journal, Donya drew a visual representation of these frameworks (see figure 4.1). In this image, the more businesslike an activity, the lower its potential for human connection, and vice versa. This is, of course, a Quaysider view, reflecting a particular set of assumptions about human nature and connection. A different set of assumptions are in operation at Kankanmori. And in

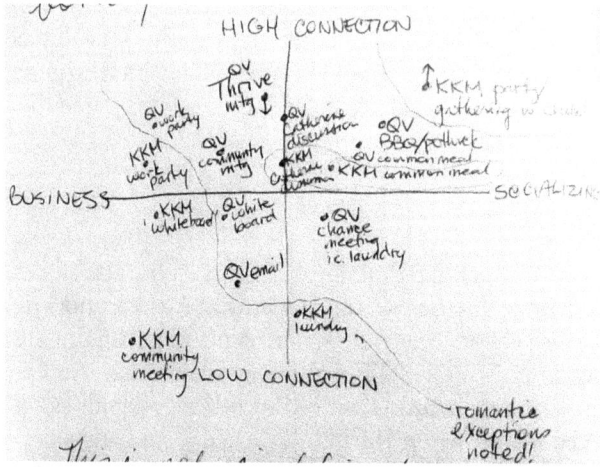

FIGURE 4.1. Donya's view of high/low connection and socializing versus business at Kankanmori and Quayside Village. Reproduced with permission of Donya Metzger.

both cases, these assumptions are more or less taken for granted, simultaneously informing and being reinforced by their organizational structures. What the exchange did, then, was open up the possibility for noticing this taken-for-grantedness.

On a smaller scale than rules about committee participation and common meal preparation—although similarly pointing to ideas about fairness—the Quayside women also felt that Kankanmori's laundry procedures would not translate well at Quayside Village. Neither Donya nor Connie could imagine that Quaysiders would tolerate regulations regarding laundry, and they felt that a payment regime would only add a cumbersome and impractical layer of bureaucracy. It did not bother them—as they felt it might Kankanmori residents—that one household might run two loads of laundry for every ten run by another household. Juhli, on the other hand, focusing in particular on the organization of space in the laundry room, wrote that "a more accountable laundry system" at Quayside Village would not go amiss: "Laundry gets left for too long, and the room often feels crowded and there are laundry baskets everywhere"—a situation that Haruko found curious, as she told her co-residents at Kankanmori:

> There are only two of each machine. We used them about four times, maybe? You don't pay anything at all. When the previous person's washing is done, you just pop it into a basket. I looked in daily, and there were plenty of people who left clothes there for three or four days. Only after they'd been through the dryer, of course. That was interesting.

Finally, the Quayside Village women did not find the idea of *mori-ken* attractive. It was, indeed, somewhat puzzling to them: "It really seemed like a lot of work for no good reason to us Quayside Villagers who generally agree that it will 'all come out in the wash'" (Donya)—a principle that applies as equally to common meals as laundry.

Although they recognized that by definition spontaneity could not be planned in advance, by the end of their stay at Kankanmori Juhli, Donya, and Connie were eager to see looser forms of socializing at Quayside Village. They were also interested in moving away from the fixed Monday night common meal schedule to allow for other possibilities on an ad hoc basis. As noted above, when Haruko returned from Quayside Village, she described to her co-residents how Juhli had copied the brunch option that Kankanmori put in place to accommodate residents whose work schedules precluded preparing evening meals. It is worth noting, however, that although this option was structured in to Kankanmori's common meal procedures, in the context of Quayside Village it would, if widely taken up, represent a loosening.

The Quayside Village women were not interested, however, in Kankanmori's regulations regarding committee participation, common meal preparation, laundry etiquette, and *mori-ken*—all of which they felt would not fit with the ethos of Quayside Village. The one exception to this had to do with the structuring of information for prospective and new residents; indeed, their encounter with Kankanmori's systematic and comprehensive approach to orientation made Quayside Village's ad hoc approach seem woefully inadequate by comparison. Thus, while some of Quayside's own practices were validated, others were held up to scrutiny and found wanting. In the end, despite feeling strongly that aspects of what they saw as Kankanmori's "rigidity" would not translate well in the context of Quayside Village's more laissez-faire ethos, the three women found much to emulate, as Donya summarized in her journal:

> Some of the clarity exemplified at KKM would be great to adopt at QV. We've talked a lot about *really* writing a handbook so newcomers can get the info they need to integrate sooner. I also really love the idea of having more social events. Working together is really important, but so is playing together. Community is built on relationships, and I think better bonds are created by play.

Connie, Juhli, and Donya's engagements with life at Kankanmori, as well as their evaluations of Quayside's practices in light of these encounters, were clearly oriented to a desire to create the best possible life. Emulating Kankanmori's more structured approach to orientation, for instance, would serve to ease the transition of new residents into the community, reducing any potential anxiety or uncertainty. In keeping with Quayside Village's spirit of informality, however, they did not want to introduce *too much* structure. There was a balance, then, between adding enough structure to be useful but not so much as to be oppressive. The emphasis on increasing social connection—"better bonds are created by play"—is similarly about improving community life. The women's curiosity about how things unfolded in another cohousing community in another culture was, in the end, oriented pragmatically, toward creating an even better life at Quayside Village.

From Quayside Village to Kankanmori

Connie, Juhli, and Donya were specific in outlining which aspects of life at Kankanmori they felt Quayside Village should adopt and which they felt would, and should, be rejected. In making these choices, they emphasized those Kankanmori practices that, in their view, would enhance well-being at Quayside Village *as it was*; the focus was on tinkering and making small improvements, not on introducing fundamental change. In contrast, Carl and Haruko, while also choosing particular practices to emulate, zeroed in on Quayside Village practices that they felt would precipitate profound changes to Kankanmori's approach to the good life.

When they returned to Tokyo, Haruko and Carl signaled their desire for change in how they structured their presentation on their experiences at Quayside Village:

> HARUKO: We visited Quayside Village. It was an excellent experience that we were very happy with. We hope to return the benefits of that experience to Kankanmori, not just through this presentation but also by treating it as an opportunity to think about how we can use what we learned going forward. If you have any questions, please feel free to speak up.
>
> CARL: We also wanted to make today's presentation in this slightly unusual place. As you'll see in the presentation, creating spaces is extremely important at QV. They live here [referring to image on screen] and are very attached to it. There's no gap between public and private. It's smooth.

The "unusual place" Carl was referring to was the section in the Kankanmori common room with couches and a library—a relatively informal space, given that meetings are usually held in the dining area, with people seated at tables arranged in a large square to face each other. In addition, both Haruko and Carl sat on the floor in relaxed postures. Their goal, then, was to recreate the informal feel of life at Quayside Village, where, as Haruko put it, "everything is casual."

By the end of their stay at Quayside Village, Haruko and Carl had come to the conclusion that Kankanmori could benefit from a more open and flexible approach to making community. In her written commentary, Haruko referred specifically to Kankanmori's committee system (*kakari*): "Maybe we can make something to look over the whole community instead of only having the divided group structure. Something like the [QV] Thriving Committee." Carl's reflections echo this sentiment:

> The Thriving Committee is the practice that has the most potential to enrich life in Kankanmori. Currently, regular monthly meetings in Kankanmori are seen rather critically by many residents as empty rituals: they mainly serve to report facts, such as the number of common meals served in the previous month, or to formally vote on decisions that are already settled in informal

pre-meetings—so-called workshops. Very rarely are there really open discussions in the meeting, and even rarer people talking about personal matters. Many residents perceive that the purpose of living in Kankanmori is mainly to perform community duties and chores in their own right, and because procedures and tasks were decided by former residents. The Thriving meeting, on the other hand, focuses directly on the question: "How can we make our lives thriving?" Thus the quality of life and well-being are in the center. After we presented about the Thriving meeting to residents of Kankanmori, many realized that life should no longer be structured by rules but rather that new rules and procedures should be developed in order to allow for more fun and a higher quality of life.

In Carl's perspective, Kankanmori's *kakari* and its formalized approach to community meetings, both ostensibly designed to produce the good life, were possibly doing the opposite. The question prompted by the mere existence of a Thriving Committee—"How can we make our lives thriving?"—led him to conclude that new systems should be put in place, the primary purpose of which would be to "allow for more fun and a higher quality of life."

What Haruko and Carl found attractive about Quayside Village's Thriving Committee was, first of all, that meetings took place in private spaces.[23] This made for an informal atmosphere that could encourage residents to share the "private" aspects of their lives, which, Carl said, "are not exposed at Kankanmori, nor do residents ever attempt that." This sharing would enable residents to be more supportive of each other—something that Quaysiders consider foundational to a flourishing community. In addition, and equally important, the Thriving model cut across existing committee divisions, creating space for general, overarching discussions about how to approach life as a whole. This would serve as an antidote to the silo-ization that Haruko and Carl felt characterized Kankanmori's *kakari*, where issues were narrowly confined to specific committees, with little opportunity to work across them or to recognize the impact of activities in one area on others. Thus, in summarizing what she learned from her stay at Quayside Village, Haruko wrote that

> I learned to think there could be a way to make our lives at Kankanmori for ourselves rather than try hard to stick to the original Swedish way [that served as a model for Kankanmori] because our way of living is so different comparing to Sweden and what is important is us, who live here right now. Change is totally fine, or we have to change. That's what I learned through my stay at QV.

These comments echo Ikuko Koyabe's view, noted in chapter 1, that "instead of just taking the ideas of Northern European countries," the goal was "to adjust their ideas to our lifestyle. We wanted to introduce something new."[24] In other words, Koyabe did not intend for the Swedish model to be determinative but generative, giving rise to approaches that would meet the unique and specific needs of Japanese. Haruko's experiences at Quayside Village prompted her to extend this perspective temporally, highlighting the importance of questioning historically sedimented habits and of adjusting models to current lifestyles and needs.

Despite their attraction to Quayside Village's more flexible approach, Carl and Haruko were initially unsure as to how acceptable it would be to Kankanmori residents. As Haruko had written, duties at Kankanmori "are provided to everyone equally, and that equality may be cultural." In other words, the structure of residents' obligations at Kankanmori reflected something about Japanese approaches to fairness—the *everybody is equal* and *fairness = sameness* frameworks outlined in chapter 3. On a smaller scale, as noted earlier, Haruko also felt that Quayside Village's practice of appointing chairs and minute takers at meetings on an ad hoc basis "wouldn't probably work in Japan because how we are educated is very different." Carl similarly wondered how well the "flexibility and deliberately emergent nature of rules and organizational structures" at Quayside would translate at Kankanmori. This was evident in the afternoon tea exchange between Carl, Donya, and Connie, included above. Thus neither Haruko nor Carl were confident that Quayside Village's laissez-faire approach to participation would fit well at Kankanmori.

∽∽∽

As was the case with Donya, Juhli, and Connie, Haruko and Carl were fundamentally oriented to using what they learned at Quayside Village to enhance the good life at Kankanmori. Their desire to change Kankanmori's committee structure mirrored concerns about the inflexibility of the system expressed by other residents, as discussed in chapter 3. At the same time, their hesitance about whether Quayside's more relaxed approach would be acceptable to Kankanmori residents was not without basis: some residents felt that Kankanmori's ordered sets of procedures provided the grounds of possibility for community, and some, in encountering Quayside Village's system, wondered if it would not give rise to concerns about fairness. Recall Junko's comment at the afternoon tea when Connie, Juhli, and Donya were at Kankanmori:

> Compared to what we heard about QV just now, Kankanmori's committees have more detailed rules, and there are other specific obligations, like common meal duty once a month, cleanup every two months, locking up. But I

wonder if that isn't what preserves the sense of fairness. It seemed to me that the greater freedom at QV might also make the things that are unfair worse. The question is whether you do think of it as unfair—and if you mind that unfairness. Or whether there's something that regulates that.

There were, then, two lines of thought at Kankanmori, one that on occasion found its organizational structure challenging and perhaps even oppressive, and another that saw it as stabilizing and comforting. As I describe below, however, the challenging/oppressive perspective prevailed in the end and, buttressed by the exchange, contributed to significant, albeit tentative, shifts in Kankanmori's approaches to community life.

One Year Later

A year after the exchanges, I asked Haruko, Carl, Connie, Juhli, and Donya to consider whether the visits had any long-term impacts on their communities. Did the exchanges lead to the introduction of any new ideas or practices? If so, what shape did these new ideas and practices take? Or, perhaps, were some or all of the orientations of their home communities validated, newly recognized not just as the way things are but as the way they should be?

Changes at Quayside Village

The Quayside women considered the more structured approach to orientation being adopted at Quayside Village to be one of the most significant long-term impacts of their time at Kankanmori. As Connie wrote:

> We have really worked on a manual for new residents and visitors. We will also be working up an orientation video, and I know that we realized the need for that from our visit to Kankanmori. We knew we need a manual, but Kankanmori lit a fire under us (that's relative, of course, because it has still been more than a year!).

This new manual and video reflected Quayside Village's desire to "improve our welcoming process for new residents" (Juhli).

As noted above, information for potential and new residents was the only aspect of what the Quayside visitors saw as the more structured life at Kankanmori that they felt their co-residents would be interested in adopting. Donya, however, wondered if a change in how monthly meetings were organized might have also been influenced, at least in part, by the exchange. Whereas facilitators and note takers for community meetings previously volunteered on an ad hoc basis, shortly after the exchange Quayside Village began trialing a meeting facilitation team of three that would remain consistent over time. Donya was unsure of the extent of Kankanmori's influence on this process, but she did note that "this greater organization has been a shift closer to the Kankanmori-style meeting, although not that far"—by which she was referring to the rigid time allocations for topics (one to ten minutes) and the lack of open discussion she noted in her journal during her stay at Kankanmori. Interestingly, in keeping with Quayside's *each-according-to-their-strengths, each-according-to-their-desires* philosophy, there is a division of labor among the team of three that reflects individual skills and proclivities. Duong, for instance, who has a background in counseling, is the main facilitator of discussions at meetings and, as Donya put it, "is finding a sweet spot of keeping everyone grounded and getting voices heard while staying on task," while Elise, who has taken up the job of seeking input into the agenda, "is great at advance communication." So, there may be slightly more structure, but not as much as at Kankanmori, and in a form in keeping with Quayside Village philosophy.

Another feature of life at Kankanmori that all three women wanted to bring back with them to Quayside Village was flexibility with regard to common meal schedules. Although in the past Quayside Village held common meals twice a week, at the time of the research for this book they were happening only once a week, on Mondays. Juhli, in particular, was interested in expanding this, since she herself was never able to participate on Mondays. She experimented with this as soon as she returned from Tokyo, making a Sunday brunch with her partner, Ian, and Donya. A year later, however, she noted that although "occasionally there have been common meals on different nights at Quayside in an attempt to include cooks that aren't able to cook on the weekly designated meal night," the pattern hasn't taken hold.

Finally, all three women were profoundly impressed with the level of spontaneous socializing at Kankanmori, and they hoped to infuse some of that energy into Quayside Village. A year later, Connie and Donya noted that Quayside Village's social life was, in fact, expanding—"thanks largely to Donya," according to Connie. Donya wrote:

> We haven't had too many more meals, but we've upped our party game! We had a New Year's party with Driftwood cohousing [a new community being built just up the road from Quayside] that was quite fun and included a "variety show"; I bet we'll make that a tradition. There is also another Oscar Party planned for this year, and several screenings of nominated movies ahead of time.

Although these parties were not impromptu—which was precisely the aspect of Kankanmori's social life that they found most desirable—the women hoped that simply increasing the number of social events, even if organized, would lay the groundwork for more spontaneity.

Although, as with the organization of monthly meetings, she was not sure about any direct connection, Donya noted that Kathy, one of the founding members of Quayside Village and a core member who contributes significant energy to community life, started doing a little less community work, at the insistence of Carol, another founding member. Since "those of us who visited Japan saw more clearly what happens when a very small group of people do much more than their share of tasks," Donya wondered if the exchange might have contributed to this shift. Whatever its actual impact, her comments point to the influence of the women's visit to Kankanmori on their own thinking. While I doubt that she would let go of the importance of "recognizing or honoring people's gifts or abilities or energy levels, so that people can be of service to the community joyfully," a point she raised with her hosts in Tokyo, the visit to Kankanmori provided, perhaps, a widescreen reflection on fairness in the distribution of labor.

Changes at Kankanmori

During her stay at Quayside Village, Haruko attended the Sunday morning yoga class held in the common room. Shortly after her return to Kankanmori, she initiated community yoga and exercise classes, drawing on another resident's connections with a yoga teacher to set up three classes a month in the common room, complemented, during the fourth week, with a general body maintenance course. The classes have been a success.[25] Although certainly not disruptive of Kankanmori's overall structure, this intervention represented precisely the kind of initiative that Quayside Village's Thriving Committee would support.

More profound in terms of its potential to reform Kankanmori's organizational framework and ethos was Carl and Haruko's introduction of a provisional committee that, mirroring Quayside Village's Thriving Committee, would incorporate all other committees under one umbrella and would be organized in such a way as to encourage, or at least invite, interpersonal sharing. During the year following the exchange, the "thrive" group (participants had not yet decided on a permanent name) met five times. Significantly, in keeping with the desire to create an informal atmosphere that would allow people, if they chose, to discuss personal difficulties or voice concerns about Kankanmori's organization, the meetings were held in someone's apartment rather than in the common room. This informal atmosphere was key, according to Carl and Haruko, since those residents who were reluctant to bring up personal hardships at the monthly community meetings might feel more comfortable doing so in a less formal context. If residents could be more open about their concerns and get more support from others to work through them, then Kankanmori might not lose members for the wrong reasons.

A Thriving model could also provide space to address the perception that "currently duties are too numerous and too demanding," as Carl put it. Although this perception was not initiated by the presence of the Quayside visitors, it was certainly validated by it, as Kankanmori residents discovered that Quayside Village had only a handful of committees and that participation in them was voluntary. After learning this, and despite opportunities for discussion provided by the many common meals and the official afternoon tea held during the Quayside women's stay, several Kankanmori residents asked to meet with Donya, Connie, and Julhi separately and privately. Some of them had work schedules that prevented them from participating in the other events, but, more importantly, they wanted to enjoy the company of the Quayside women in a smaller, more intimate setting—*and* to have time to learn more about how community participation happened at Quayside Village. During her time at Quayside Village Haruko had paid close attention to this issue, later writing that

> as soon as we were back from QV, we started talking about no set obligations at QV and that's also a community seemingly working. I wasn't saying we should completely copy them, but giving everyone the equal amount of chores may not necessarily be fair. There are different stages in life, and if we want us to live here for a longer time, we need to accept those times when you are very busy with raising children/work/taking care of your family, etc.

More generally, she wrote, "I now am vocal about having more diversity or flexibility, not based on because [this is] how it has been since Kankanmori's foundation, but it's totally natural that we change and modify ideas and rules accordingly as residents change." Some of the residents who wanted to meet with the Quayside women in a small group shared Haruko's sentiment and were consequently supportive of Haruko and Carl's "thrive" initiative.

Thus, although Carl and Haruko were initially concerned that Quayside Village's looser, more flexible approach to community life would not translate well in Kankanmori for cultural reasons, they eventually changed their minds. Several months after the exchange visit, and before the first "thrive" meeting at Kankanmori, Carl wrote that "not a single practice of QSV would be inappropriate for Kankanmori. If properly framed and explained and if responding to a real need, any practice can be transferred." And so, a year and a half after the exchanges, and after a number of "thrive" meetings and a great deal of discussion, Kankanmori residents launched a two-pronged experiment. First, they reduced the number of main committees to five: Communications, Common Meal, House Maintenance, Gardening, and Treasurer. The tasks remain the same—they are just combined into fewer groups—but residents are only required to sit on one of the committees. (There are still five subgroups, but Wood Shop subgroup was dropped and a Senior subgroup introduced, charged with "discussing the life of seniors at Kankanmori and setting rules.") Second, they eliminated *mori-ken*. People can now pay for common meals in advance, through a cash deposit system, and guest room usage is also paid for directly with cash. Payments for laundry were initially eliminated altogether, but in the first six months utility costs increased significantly, and so charges were reinstated, but at a reduced rate, and in the form of a pay-later system. All of these changes were instituted on a trial basis, to be revisited yearly at the AGM.

How the ideas and practices the visitors brought back to their home communities unfold in the longer run remains to be seen. This is especially the case for Kankanmori, given the experiments with committee structures and *mori-ken* that they launched after the exchanges. Although a description of how these changes are taking shape is beyond the scope of this book, that they are occurring at all indicates that Kankanmori's relatively rigid and systematic organizational structure, as described in chapter 3 and experienced by the Quayside Village visitors, is not itself as fixed or rigid as it might seem. On the contrary, Kankanmori's experiments with change point to a community that is flexible and open to exploring new, alternative approaches to increasing the happiness and well-being of its members.

Conclusions

One of the lessons learned by those who participated in the exchanges is that urban cohousing manifests itself in unique ways in distinct contexts, depending on history, culture, political and policy realities, material resources, and the knowledges, skills, and proclivities of those involved. All cohousers know this intellectually, of course, but to experience it, viscerally, is another matter. Recognition of this variation underscores the inherent flexibility and malleability of cohousing, which is precisely what gives it power as a collaborative approach to well-being.

This flexibility is required, of course, if cohousing is to be workable in different societies and capable of adapting to new conditions, be they changes in residents or in political, economic, or environmental circumstances. Circuits for the flow of information and the exchange of ideas are paramount to these adaptive efforts: thus the existence of numerous web networks, conferences, publications, and study centers devoted to learning and sharing information about intentional community. In-person exchanges, of the type that occurred between Quayside Village and Kankanmori, provide specifically *embodied* encounters, enhancing opportunities for all involved to reflect on the unique features of their own communities and to learn directly from others who are practicing cohousing in other ways in other places. It is worth remembering that the exchange participants included not only those who visited the other community but the entirety of both communities: residents of Kankanmori had an immediate, embodied encounter with Quayside Village by means their encounters with Juhli, Connie, and Donya, and vice versa for the residents of Quayside Village: Haruko and Carl's visit made Kankanmori immediately present to Quaysiders. In both cases, residents came out en masse to organized events with the visitors and also interacted with them informally throughout their stays. As Patrick said to Carl and Haruko during their presentation on life at Kankanmori, "It's interesting, having you guys here and hearing how you arrange and run your business as compared to us. I always thought we were loosey-goosey in the way that we did things, but now I realize how loosey-goosey we are."[26] These comments point to the particular nature of information-sharing engendered by the exchanges—one based on co-presence and active engagement, and one that provided the grounds of possibility for the kind of insight that Patrick expressed, a bringing to the surface of something previously more or less taken for granted.

In explaining why he wanted to visit Quayside Village, Carl wrote that he was "interested in building up direct relationships with cohousing activists in other parts of the world and in establishing lasting relationships between like-minded people in Japan and Canada"—like-minded people, that is, who may nevertheless also do things differently. In this case, residents of Kankanmori and Quayside Village, living in communities situated in different cultural contexts, practiced unique ways of working collectively to produce the good life, giving rise to unique cohousing formations. And, during the exchanges, they collaborated across their communities to reflect on this.

What residents attended to during the exchanges reveals something about how they view cohousing's place in the creation of happiness and the good life. The lenses through which Haruko, Carl, Connie, Juhli, and Donya interpreted and participated in the community they visited all circled around the assumption that connection is a crucial determinant of happiness and well-being. More specifically, they focused on practical, collaborative engagements in the business of building and maintaining the connections that create community, and on *how*, in particular, that collaboration is organized. Recall that Connie's key focus when visiting Kankanmori was to "see if we're really doing things the best way." The ways in which residents of the two communities encountered each other thus underscores two additional points about cohousing as a model. First, as Kankanmori's experiment with fewer committees and the elimination of *mori-ken* indicates, cohousing is fundamentally emergent and unfolding rather than fixed. This is because, second, and relatedly, cohousing is something that people *do*—it is a creative process that residents undertake, actively and deliberately.

A passage from Juhli's reflections just after the exchange perhaps best captures the promise of collaboration across as well as within communities:

> In a way, seeing the love and dedication to cohousing through the eyes of Yoshie and Emiko gave me more appreciation and love for the founders of QV. I could see that it takes a huge commitment to develop a multiunit building for yourself and strangers. Perhaps that's one of the reasons there are many rules and systems at KKM. It must be such a challenge to create something and keep the integrity of the original vision, and then let it go to people who will inevitably inhabit the space and add their life and expectations to the space, their home.
>
> This opportunity has made me more considerate of how I am in community, what I like about community, and what I would miss if I weren't in a community like QV. I also appreciate how easy going it is, generally, and how much there is to learn from my neighbors. I think I will be more involved in my community now that I have more of an understanding and appreciation for what a unique opportunity it is to live in a place like this.

Notes

1. During the course of this project, ten Kankanmori members, including Yoshie, who had been on the first trip, returned to Sweden to compare notes with the communities they visited in 2002.
2. McCamant and Durrett, *Cohousing*.
3. Thin, "Qualitative Approaches," 2.
4. Kavedžija, "Good Life," 87.
5. Thin, "Qualitative Approaches," 2; Harry Walker and Iza Kavedžija, "Introduction: Values of Happiness," in *Values of Happiness: Toward an Anthropology of Purpose in Life*, ed. Harry Walker and Iza Kavedžija (Chicago: HAU Books, 2016).
6. This potential was never realized in any traditional research sense (e.g., through what they said). Although I was able to have a discussion with the younger residents at Quayside Village about what it was like to grow up in cohousing (see chapter 2), Kankanmori's children were too young to engage in this kind of process. Rather, Anna's and Lisa's perspectives are revealed visually, in the free-

dom of movement and play that they engaged in with those they encountered at Quayside Village.
 7. See *Exchange at Kankanmori*, "Quayside Visitors Tour Kankanmori," 0:05, and *Exchange at Quayside Village*, "Haruko Explores Quayside Village," 0:07.
 8. See *Exchange at Kankanmori*, "The Quayside Visitors Give a Presentation," 2:27, and *Exchange at Quayside Village*, "Carl and Haruko Give a Presentation," 8:03.
 9. See *Exchange at Kankanmori*, "Afternoon Tea with the Quayside Visitors," 2:49.
 10. See *Exchange at Kankanmori*, "Having a Traditional Japanese Meal," 7:42.
 11. See *Exchange at Kankanmori*, "Building Outdoor Planter Boxes," 8:44.
 12. See *Exchange at Quayside Village*, "Carl and Haruko Attend a Thriving Meeting," 5:21.
 13. Jerome L. Garciano, "Affordable Cohousing: Challenges and Opportunities for Supportive Relational Networks in Mixed-Income Housing," *Journal of Affordable Housing & Community Development Law* 20, no. 2 (2011); Lietaert, "Cohousing's Relevance to Degrowth"; Alan O'Hashi, "Bridging Social and Cultural Divides in Cohousing," *Communities* 178 (2018); see conclusion.
 14. See *Exchange at Kankanmori*, "The Quayside Visitors Make a Meal," 3:46, and "Common Meal Accounting," 5:33.
 15. See *Exchange at Kankanmori*, "The Visitors Attend a Community Meeting," 1:46.
 16. See *Exchange at Quayside Village*, "Carl and Haruko Attend a Thriving Meeting," 5:21, and "Kankanmori Visitors Attend a Community Meeting," 6:30.
 17. He did note that a form of check-in/check-out is practiced in Seseki, one of the other collective housing communities in Tokyo. However, he felt that in addition to a tendency to avoid discussions of personal well-being, residents of Kankanmori would find such a practice too time-consuming.
 18. E.g., Clancy, "Acquisition of Communicative Style."
 19. See *Exchange at Kankanmori*, "After Dinner Drinking Party," 5:56.
 20. See *Exchange at Kankanmori*, "Karaoke Night," 10:10.
 21. See *Exchange at Quayside Village*, "Kankanmori Visitors Attend a Community Meeting," 6:30.
 22. See *Exchange at Kankanmori*, "Afternoon Tea with the Quayside Visitors," 2:49.
 23. See *Exchange at Quayside Village*, "Carl and Haruko Attend a Thriving Meeting," 5:21.
 24. Kankanmori Residents, *Collective House*, 12.
 25. See *Life at Kankanmori*, "Community Yoga," 5:53.
 26. See *Exchange at Quayside Village*, "Kankanmori Visitors Attend a Community Meeting," 6:30.

CONCLUSION
Policies of Well-Being

> Community living that engages the individual, younger as well as older people, improves the health and wellbeing of everyone.
> —Toni C. Antonucci et al., "Society and the Individual at the Dawn of the Twenty-First Century"[1]

> Even if only a tiny percentage of the population eventually live in cohousing, strategies it is currently pioneering have the potential to radically influence urban growth, community development and social change processes. As such, cohousing may well be the first manifestation of communitarian endeavour with relevance for global sustainability and the linked problems of rapid urban sprawl, continued environmental degradation, excessive resource consumption and increasing social disorder.
> —Graham Meltzer, "Cohousing"[2]

RESIDENTS OF KANKANMORI AND QUAYSIDE Village live their lives in ways that challenge the narrow focus on individual selves characteristic of contemporary society. Indeed, it was precisely the negative aspects of hyper-individualism—loneliness and isolation being at the top of the list—that prompted founding members to create Quayside Village and Kankanmori in the first place and that motivate residents to move in and stay. As I noted at the end of chapter 3, Ikuko Koyabe, the "mother" of collective housing in Japan, once explained to me that individual well-being depends on being part of a community and developing bonds with multiple and diverse others; thus her support for collective housing. This is a far cry from the myopic focus on one's own needs and internal life advocated by some positive-psychology-influenced and popular-culture approaches. In Koyabe's perspective, in contrast, the individual and collective are inextricably tied.

One immediately evident outcome of engagement with community is a more "fruitful" and "colorful" life, as Shoko explained:

> In my case, living in a regular apartment I had no opportunities at all to get to know my neighbors. And since I'm single on top of that, living alone, there's really no solidarity. There's an aloneness. You're home alone. Of course there

are parts of that that are enjoyable in a sense, but I also thought, "Am I going to be alone forever?" When I considered my future living arrangements, rather than enjoying life alone, I thought that moving somewhere with people I could share things with would bring more color to my life. A more fruitful life! A more colorful, fruitful life! Even if you really enjoy your time alone, it gets very lonely sometimes. At Kankanmori, everyone comes here to talk in the evening, and you can join in. That's something I couldn't do when I was living alone.

This "more colorful, fruitful life" involves not only the pleasures of "joining in" but also the deeper changes in individual selves that can be generated by actively engaging in the solidarity Shoko valorizes. Several examples will serve to make the point. Keiichi, whose personal narrative is included in chapter 1, initially joined Kankanmori out of simple curiosity. His participation in Kankanmori's social events, however, and in the practical group work of community maintenance, soon prompted him to reflect on how he was living his life as a whole. He realized that he needed to "treasure my life more," and so he quit a job that he now felt took up too much of his time; found another, more flexible job; and even dropped some of his friends who were critical of collective housing in favor of new friends who were more supportive of his new living situation. Hiroshi, whom I referred to at the end of chapter 3, also experienced a change in perspective after joining Kankanmori: like Keiichi, he became more reflective and deliberate in his decisions and actions, and he found himself developing an appreciation for the little things in life, like curtain design, for instance—not just "work, work, work." His perspective that "living together is better" than living alone, similar to Shoko's point about solidarity, provides insight into the impact that living in collective housing has on every aspect of one's being in the world. Phil, at Quayside Village, whom I quoted at the end of chapter 2, similarly made connections between the dailiness of living in cohousing and "something bigger":

> The idea of what it means to live in this type of experience, I would say it's not because it works, which it does, it's because we celebrate life, we create life with each other, there's a larger force at work here. A sense of, you know, meals together, and you know, Peter's dog dies and the whole community rallies around him, and Marylee does her solo show at the Fringe Fest, and everybody goes, and Juhli had the concert at Ambleside, and we ran into you guys there, and half the building was down at her concert! And that to me is cohousing. You know, yeah, we get the garbage out together, and, yeah, we get the recycling done together, but something bigger is happening here.

This "something bigger" goes beyond the mere fact of contact with others to what emerges from the kinds of repeated daily interactions that unfold in cohousing: "We create life with each other."

CONCLUSION *187*

Just as residents of Kankanmori and Quayside Village joined their communities out of a dissatisfaction with hyperindividualism, so this book began with a frustration with individualistic approaches to well-being. This exasperation prompted me to look for approaches to the good life that were not focused exclusively on what goes on inside people's heads. Nor were hypercollectivist practices—in which, for instance, private property and space are completely eliminated—viable candidates, since they also erase half of the story. Instead, I wanted to find an alternative model of the good life that recognizes both the individual, or subjective, aspects of well-being *and* the social, or collective, aspects. I was, in addition, looking for an approach that had the capacity to address environmental concerns as well as those associated with disconnection and isolation—*and* that would be both attractive and feasible in an increasingly urban global society. This led me to urban cohousing. Once there, it became clear that the project required a collaborative methodology in order to mirror the collaborative framework of cohousing itself. It also seemed to me that gauging the flexibility and adaptability of cohousing as a model was best accomplished by comparing cohousing communities located in different cultural contexts.

So, what can Kankanmori and Quayside Village and, by extension, places like them teach us about social and environmental sustainability? What are the potential upward ripple effects of cohousing, into how governments think; downward, into the most mundane and intimate aspects of individual lives; and sideways, into neighborhoods and the wider society? And what kind of vision of the good life—of utopia—does collective housing represent?

Urban Cohousing: Building the Good Life

Kankanmori's and Quayside Village's shared agendas reveal what their residents consider foundational to building a good life: social connection and mutuality (both within and external to the community), autonomy and agency, trust and self-governance, diversity, and environmental sustainability.

Connection, Autonomy, and Trust

At the base of Kankanmori's and Quayside Village's approaches to the good life lies what is perhaps the most obvious benefit of community: social connection. At the same time, residents consider individual autonomy—that is, freedom and control over one's own life—equally essential.

Residents work assiduously to harmonize these two requirements. The balance is evident, first of all, in their built environments. Shared spaces, such as common rooms, laundry rooms, and gardens all serve to encourage interaction among residents, while individual apartments provide privacy and autonomy. Similarly, shared property—kitchen, laundry, and garden equipment—encourages contact, while private property—apartments and their contents, and individuals' control over their personal finances—allows for independence. Finally, both informal social events and activities focused on community maintenance, whether obligatory, as at Kankanmori, or voluntary, as at Quayside Village, work to create linkages, but they take up a limited proportion of residents' lives, which they are then otherwise free to do with as they wish. This desire for and structuring of both independence and connectivity—autonomous connectivity, perhaps, or collective individualism—is one of the reasons why residents wanted to move into Kankanmori and Quayside Village in the first place, a motivation that they share with denizens of cohousing in general.[3]

Autonomy and independence point to self-governance at the scale of the community as well as in relation to the freedom of individuals to govern themselves. While community self-governance takes different forms at Kankanmori and Quayside Village, in both cases residents have devised specific values and processes of decision-making in order to govern space, finances, and social life, and all residents have an opportunity to participate in constructing and practicing community self-governance. Significantly, these structures and processes underscore a reciprocal relationship between self-governance and trust, the sense that each member of the community is acting in good faith and doing their best. Recall Kankanmori's principles that *there needs to be a focus on communication and diversity: we need to grow and learn from each other*, and that *we believe our lives are enriched by developing relationships with our neighbors*. Both values assume, and encourage, trust in each other's good intentions. Residents of Quayside Village are even more explicit in their foregrounding of trust: *We trust the wisdom of our collective diversity of attitudes, beliefs, and cultural traditions. Through this approach we create a community that is safe—physically, emotionally, socially, and spiritually*. Thus Quayside Village's and Kankanmori's organizational principles, and the sets of procedures they generate, work to shape residents' behavior in the direction of the kinds of trusting persons they would like to be. This, in turn, supports an environment of mutuality and effective self-governance.

Connection with the World: Integration with Rather Than Segregation from Society at Large

As residents of Quayside Village and Kankanmori conceptualize it, connection entails engagements with people outside of the community as well as with those inside; residents desire to be a part of society rather than removed from it. Among Kankanmori's organizing philosophies is the idea that *life needs to be open to the outside world*, while, for their part, Quayside Villagers *value participation in the wider community to build a better world*. In keeping with these principles, both communities make themselves accessible to, and even actively encourage, media and research-related inquiries that help to make cohousing visible to members of society at large. They also host tours and orientation sessions and put on special events to which residents of the surrounding neighborhoods, as well as others from farther afield, are invited. In other words, they open their doors, enthusiastically, to those who are interested in learning about cohousing. In addition, they themselves also venture out to engage in various organizations and activities. In contrast to those intentional communities that have clear boundaries between inside and outside, where residents tend to stay on site and economic and social activities are for the most part internal, residents of Quayside Village and Kankanmori have full and complicated work and social ties in the outside world.

These outward-looking philosophies and practical connections with society are characteristic of cohousing communities. In Sargisson's cross-national study, for instance, residents cited their external involvements, ranging from interactions with people living in the surrounding neighborhoods to civic participation more widely, as one of the benefits of living in cohousing.[4] In places where radical individualism has taken hold, and where ties of extended family, neighborhood, workplace, and so on have accordingly been loosened, cohousing gathers people together, orienting them inward and closer to each other in the project of creating community—of building bonds "not based on blood," as Carl at Kankanmori put it. But cohousing also works to expand these bonds outward, encouraging wide-ranging connections at ever-larger scales.

The concept of what social scientists refer to as *social capital* provides a useful tool for thinking about the forms of connection practiced by urban cohousers. The Organisation for Economic Co-operation and Development (OECD) defines social capital as "social networks, together with shared norms, values and understandings that facilitate cooperation within and among groups."[5] The emphasis here is not on social capital as something that is owned by individuals or socioeconomic classes and that works to create hierarchies of difference and privilege[6] but, rather, as something that brings people together across differences. In the case of urban cohousing communities, this bringing together does not rely on already existing shared norms and understandings in any homogenous sense. Rather, it involves negotiating connections across differences in a way that does not require their erasure but instead capitalizes on them as resources that enrich the collaborative production of the good life.

Robert Putnam and Lewis Feldstein distinguish between *bonding social capital*, which is inward-looking, insofar as it links people "who are similar in crucial respects," and *bridging social capital*, which "encompasses different types of people and tends to be outward-looking."[7] Communities such as Kankanmori and Quayside Village build both: they cultivate bonding social capital by means of collaborative processes of design and self-governance, and they produce bridging social capital via their engagements with society, including especially in the neighborhoods within which they are situated. Maria Laura Ruiu also refers to *linking social capital*, which is about creating connections between cohousing communities and people or organizations beyond the immediate neighborhood.[8] Residents of Kankanmori and Quayside Village create this kind of capital through their connections with other cohousing communities and organizations, and, at Quayside Village, effort is also put into fostering relationships with government bodies, such as municipal authorities. Ruiu sums up the benefits of these forms of social capital as they unfold in cohousing communities:

> The social capital of cohousing groups promotes a sense of community and belonging, mutual support networks inside and outside the communities, a sense of safety exercised by a social control (in relation to the constant presence of people on the site), and a high civic engagement. Differently from an "ordinary" condominium, in cohousing communities the bonding social capital is guaranteed by internal cohesion, trust among members, shared goals, internal rules; the bridging social capital depends on the willingness to be open to the outside, and on creating friendly relationships with the wider neighbourhood; the linking social capital is built in relation to cohousers' ability to create partnerships with external actors (institutions or external organizations), which may help groups to reduce the length of the development process and promote a higher degree of heterogeneity within communities (in terms of economic, cultural and social capital).[9]

It is worth stressing here that social capital is not fixed: it consists not only of structures for bonding, bridging, and linking but also of the processes that are involved in realizing these structures in everyday life. It is, in other words, a set of emergent practices. Thus Helen Jarvis points out that

> the infrastructures of daily life in cohousing include not only mechanisms for reciprocity and exchange but also, crucially, circuits of learning, doing, being, and becoming.... We learn from these communities that social networks alone are insufficient: a meshwork of social, spatial, material, and institutional infrastructures all contribute to lived experience.[10]

This living meshwork, always under construction, underscores one of the defining characteristics of the good life at Kankanmori and Quayside Village and, by extension, of urban cohousing in general: namely, that it is always unfolding and contingent on both cultural context, in the widest sense, and the particular configuration of residents at particular moments in time.

Diversity

Connection, whether with those inside or outside of the community, inevitably points to diversity. Indeed, Kankanmori is oriented to the idea that *everyone from single people to large families can enjoy Kankanmori*, and Quayside Village's original mission statement calls for *a community that is diverse in age, background, and family type*. While it could be said that communities like Quayside Village and Kankanmori are attempting to re-create aspects of traditional neighborhood and extended family ties, this would be to misread what are in fact significantly more complicated and nuanced situations. Residents are not oriented to a "return"—to replicating idealized forms of relatively homogenous approaches to community living that existed in the past. On the contrary, diversity of geographic origin, profession, and philosophical orientation are considered central by residents of both communities. This foregrounding of diversity reveals residents' recognition of the complex realities of contemporary life while at the same time marking a desire, a perspective that diversity is something from which everyone stands to gain. Thus, Quaysiders believe that differences enhance rather than undermine productive decision-making processes and the formation of rich interpersonal bonds, and Kankanmori residents position diversity at the root of personal growth and expansion. As Junko at Kankanmori put it, residents are neither friends nor family but "something different, something new." Life in these communities does not just reflect nostalgia, then—although there certainly is an element of that. It also, and perhaps more importantly, embodies an attempt to graft imaginaries of what life was like in the past with contemporary realities and aspirations. Thus, Kankanmori and Quayside residents hail from everywhere and anywhere and bring to their communities a range of experiences and orientations.

Both communities have been successful in encouraging multigenerationalism. Neither Kankanmori nor Quayside residents wanted their communities to become retirement communities or, at the other end of the spectrum, sharehouse facilities, increasingly common in Japan, which provide housing for young professionals who are primarily interested in convenience and efficiency rather than in building relationships with others. On the contrary, residents feel strongly that everyone—young, old, and anywhere in between—benefits from being part of a mixed-age community. This fits the pattern of cohousing in general: the vast majority of communities registered with the Canadian Cohousing Network, the Cohousing Association of the United States, and the UK Cohousing Network,[11] for instance, are multigenerational; and there are no single-generation collective housing communities in Japan. Multigenerationalism is, nevertheless, deliberate rather than natural or accidental: recall that Kankanmori alters rental prices in order to attract residents in particular age groups when residents feel that its age distribution is unbalanced; in addition, discussions of the need for more babies and children do occur at Quayside Village, even if no formal efforts to make this happen are put into place. Both communities have also been successful in attracting single-parent families, as well as single people in general—both exceptions to normative ideals of the nuclear family. This, too, has been deliberate, as is evident in built environments that include units of various sizes and configurations. In addition, the pooling of resources in both communities makes it more possible for those with limited economic resources to join, as do the affordable units at Quayside Village. Finally, both communities have elevators, and Kankanmori's apartments are all one floor, as are a number of units at Quayside Village, thus accommodating residents of varying physical abilities.

Diversity provides opportunities for residents to have intimate, meaningful encounters with others different from themselves. This was something that parents, in particular, wanted for their children, but it was a desire that everybody shared to one degree or another. Recall, for instance, Yoshie's experience, mentioned in chapter 1:

> A prosperous resident in his seventies used to drive a red car and I, who was busy doing protesting about government policies, would not usually become friends with someone like him but because we both lived in Kankanmori we did.[12]

As Koyabe wrote, reflecting on Kankanmori's name (*mori* = forest): "A forest can only be a healthy forest if there is a variety of trees of all sizes, not just one."[13]

Despite these measures, however, heterogeneity remains an aspiration yet to be fully achieved. This is the case in cohousing in general. As Alan O'Hashi, a board member of the U.S. Cohousing Association, points out, while "cohousers may intellectually 'value diversity' ... diversity doesn't always play out, considering that the typical cohouser is white [or a member of the dominant ethnic group], educated, high income and high perceived social class, and, about 70 percent of the time, a woman."[14] Cohousers recognize this challenge. In 2018, for instance, *Communities*, the flagship magazine of the Foundation for Intentional Community, published a special issue on "Class, Race, and Privilege."[15] Articles on race, class, and ability have also appeared in other issues of *Communities*.[16]

Journalists writing in the popular press have similarly pointed to the relative homogeneity of cohousing communities,[17] as have scholars. Francesco Chiodelli and Valeria Baglione, for example, note that in many cases cohousing can be considered "a kind of private residential community,"[18] marked by "social, ethnic and ideological homogeneity" and a "lack of integration with surrounding neighbourhoods."[19] Others point specifically to the class-based nature of cohousing.[20] These patterns clearly limit cohousing's potential for society at large.[21]

Joanna Winter and Charles Durrett, key figures in the US cohousing movement, counter images of class exclusivity, claiming that they represent "only one segment of the cohousing movement—the segment that gets the most press."[22] On the contrary, they argue, "cohousing is intrinsically an affordable model: one of its main purposes, outside of a strong sense of community, is limiting resource consumption by sharing resources. The savings in energy, maintenance costs, and food outweigh the apparent upfront costs due to new construction."[23] Nevertheless, diversity remains a challenge. The scholarly literature addressing this problem, however, and, perhaps more importantly, the concerns expressed by cohousing residents themselves—as evidenced by the numerous articles on the topic published in *Communities* and the stated desires of Kankanmori and Quayside Village residents—point to a clear aspiration for heterogeneity, which, in turn, reflects recognition that diversity is a necessary ingredient of the good life.

Environmental Sustainability

Residents of Quayside Village and Kankanmori alike consider environmental sustainability an essential component of any conception of the good life that is viable in the long term; indeed, many see it as the foundation of all other possibilities. Kankanmori has among its guiding principles the idea that *living at Kankanmori needs to be both practical and ecological*; and similarly, Quayside Village residents *value acting as stewards of all elements of our environment*. Residents put these values into practice by pooling material resources, recycling and composting, and growing a certain portion of what they eat—all of which serve to limit consumption, reduce environmental footprints, and, significantly, require collaborative efforts that in turn enhance social connection. The locations of Quayside Village and Kankanmori also contribute to environmental sustainability: because the communities are situated in densely urban areas, the need for cars decreases, thereby increasing possibilities for walking, cycling, and using public transit.

Recognition of the links between social and environmental sustainability is a hallmark of contemporary cohousing: recall Graham Meltzer's observation, noted in the introduction, that "the quality of our social relationships and our 'sense of community' are major determinants of our capacity for pro-environmental behavioural change."[24] This connection has also been taken up by key international organizations. The OECD, for instance, has developed a policy framework that explicitly integrates environmental and well-being goals.[25] Based on the idea that policies for climate change mitigation are more likely to be successful when they articulate with those oriented to well-being more generally, the framework calls for replacing policies "focused on reaching a single, or very narrow range of objective(s) independently of others" with those addressing "*multiple well-being objectives.*"[26] Echoing Jeffrey Sachs's claim that "our societies are not well organized to promote happiness. The global market economy is good at producing wealth, but not at sharing it fairly or protecting the environment from vicious greed,"[27] the OECD's approach focuses on what is eclipsed by GDP and on what cannot be easily commodified: social connection and a clean environment.[28]

Urban cohousing communities, like other intentional communities, realize, albeit at a smaller scale, the OECD's template. The cooperative sharing of resources among members, along with such communities' commitments to local places, highlights their viability as an alternative model of living that contributes simultaneously to increased social connection and reduced environmental impacts:

> [Intentional community] experiments include participatory governance and community design processes and a great variety of institutions for cooperative economic behavior. These social, political and economic institutions have the potential to create not only greater ecological sustainability and social equity, but also the development of greater social bonds based upon trust, mutual understanding, cooperation and shared knowledge of and relationships with particular places. Even if these communities fail to achieve all of their goals, their attempts to do so situate them as unique entities, striving to address the sustainability challenge by acting at the disjuncture between sustainability ideals and actions toward sustainability.[29]

In shifting practices of consumption from individuals to collectives, even if only in part, cohousing communities contribute to degrowth initiatives.[30] As such, they provide a blueprint for how we can successfully move away from the taken-for-granted idea that constant and accelerated economic expansion is essential to happiness and well-being.

The range of values outlined above, widely shared among cohousers, frame how cohousing residents imagine well-being. These values are of course articulated and practiced in different ways in different communities, and they may also wax and wane in importance across time as residents focus on them more or less, and as residents are more or less successful in bringing them to fruition; thus my reference to cohousing as a *model*, and my use of the term *building*, to mark process and creativity.

As I documented in chapters 2 and 3, the creative process that is urban cohousing takes the form of "conversations" between philosophy and practice—between ideals and aspirations, on the one hand, and the contingencies of everyday life, on the other. The orientations of the exchange participants, described in chapter 4, further highlight cohousing as an emergent, creative practice. After visiting Kankanmori, Juhli, Connie, and Donya were eager to improve the clarity and transparency of Quayside Village's procedures, and they also wanted to increase the frequency and spontaneity of social events. The first, they felt, would work to augment new residents' sense of stability and security as they settled in, while the latter would intensify the pleasures of social connection, further solidifying interpersonal bonds among community members. Upon their return from Quayside Village, Haruko and Carl wanted to find ways to open things up at Kankanmori so that people would feel comfortable sharing more of their personal lives with others. Their goal was to increase possibilities for mutual care, which they felt might enable those residents who needed extra support to stay at Kankanmori for longer periods of time. Carl and Haruko also wanted to loosen the rigidity of community obligations, in order to produce a richer and more enjoyable set of social connections. Years after their communities were established, then, Quayside and Kankanmori residents continued to seek ways to enhance their approaches to the good life. This is a common feature of cohousing communities.

As independent and self-governing collectivities, urban cohousing communities constitute "a form of civic association."[31] The sets of values and organizational procedures they devise are their policies (with a small "p"), their charters for social action—that is, for how to go about the business of associating with each other and with the wider societies within which they are embedded.[32] These orienting frameworks both reflect and reproduce particular ideologies of what it means to be a human being, of how humans should ideally interact with each other, and of what happiness and well-being look like. The practices that mark daily life—common meals, community meetings, group projects, social events, and periodic reevaluations of how community life is unfolding—provide insight into how these policies are realized or not, directly or indirectly, partially or completely, in pure or modified forms. Significantly, none of this is given. Rather, values and organizational frameworks, whether overt or taken for granted, are produced collaboratively, via discussion, explicit or implied agreement, and myriad everyday practices that serve to realize particular principles, or that work to challenge and modify them. How might these policy practices—these orientations to what the good life looks like and how to go about producing it—inform government policy, policy with a capital "P"?

Policy

> Experiments and innovations in collective housing may not prove to be the most "radical" solutions in the long term, but they do represent a necessary shift toward fundamentally rethinking how and where people live, to promote sustainability, in the future. The energy-efficient arguments alone (fewer building materials, combined heat and power) are compelling; added to these are the need to address the social isolation and absence of reciprocal welfare characteristic of the rising number of smaller households, many with high support needs.[33]

Encouraged by intergovernmental organizations such as the United Nations and the OECD, the renewed concern with happiness and well-being that emerged in the second half of the twentieth century radiated out from academia to influence not only popular culture but also governments. In 2011, the United Nations put out a press release calling on member states "to pursue the elaboration of additional measures that better capture the importance of the pursuit of happiness and well-being in development with a view to guiding their public policies."[34] In keeping with this request, the UN encourages governments to use its Human Development Index "to question national policy choices" and to "stimulate debate about government policy priorities."[35] The OECD's Better Life Index and the New Economics Foundation's Happy Planet Index are similarly geared to informing national policy-making. And governments have responded: France, Britain, Italy, Germany, the Netherlands, Thailand, the United Arab Emirates, Ecuador, Bolivia, Israel, Aotearoa/New Zealand, Australia, Japan, and Singapore, among others,[36] have each incorporated happiness and well-being into their policy frameworks in one way or another.[37]

These moves represent an expansion in frameworks of governance to encompass not only the amelioration of suffering but also a focus on creating the conditions of possibility for flourishing. Today, well-being is not only an *appropriate* goal of government but also a *necessary* one; thus, Clark et al. refer to "a new role for the state—not wealth creation but well-being creation."[38] In his introduction to the 2019 *Global Happiness and Well-Being Policy Report*, Jeffrey Sachs writes that "the 'pursuit' of happiness should no longer be left to the individual or the marketplace alone. Happiness and well-being should be of paramount concern to all of society, engaging governments, companies, healthcare systems, and other sectors of society."[39] Along with the happiness indexes mentioned above, the very existence of the annual *Global Happiness and Well-Being Policy Report*, launched in 2018, along with others, such as the *World Happiness Report*, launched in 2012 in response to "a new worldwide demand for more attention to happiness and absence of misery as criteria for government policy,"[40] tells us that happiness and well-being have become increasingly central to governmental imaginaries and practices. Supported by the UN's Sustainable Development Solutions Network and the Global Happiness Council, in collaboration with a number of academic centers, such as the Center for Sustainable Development at Columbia University, Oxford's Wellbeing Research Centre, and the School of Economics at the University of British Columbia, these reports provide a comprehensive resource for governments, representing overarching, global perspectives on well-being and how best to produce it. They are also in conversation with handbooks that bring together the work of an array of scholars and that similarly serve as resources for policy-makers, such as the *Oxford Handbook of Happiness*[41] and the *Handbook of Well-Being*.[42]

These reports and handbooks outline a range of policy approaches spanning the macro, the meso, and the micro, including everything from policies related to budgeting, taxation, and the creation of new institutional structures (such as a Ministry of Happiness) to those focused on individualized interventions designed to increase interpersonal and parenting skills, physical fitness, and mental health more generally.[43] Many of these potential interventions, based on large-scale, often survey- and statistics-based studies, coupled with illustrative case studies of particular place-based initiatives, reflect orientations similar to those articulated by residents of Quayside Village and Kankanmori: namely, that well-being requires a balance of connection and autonomy; forms of governance that are transparent, inclusive, and enabling rather than constraining; and approaches to social organization that foster connection not only at the level of interpersonal relations but also at the larger scales of neighborhood, city, and nation.[44]

There are two overarching frames to these large-scale, global discussions. First is the call for cross-sector cooperation in order to integrate policy arenas holistically under a unifying framework of happiness and well-being.[45] The OECD's approach to combining well-being and environmental goals, mentioned above, provides an example of this. Second is the recognition that incorporating all "stakeholders" in policy-making processes, as opposed to undertaking top-down interventions "designed far away and dropped from above," increases the likelihood of policy success.[46]

This speaks to the relationship between civic participation, at all scales, and well-being.[47]

Of course, the rolling out of the frameworks and approaches outlined in policy reports and handbooks is messy and uneven. The grounds of possibility for happiness and well-being are read and invested in differently by different government bodies, with some focusing on increasing democratic participation and trust in government and others emphasizing individual capacity building. There is also a tension, which I noted in the introduction, between a focus on human welfare, an idea that, as Wendy James puts it, "can only be imagined, and put into practice, in the context of a clear social whole,"[48] and the individualized focus that dominates some programs targeting individual selves abstracted from any social context. The latter can all too easily be captured by agendas of austerity and restructuring, using the language of happiness and well-being to shift focus away from social context and government responsibility for the structural conditions of possibility for the good life and instead placing all responsibility on individuals (see discussion in introduction). In other words, an emerging *conversational* consensus among governments and international agencies, and in the policy reports and handbooks that inform them, does not necessarily mean that all governments have the same agenda in framing policy in terms of happiness and well-being, or that they are all heading in the same direction in the same way. Still, if neoliberal, market-based, and ultimately asocial elements can be successfully challenged, the general shift in orientation, even if piecemeal and fragmented, is nevertheless hopeful and suggests movement in a positive direction.

Although the overwhelming emphasis in policy reports and handbooks is placed on the macro or the micro, there are some signs that the meso—that in-between space where cohousing sits—is gaining traction in some policy-making circles. The changing nature of the family—fewer children, relatives scattered far and wide—bolsters the case "for government to support different sorts of community engagement, civil social organizations and spaces."[49] "Community" is, of course, a more ambiguous target than the big things like taxation policy or, at the other end of the spectrum, programs oriented to the development of parenting skills. Nevertheless, given the inherently social nature of human beings, some have claimed that "social policies take on an importance matching the economic agenda"[50]—or at least that they should.

This remarkable attempt to place the social on par with the economic has given rise to a wide array of proposed mesolevel planning and design interventions, including changes to zoning regulations; initiatives that work to enhance affordability, mobility, and access to green spaces and cultural sites; and the development of neighborhood programs—all with the goal of building and expanding inclusivity, trust, belonging, and environmental sustainability.[51]

Attention to the meso level of community also opens up space for consideration of cohousing as a policy intervention. In keeping with the ideas that "housing is more than shelter; it is deeply connected to a person's identity, psychology, and—ultimately—well-being," and that "the architectural and social aspects of housing are intertwined," Diener and Biswas-Diener make a case for state support of cohousing on the grounds of its potential to both lower housing costs and increase social connection and, in particular, mutual care and support.[52] This expands the framework for housing policy to include not only issues of accessibility and affordability but also recognition of house as *home*, or *dwelling*, in the expansive sense I outlined in the introduction.[53] Here, home operates as a kind of hub, a connecting point where just about every aspect of social, economic, political, and policy organization plays out to one degree or another—and from which much radiates out into society at large.

Some Northern European governments, zeroing in on cohousing as a key contributor to social and environmental sustainability, have acted to encourage its development.[54] Many Swedish cohousing projects, for instance, take the form of municipal housing corporations,[55] and, in the North American context, Lubik and Kosatsky argue for municipal government support for cohousing developments as a public health intervention.[56] As I noted in the introduction, a number of studies have documented an association between living in cohousing and experiences of well-being—not only in terms of residents' feelings of satisfaction, but also in relation to health more generally, to civic engagement, and to the state of the environment. Government investment in cohousing, whether at the national, provincial/prefectural, or municipal level, thus has the potential to produce a raft of positive outcomes. It could provide cost savings in healthcare, including in mental health. It could provide social support for elderly, low-income, and disabled people, as cohousing communities are designed to accommodate more diverse populations with diverse needs. It would contribute to reductions in a society's environmental footprint. And it has positive impacts on citizens' civic participation. Cohousing, in other words, is good not only for its residents but also for society as a whole—financially, socially, and environmentally. This is not to argue that everyone needs to live in cohousing. Rather, it is to claim that cohousing provides a practical, feasible, and, to many, an attractive alternative to current social arrangements, one option to be considered. Indeed, cohousing has been on the radar of the UN-associated World Habitat Award: Quayside Village was a finalist in 2003.

Diener and Biswas-Diener's argument in favor of state support for cohousing is, however, the only mention of cohousing in any of the *Global*

Happiness or *World Happiness* reports. It thus remains relatively marginal to the discussion. This speaks directly to one of the four dimensions of well-being that Gordon Mathews and Carolina Izquierdo propose as foundational to the study of happiness, namely the arena of national institutional and global forces that shape how well-being is understood and practiced.[57] Housing and zoning policies reflect, and serve to realize, ideas about the nature of human beings and how they relate to each other, about house and home, and about space, property, interdependence, and privacy. The spread of cohousing as a model, and its success in increasing levels of social and environmental sustainability, then, does not depend exclusively on the agency and motivation of those who live, or want to live, in cohousing; it relies, as well, on the frameworks and resources of governments that enable or constrain the development of such communities.

At the same time, government support for cohousing initiatives, while certainly useful, and perhaps essential—particularly with regard to efforts to increase the availability of affordable and accessible living arrangements, for instance—raises issues of autonomy. To a large degree, it is precisely cohousing residents' collaborative processes of community building and maintenance that make cohousing work. Thus Yoshie, at Kankanmori, valued the idea of government support but was simultaneously suspicious of it. During one of my stays there, for instance, a group of Tokyo city officials came by for a tour. Afterward, Yoshie told me that while she theoretically welcomed government support for collective housing, she also feared that governments would tie such support to particular forms of organization, including not only architectural designs, which would likely focus more on cost efficiencies than on enhancing social interaction, but also procedural frameworks for managing everyday life. This would undermine the freedom of cohousing communities to devise their own, unique approaches to living collectively, thereby undermining the very idea of collective housing itself.

Cohousing can enhance happiness and well-being, as numerous studies have shown, and it can save money in the long run—in terms of physical and mental healthcare costs, the costs of poverty, and the costs of environmental degradations associated with private property ownership and overconsumption. As Yoshie's concerns indicate, however, government support needs to be limited to providing the conditions of possibility for cohousing to develop—by means of zoning interventions,[58] for example, or financial support for affordable or accessible units. It would mean incorporating residents of cohousing communities as "stakeholders," as knowledgeable insiders who best know how to integrate policies holistically under a unifying framework of happiness and well-being. This is precisely what happiness economists and statisticians such as John Helliwell, Martine Durand, and Carrie Exton call for.[59]

◆◆◆

Broad agreement between the orientations of Quayside Village and Kankanmori, on the one hand, and those articulated in the happiness reports and handbooks discussed above, on the other, does not translate into detailed agreement or the capacity to create a template that can be applied in any context across time and space. Gordon Mathews makes a parallel point in his discussion of statistically based, supposedly universal measures of happiness: "Statistical findings have, no doubt, a broad accuracy. At a subtler level, however, their accuracy is arguable."[60]

Anthropological analyses of happiness and well-being in a range of milieus do of course point to cross-cultural, human commonalities.[61] *Connection* is one of these: the good life is, just about everywhere, conceived as "not only highly relational . . . but *other-oriented*."[62] As Michael Jackson argues, a "sense of being-with-others . . . [is an] existential precondition for well-being."[63] *Autonomy*, variously referred to as *freedom*, *control*, *agency*, and *self-governance*, emerges as similarly central—and, moreover, as articulated in balance with connection. Mathews and Carolina Izquierdo write in this regard of the universal human requirement for "*both* individual freedom and social relatedness."[64] Finally, *meaning* and *purpose*—as Mathews's work on *ikigai*, or what makes life worth living, indicates[65]—play a key role. Mathews and Izquierdo summarize these requirements as follows:

> Human beings need the support of, if not necessarily their families, then very definitely their human social world. Human beings also tend to seek freedom from coercive control, especially if that control is thought to be not intrinsic to oneself but externally imposed—human beings need some sense of control over and efficacy in their lives. Human beings also need a sense of life being worth living in a given society.[66]

What shapes do these ingredients take, in general, in cohousing communities such as Kankanmori and Quayside Village? First, cohousers' practices of connection encompass both others within their communities and those outside of it, in neighborhoods and workplaces, in schools and gyms, and in governmental and social movement organizations. These types of connection imply association with differently situated others—with those of various ages and abilities, and occupying specific ethnic, cultural, sexual, class, or professional positionalities. There is, in addition, a particular valence to the form that connection takes in cohousing: it is not just about contact but about mutual care and reciprocity—and about *responsibility*, a keystone of the other-orientedness that Harry Walker and Iza Kavedžija identify.[67] The responsibility for one's own happiness that marks contemporary, positive-psychology-informed, Western approaches is, as I noted earlier, culturally and historically unique. The more cross-culturally common other-orientation that Walker and Kavedžija refer to highlights instead commitment to others. This mirrors precisely the forms that connection takes in cohousing, where residents hold themselves responsible for the care of each other and of their community: they work together to maintain their shared buildings and gardens, make decisions, and solve problems; they support each other in times of trouble; and they build camaraderie and have fun together. The model provided by cohousing thus represents a shift away from obligation only to oneself to responsibility for one another. This commitment is not, however, dry or tedious. Certainly, there is effort involved in planting a garden, calculating finances, cleaning a common room, or taking care of a sick neighbor. But this joint work, including that related to challenges and conflicts, also helps to create a sense of belonging, of *communitas*, in the most general sense of togetherness—and, on occasion, of effervescence, of instances when "the endorphins flow," as Donya wrote about the Saturday Night Fever party at Kankanmori, when the subjective experience of well-being, or even of euphoria, is collective. In the context of cohousing, the longing for connection and the amelioration of loneliness does not translate into a desire to participate in community simply in order to boost one's own personal level of happiness. Instead, it is oriented to experiencing well-being *together*.

The value of autonomy also takes on a particular flavor in communities like Quayside Village and Kankanmori. Here, freedom and autonomy are not about *separation* from others; rather, they manifest as particular forms of engagement *with* others, the general parameters of which are provided by communities' stated principles and organizational structures. The goal of cohousing is to build a healthy Community with a capital "C"—that is, the Community that, as Katsuji at Kankanmori put it, is a "basic characteristic of humanity." This Community with a capital "C" does not require the dissolution of the autonomy or integrity of the individual. On the contrary, in creating a balance of interdependence and independence, neither the community nor the individual cannibalize the other; instead, both are constructed, and practiced, as inextricably tied: each not only tempers but also is essential to the other. Finally, situated in societies that increasingly value *individual* agendas and orientations, Kankanmori and Quayside Village also provide opportunities to participate in *shared* meanings and purposes: the creation of places of belonging and reciprocal care, of fun and enjoyment, and of approaches to life that can help to make the world a less lonely, happier, and more sustainable place, one step at a time.

It is these specifics about how connection, autonomy, and meaning-making are practiced in cohousing communities that lend it force as a model of the good life. None of these specifics can be articulated, in anything resembling nuance, in large-scale, statistically based studies, however much they point in their direction. Indeed, if there is a *fact* that emerges from anthropological studies, based as they are on qualitative methods attuned to detail and subtlety, it is that *happiness*, *well-being*, and *the good life* are empty signifiers, meaning that they are ambiguous, imprecise categories that are imagined and "filled" differently, according to time and place; and that whatever shapes they take are embedded in, and therefore inseparable from, wider systems of values.[68] *Connection*, *autonomy*, and *meaning-making* are also empty signifiers, practiced differently in different times and places, even as they remain central, in whatever form they take, to the good life, in whatever form it takes. Indeed, the valences and particular shapes of connection, autonomy, and meaning-making that I claim characterize cohousing in general are at the same time different in Kankanmori and Quayside Village. The conversation between philosophy and practice that takes place in each community thus points to the kind of conversations required between the general well-being frameworks of those informed by globally oriented happiness reports and handbooks—to connection, belonging, trust, governance, etc.—and actual policies and practices in particular places and times.

A Note on Utopia

> A general shortcoming of utopian projects is that they are not aimed at proposing specific transformations to the system that would shift current conditions towards a position elsewhere; instead they propose *fait accompli* visions (i.e. finished products) that would per se represent a better way to live. Collaborative housing . . . however, is a concrete reality with the potential of becoming instrumental in changing the current situation of housing and the city.[69]

Given their aspiration to create the good life, and the implications of their approaches for social and environmental sustainability, urban cohousing communities represent utopic models. Thomas More coined the term *utopia* in 1516 in the now-famous book by that title. *Utopia* is a combination of the Greek terms *outopia*, meaning "no place," and *eutopia*, or "good place." The term thus conjures up images of both perfection and impossibility, of a "wishfully constructed place which does not and cannot exist."[70] Imagination, then, is a hallmark of utopianism.

There have, of course, been numerous attempts to put such visions into practice, not the least of which have been Marxist-inspired utopian socialisms and a range of religious and spiritual communities. Many have been short-lived, while others have endured for longer periods of time; and membership in some has been voluntary while in others it was not. Many have also prompted criticisms of utopianism as potentially authoritarian or totalitarian. This potential is linked to "utopia's imputed belief in the perfectibility of humankind"[71]—a belief that can lead to violently repressive impositions, as in, among others, Mao's China and Stalin's Soviet Union, the horrors of which have been amply documented.[72] Early on in my research, when I visited a number of intentional communities in search of potential sites for this project, I was exposed to a set of relatively mild authoritarian practices: I spent a week in a community in Japan in which there was no private property (other than clothes and toiletries); residents were required to surrender all their finances when they joined; no one other than the leader had their own room; roommates were chosen by the leader and rotated on a periodic basis; residents who wished to couple had to seek the approval of the leader; children were raised together in a separate building; all meals were eaten together; and after each evening meal one community member was chosen to be evaluated by others and thereby helped to better themselves.

This is not the kind of utopia represented by urban cohousing communities. They do not attempt to put into place fully formed models of the good life, and they do not revolve around a charismatic leadership that controls residents' lives in any kind of totalizing way.[73] Instead, they work in the *direction* of something "better," following a path that residents recognize is unfolding and contingent. In this sense, they constitute what Ruth Levitas refers to as *utopia as method*,[74] or what Lucy Sargisson would characterize as *practical, pragmatic* utopia.[75]

Two features of utopia as method are shared by utopic visions and practices more generally. First, both arise from dissatisfaction with current social arrangements. Thus they are inevitably critical in nature, pointing to what is wrong with society. Second, they are inherently collective: they concern "*social* dreaming,"[76] focused on collaboratively producing particular *social* arrangements or systems. They therefore challenge the individualistic, overly subjective orientations of some mainstream and many popular culture approaches to happiness and the good life.

Despite these shared features, urban cohousing communities orient to current social arrangements differently from grand utopic schemes that imagine entirely new worlds and attempt to realize them fully formed. Cohousing communities *are* inherently critical of contemporary social arrangements, but they also remain close to them; they do not reject society as a whole, and they do not separate themselves off from it, either physically or socially. In describing what she calls "everyday utopias," Davina Cooper notes that "while they may ambitiously seek to actualize counter-hegemonic practices, they draw on many aspects of mainstream culture."[77] They are, in other words, *heterotopias*, alternative enclaves that exist *within* mainstream society.[78] Cooper cites French social theorist Michel Foucault, who described the utopian "attitude" as "a mode of relating to contemporary reality ... in the end, a way of thinking and feeling; a way, too, of acting and behaving that at one and the same time marks a relation of belonging and presents itself as a task."[79] In my reading, the "belonging" to which Foucault refers marks a relationship to society *as it is*—not to some other, purely imaginary world—while the "task" is to take what is already present and transform it, by means of practical imagination, into a more perfect future. Working with what is available, then, utopia as method is composed of both an orientation, or attunement, and a set of unfolding, creative practices that embody "a mode of striving toward something else that is better."[80]

This is why places like Kankanmori and Quayside Village can share a set of characteristics and at the same time differ in fundamental ways. The model of cohousing that residents draw on is not rigid but open and flexible, and, as I outlined in the introduction, there are a number of frameworks, circulating both locally and globally, that they can explore as they envision and construct their own communities. Local imaginaries of more socially cohesive pasts, for instance, provide key sources of input. In the case of Kankanmori, *nagaya*, a form of pre–Meiji Era row-house architecture and community organization, provided this historical reference point,[81] while Quayside Village, for its part, emerged in a historical context rich with a co-op movement and counterculture-era experiments in communal living.[82] In participating in global networks through which alternative approaches to the good life circulate—all of which may be situated in the context of growing interest in and practices of commoning—the creators of Quayside Village and Kankanmori also had at their disposal a range of models from the intentional community movement to build on in determining the initial shape of their communities, and current residents continue to turn to these networks when seeking solutions to emergent problems or information on novel initiatives. Collective housing communities are thus hybrid from the start: in drawing on a variety of local and global resources, they construct approaches to living that work for *them*, that articulate with local contingencies and the needs and proclivities of their residents, and that can be modified as circumstances change.

As the historical models on which they drew indicate, Quayside Village and Kankanmori, like other cohousing communities, are situated in societies with unique historical, cultural, and ideological trajectories. Even the popularity of cohousing in the two countries differs: perhaps counterintuitive in the face of stereotypes of a collectivist Japan, cohousing is less popular there than in Canada, where, in places like Vancouver, waiting lists are long and the development of new cohousing communities continues apace. More relevant to my discussion here are the different, sometimes diametrically opposed, orientations to the individual and the collective characteristic of the Japanese and Canadian cultural contexts. Quayside Village's philosophy of *each-according-to-their-strengths, each-according-to-their desires* reflects the centrality of the individual in Canadian society and gives rise to relatively loose practices of participation that are by invitation rather than obligation. In contrast, Kankanmori's philosophy of *everyone is equal* reflects the ideological centrality of collectivity in Japan, despite recent incursions of Western forms of individualism. This has resulted in more obligatory practices of participation focused on *fairness*, which in this context translates as *sameness*, the idea that everyone should contribute in equal measure. Different cultural approaches to the individual and collective also influence the relationship between the public and the private in terms of both property and space, one marked by relative fluidity and permeability in Quayside Village, in contrast with Kankanmori, where there is greater segregation between personal and public spaces and property.

This back-and-forth between similarity and difference reveals the basic building blocks of cohousing that the two communities share, on the one hand, and the nuances of collaborative community building in the context of particular cultural configurations, on the other. Urban cohousing, then, provides a singularly flexible model that can accommodate a range of desires and cultural frameworks. The differences between Quayside Village and Kankanmori also highlight what lies at the foundation of utopia as method: it is not, Levitas writes, "about devising and imposing a blueprint. Rather, it entails holistic thinking about the connections between economic, social, existential and ecological processes in an integrated way."[83] This holistic thinking is oriented, in turn, to imagining and heading in the direction of forms of living that are "ecologically and socially sustainable and enable deeper and wider human happiness than is now possible."[84] The specific shapes that these processes take inevitably vary by context.

In some ways, and especially when put into global context, urban cohousing communities like Quayside Village and Kankanmori represent what Lucy Sargisson refers to as "piecemeal utopianism."[85] She remains skeptical of their reconstructive potential, arguing that their criticism of society "is limited and its scope is local, generally restricted to the domestic sphere, household and/or local neighborhood."[86] She does note that cohousers report that their lives in cohousing are better than their lives previously.[87] Nevertheless, she claims, cohousing is a form of "modern utopia" that "seeks the good life without challenging mainstream values."[88] In her view, it does not, for instance, challenge regimes of either private property ownership or nuclear family formation.[89] At the same time, she recognizes the potential of cohousing to spill over the confines of its "pockets," particularly as its philosophies and organizational frameworks encourage greater civic engagement, and to the extent that residents actively share their way of living with society at large, either by opening their doors to others in their neighborhoods or, via the work of reporters and scholars, to those beyond their immediate locales. The very existence of cohousing communities in widely varying contexts, and of circuits for the travel of information about them, indicates that they in fact comprise a global social movement—inchoate, perhaps, but also growing in visibility and influence. In addition, given that they emerge from a critique of society—from the estrangement that comprises a key characteristic of intentional communities[90]—cohousing communities offer the benefits of critical reflection, embodying an alienation from society that has the potential to be productive. Their criticisms of contemporary social arrangements "serve as a means for destabilizing and relativizing the present, setting it in a context in which its fundamental elements must compete with alternative orders."[91] Urban cohousing communities may, then, function as "catalysts for change, points of inspiration, and vehicles for political critique."[92]

Sargisson's simultaneous highlighting of current limitations and future potentials indicates that the very idea of utopia as method, of practical utopia, means that there is still work to be done. Along with Sargisson, for instance, Jo Williams refers to some cohousing communities' lack of integration with their surrounding neighborhoods,[93] suggesting that *participating in the wider community to build a better world*, as the Quayside Village value statement puts it, is not always fully realized. There are other challenges as well. While lauding cohousing's contributions to degrowth initiatives—in particular, the pooling of resources that serves to reduce levels of consumption—Matthieu Lietaert concedes that cohousing may require public assistance in order to become a truly viable mainstream alternative: "If the cohousing movement is to become a widespread way of life it will need a much more significant involvement and support from public authorities to help low income families and individuals."[94] This speaks directly to the challenges of diversity and the importance of configuring government support in ways that encourage rather than undermine community autonomy.

In keeping with the idea of utopia as method, these criticisms do not require that urban cohousing, in its current forms, be abandoned in favor of perfect, fully formed models of the good life. Rather, they underscore the point that there will always be problems that need to be addressed, that the project will never be finished. Davina Cooper accordingly invites us to reject impossible ideas of perfection to focus instead on the "dynamic, improvised, often flawed quality" of places like Quayside Village and Kankanmori,[95] which are oriented not only to what is more desirable, but also to what is *viable*—that is, to what is possible given current conditions.[96] Such an approach allows us to transcend an all-or-nothing, utopia/nonutopia binary,[97] to focus instead on both/and—on working-toward.

As practical utopias, urban cohousing communities are always already imperfect and unfinished; and yet they are also always reflexive and always striving, representing one attempt, simultaneously critical and hopeful, imaginary and practical, fantastical and realistic, to collaboratively move in the direction of a happy, good life. Urban cohousing is not about the perfect life; it is not about some imaginary future or place where there are no problems and everyone is completely fulfilled and lives in complete harmony with others. Rather, it is about a *good* life, a way of living that turns away from the ravages of social isolation and environmental degradation to move instead in the direction of social and environmental sustainability.

Conclusions

At the same time that loneliness, on the one hand, and happiness and well-being, on the other, have been taking up more and more space in our scholarly, policy, and everyday imaginations, intentional communities have been gaining in popularity across the globe as an approach to living that enhances both social and environmental sustainability. This is, perhaps, not surprising: Susan Brown notes that periods of growth in the development of intentional communities "tend ... to cluster numerically in times of extreme stress caused by cultural confusion usually generated by radical changes in the social and cultural environment"[98]—in these times, patterns of loneliness and isolation, and of growing concerns about climate change. Cohousing, a form of intentional community uniquely suited to an increasingly urbanized world, offers one potential response to these stresses.

Residents of Kankanmori and Quayside Village work to build the good life *collaboratively*. In their frameworks, individual happiness and well-being, and the well-being of our societies and the planet we live on, are joint endeavors, things that go together and that we do together by means of our connections with each other. These connections are sustained, daily, and often mundane. They are oriented to shared visions of meaning and purpose that point simultaneously to the importance of caring for each other and of creating space for individual expression and autonomy. Given what we know about the enhanced well-being of those who live in cohousing, and about the contributions that it makes to environmental sustainability, cohousing is a model worth experimenting with. In providing insights into the relationships between well-being and a range of phenomena—arrangements of space and of the public and the private, orientations to connectivity and independence, and engagements with the environment—urban cohousing is, at the very least, good to think with. In positioning personal, social, and planetary well-being as collaborative processes, it provides opportunities to reflect on how we reflect on and go about the business of producing happiness and the good life.

Perhaps just as the environmental movement traveled from the fringes of society to its center, urban cohousing will become increasingly recognized as a viable alternative to unsustainable forms of living. The "global cultural supermarket"[99] by means of which a range of "products" for well-being circulate includes not only mainstream cultural formations that take individualism and endless economic growth as foundational to happiness and well-being but also alternative approaches, such as urban cohousing, that focus instead on the social good and on the production of a healthy environment. The marketplace of alternative approaches may not be flashy or well-resourced, but the more we pay attention to it, the more we expand our "tool-kit"[100] for collaboratively producing the good life.

A Covid-19 Postscript

I worked on the final revisions for this book while sitting in my apartment at Quayside Village. I periodically stopped to look out my wall of windows at the city across Vancouver Harbor, and each time I felt a jolt of surprised pleasure that this was now my home too. Two years into the research for this book, I decided that I wanted to do more than study cohousing: I wanted to be a part of it. Luckily, a unit—my favorite in the building—became available, and I was able to purchase it shortly before retiring from my university position. My move to Vancouver in late summer 2020 coincided with the dip between the first and second waves of Covid-19.

In exacerbating loneliness, Covid-19 has prompted us to recognize how interdependent we are, how much we need—and want—each other. Like so many, residents of Kankanmori and Quayside Village have made extensive use of electronic forms of contact, holding meetings via Zoom and relying more on email than on face-to-face encounters for information and social connection. But they have also found ways to maintain physical co-presence, albeit in scaled-down forms. At Kankanmori, for instance, small groups of residents gather for tea-at-a-distance in the common room, just as groups of two or three have continued to meet in the courtyard at Quayside Village. Quaysiders also began a new tradition: beginning in spring 2020, at 9:30 each morning residents brought chairs to the third-floor walkway in order to enjoy morning coffee and conversation together, even while sitting well apart. They have also had the occasional balcony singalong. When Marylee wrote that she would have to self-isolate for two weeks because someone on the hospital ward she visited had tested positive for Covid-19, a roster of volunteers for her dinners was set up within hours. In the meantime, at Kankanmori, twenty-seven people, including six children, enthusiastically signed up for the first (physically spread out) common meal after their self-imposed lockdown was lifted. And everyone was excited about the impending birth of the Nakatogawas' third child: new life and new energy for everyone to enjoy and nurture as they endeavor, together, to provide mutual pleasure and support in these times. These aspects of life in cohousing never shut down.

Teppei, a healthy boy, was born on 2 September 2020.

Notes

1. Toni C. Antonucci et al., "Society and the Individual at the Dawn of the Twenty-First Century," in *Handbook of the Psychology of Aging*, 2nd ed., ed. K. Warner Schaie and Sherry L. Willis (Oxford: Academic Press, 2016), 57.
2. Meltzer, "Cohousing Sustainability," 85.
3. See, e.g., McCamant and Durrett, *Cohousing*; Meltzer, *Sustainable Community*; Sargisson, "Second-Wave Cohousing."
4. Sargisson, "Second-Wave Cohousing"; Sargisson, *Fool's Gold*.
5. Organisation for Economic Co-operation and Development, *The Well-Being of Nations: The Role of Human and Social Capital* (Paris: OECD Publishing, 2001), 41.
6. Pierre Bourdieu and Löic J. Wacquant, *An Invitation to Reflexive Sociology* (Chicago: University of Chicago Press, 1992).
7. Robert D. Putnam and Lewis M. Feldstein, *Better Together: Restoring the American Community* (New York: Simon & Schuster, 2003), 2.
8. Maria Laura Ruiu, "The Social Capital of Cohousing Communities," *Sociology* 50, no. 2 (2016).
9. Ibid., 410.
10. Jarvis, "Saving Space, Sharing Time," 574.
11. Canadian Cohousing Network, website, 2020, retrieved 4 May 2020 from https://www.cohousing.ca; Cohousing Association of the United States, website, 2020, retrieved 4 May 2020 from https://www.cohousing.org; UK Cohousing Network, website, 2020, retrieved 4 May 2020 from https://cohousing.org.uk.
12. Kankanmori Residents, *Collective House*, 3.
13. Ibid., 131.

14. O'Hashi, "Cultural Divides in Cohousing," 22.
15. For a representative sample, see Chris Roth, "Undressing and Addressing the Elephant in the Room," *Communities* 178 (2018); Crystal Farmer, "Barriers to Diversity in Community," *Communities* 178 (2018); Kara Huntermoon, "Why Diversity is Good for Intentional Community," *Communities* 178 (2018).
16. See, e.g., Yana Ludwig, "Cross-Class Cooperation and Land Access," *Communities* 182 (2019); Betsy Morris, "Making Cohousing Affordable: Strategies and Successes," *Communities* 158 (2013); Laird Schaub, "The Paralysis of Racism in Social Change Groups," *Communities* 155 (2012); Allison Tom, "Inclusivity and Disability," *Communities* 180 (2018).
17. Amanda Abrams, "Cohousing's Diversity Problem," *CityLab*, 9 August 2017, retrieved 21 April 2020 from https://www.citylab.com/equity/2017/08/cohousings-diversity-problem/536337/.
18. Francesco Chiodelli and Valeria Baglione, "Living Together Privately: For a Cautious Reading of Cohousing," *Urban Research & Practice* 7, no. 1 (2014): 24.
19. Ibid., 27.
20. Garciano, "Affordable Cohousing"; Peter Jakobsen and Henrik Gutzon Larsen, "An Alternative for Whom? The Evolution and Socio-economy of Danish Cohousing," *Urban Research and Practice* 12, no. 4 (2019); Lubik and Kosatsky, "Public Health"; Lidewij Tummers, "The Re-emergence of Self-Managed Co-housing in Europe: A Critical Review of Co-housing Research," *Urban Studies* 53, no. 10 (2016).
21. Lietaert, "Cohousing's Relevance to Degrowth," 580.
22. Joanna Winter and Charles Durrett, "Achieving Affordability with Cohousing," *Communities* 158 (2013): 34.
23. Ibid., 34.
24. Meltzer, *Sustainable Community*, 1; see also Lietaert, "Cohousing's Relevance to Degrowth"; Lockyer, "Intentional Communities and Sustainability"; Meltzer, "Cohousing Sustainability"; Meltzer, "Cohousing Environmentalism"; Meltzer, "Urban Biotope"; A. Whitney Sanford, *Living Sustainably: What Intentional Communities Can Teach Us about Democracy, Simplicity, and Nonviolence* (Lexington: University Press of Kentucky, 2017).
25. Organisation for Economic Co-operation and Development, *Accelerating Climate Action: Refocusing Policies through a Well-Being Lens* (Paris: OECD Publishing, 2019); Organisation for Economic Co-operation and Development, "Climate Change Mitigation through a Well-Being Lens: 'Putting People at the Centre of Climate Action,'" *Organisation for Economic Co-operation and Development*, 2019, retrieved 21 April 2020 from https://www.oecd.org/environment/cc/flyer-climate-change-mitigation-through-a-well-being-lens.pdf.
26. Organisation for Economic Co-operation and Development, "Climate Change Mitigation"; emphasis added.
27. Jeffrey D. Sachs, "Introduction to the 2019 Global Happiness and Wellbeing Policy Report," in *Global Happiness and Wellbeing Policy Report 2019*, ed. Global Council for Happiness and Wellbeing (2019), 5, retrieved 21 April 2020 from http://www.happinesscouncil.org.
28. Organisation for Economic Co-operation and Development, "Climate Change Mitigation."
29. Lockyer, "Intentional Communities and Sustainability," 27.
30. Lietaert, "Cohousing's Relevance to Degrowth."

31. Heidi M. Berggren, "Cohousing as Civic Society: Cohousing Involvement and Political Participation in the United States," *Social Science Quarterly* 98, no. 1 (2017): 67.
32. Malinowski, *Myth in Primitive Psychology*.
33. Jarvis, "Saving Space, Sharing Time," 574.
34. United Nations, "Happiness Should Have Greater Role in Development Policy—UN Member States," *UN News*, 19 July 2011, retrieved 1 May 2020 from https://news.un.org/en/story/2011/07/382052.
35. United Nations, "Human Development Reports," *United Nations Development Programme*, retrieved 2 May 2020 from http://hdr.undp.org/.
36. In countries whose governments do not address happiness and well-being directly, other bodies are filling in the gaps. In Canada, for example, the Canadian Research Advisory Group at the University of Waterloo; the Program on Social Interactions, Identity and Well-being of the Canadian Institute for Advanced Research; and the nonprofit Centre for the Study of Living Standards are all engaged in studying well-being and in efforts to influence policy directions.
37. Derek Bok, *The Politics of Happiness: What Government Can Learn from the New Research on Well-Being* (Princeton, NJ: Princeton University Press, 2010); Davies, *Happiness Industry*; Paul Dolan, Tessa Peasgood, and Mathew White, *Review of Research on the Influences on Personal Well-Being and Application to Policy Making* (London: Defra, 2006); Martine Durand, "Countries' Experiences with Well-Being and Happiness Metrics," in *Global Happiness Policy Report 2018*, ed. Global Happiness Council (2018), retrieved 3 September 2018 from http://www.happinesscouncil.org/report/2018/; John Keenan, "Dubai Wants to Be 'World's Happiest City.' Report Says It Has a Long Way to Go," *The Guardian*, 16 March 2016, retrieved 20 July 2017 from https://www.theguardian.com/cities/2016/mar/16/world-happiest-city-dubai-happiness-index-report; Joseph E. Stiglitz, Amartya Sen, and Jean-Paul Fitoussi, *Report by the Commission on the Measurement of Economic Performance and Social Progress* (Paris: Commission on the Measurement of Economic Performance and Social Progress, 2009); Uchida, Ogihara, and Fukushima, "Cultural Construal of Wellbeing"; see also Henrietta L. Moore, *Still Life: Hopes, Desires and Satisfactions* (Cambridge: Polity Press, 2011); Walker and Kavedžija, "Introduction."
38. Andrew E. Clark et al., *The Origins of Happiness: The Science of Well-Being over the Life Course* (Princeton, NJ: Princeton University Press, 2018).
39. Sachs, "Introduction," 4.
40. John F. Helliwell, Richard Layard, and Jeffrey Sachs, eds., *World Happiness Report 2012* (2012), retrieved 21 April 2020 from https://worldhappiness.report/ed/2012/.
41. Susan David, Ilona Boniwell, and Amanda Conley Ayers, eds., *The Oxford Handbook of Happiness* (Oxford: Oxford University Press, 2013).
42. Ed Diener, Shigehiro Oishi, and Louis Tay, eds., *Handbook of Well-Being* (Salt Lake City, UT: DEF Publishers, 2018).
43. See, e.g., Bin Bishr, "Happy Cities Agenda"; Bok, *Politics of Happiness*; Diener and Biswas-Diener, "Social Well-Being"; Ed Diener and Robert Biswas-Diener, "Well-Being Interventions to Improve Societies," in *Global Happiness and Wellbeing Policy Report 2019*, ed. Global Council for Happiness and Wellbeing (2019), retrieved 21 April 2020 from http://www.happinesscouncil.org; Martine Durand and Carrie

Exton, "Adopting a Well-Being Approach in Central Government: Policy Mechanisms and Practical Tools," in *Global Happiness and Wellbeing Policy Report 2019*, ed. Global Council for Happiness and Wellbeing (2019), retrieved 21 April 2020 from http://www.happinesscouncil.org; John F. Helliwell, "Global Happiness Policy Synthesis 2018," in *Global Happiness Policy Report 2018*, ed. Global Happiness Council (2018), retrieved 3 September 2018 from http://www.happinesscouncil.org/report/2018/; Max Norton, "Appendix: Inventory of Policy Ideas from Theme Chapters," in *Global Happiness Policy Report 2018*, ed. Global Happiness Council (2018), retrieved 24 August 2019 from http://www.happinesscouncil.org/report/2018/; Oishi, "Subjective Well-Being"; Hetan Shah and Nic Marks, *A Well-Being Manifesto for a Flourishing Society* (London: New Economics Foundation, 2004).
44. Lara B. Aknin et al., "Happiness and Prosocial Behaviour: An Evaluation of the Evidence," in *World Happiness Report 2019*, ed. John F. Helliwell, Richard Layard, and Jeffrey D. Sachs (2019), retrieved 21 April 2020 from https://worldhappiness.report/ed/2019/; Bok, *Politics of Happiness*; Diener et al., *Well-Being for Public Policy*; Diener and Biswas-Diener, "Social Well-Being"; Helliwell, "Global Happiness Policy Synthesis"; John F. Helliwell and Robert D. Putnam, "The Social Context of Well-Being," *Philosophical Transactions of the Royal Society of London* 359, no. 1449 (2004); Robert MacCulloch, "How Political Systems and Social Welfare Policies Affect Well-Being," in *Handbook of Well-Being*, ed. Ed Diener, Shigehiro Oishi, and Louis Tay (Salt Lake City, UT: DEF Publishers, 2018); Shah and Marks, *Well-Being Manifesto*.
45. Durand and Exton, "Well-Being in Central Government"; Helliwell, "Global Happiness Policy Synthesis."
46. Helliwell, "Global Happiness Policy Synthesis," 20.
47. See, e.g., Aknin et al., "Happiness and Prosocial Behaviour"; Helliwell, "Global Happiness Policy Synthesis"; MacCulloch, "Political Systems"; Shah and Marks, *Well-Being Manifesto*; see also Helliwell and Putnam, "Social Context of Well-Being."
48. James, "Well-Being," 69–70.
49. Shah and Marks, *Well-Being Manifesto*, 16; see also Webster, Ajrouch, and Antonucci, "Living Healthier, Living Longer," 31.
50. Diener and Biswas-Diener, "Social Well-Being," 131–32.
51. Bin Bishr, "Happy Cities Agenda"; see also Tzu-Yuan Stessa Chao et al., "Delivering Community Well-Being from the Happy City Concept: A Practical Approach to Urban Planning and Design," in *Handbook of Community Well-Being Research*, ed. Rhonda Phillips and Cecilia Wong (Dordrecht: Springer, 2017); Diener and Biswas-Diener, "Social Well-Being."
52. Diener and Biswas-Diener, "Social Well-Being," 140–41; see also Scott Cloutier and Deirdre Pfeiffer, "Happiness: An Alternative Objective for Sustainable Community Development," in *Handbook of Community Well-Being Research*, ed. Rhonda Phillips and Cecilia Wong (Dordrecht: Springer, 2017).
53. Clapham, "Well-Being and Housing Policy"; Samanani and Lenhard, "House and Home."
54. Williams, "Predicting an American Future."
55. Guillermo Delgado, "Collaborative Housing at a Crossroad: Critical Reflections from the International Collaborative Housing Conference," in *Living Together—Cohousing Ideas and Realities around the World: Proceedings from the International Collaborative Housing Conference in Stockholm 5–9 May 2010*, ed. Dick Urban Vestbro

(Stockholm: Division of Urban and Regional Studies, Royal Institute of Technology, in collaboration with Kollektivhus NU, 2010), 217.
56. Lubik and Kosatsky, "Public Health," 123.
57. Mathews and Izquierdo, "Anthropology of Well-Being," 261.
58. Lubik and Kosatsky, "Public Health," 123.
59. Durand and Exton, "Well-Being in Central Government"; Helliwell, "Global Happiness Policy Synthesis."
60. Mathews, "Happiness and the Pursuit," 147.
61. Mathews and Izquierdo, "Anthropology, Happiness, and Well-Being," 2.
62. Ibid., 18; see also Fischer, *Good Life*, 208; Mathews and Izquierdo, "Anthropology of Well-Being," 254, 262.
63. Jackson, *Life within Limits*, 184.
64. Mathews and Izquierdo, "Anthropology, Happiness, and Well-Being," 15; emphasis added; see also Fischer, *Good Life*, 202.
65. Mathews, *Life Worth Living*; Gordon Mathews, "Finding and Keeping a Purpose in Life: Well-Being and *Ikigai* in Japan and Elsewhere," in *Pursuits of Happiness: Well-Being in Anthropological Perspective*, ed. Gordon Mathews and Carolina Izquierdo (New York: Berghahn Books, 2009).
66. Mathews and Izquierdo, "Anthropology of Well-Being," 254.
67. Walker and Kavedžija, "Introduction," 12–13.
68. Ibid., 8.
69. Delgado, "Collaborative Housing," 212.
70. Levitas, *Utopia as Method*, 3.
71. Ibid., 9.
72. Ibid., 176.
73. Brown, *Intentional Community*.
74. Levitas, *Utopia as Method*.
75. Sargisson, "Second-Wave Cohousing," 44–45.
76. Ibid., 31; emphasis in original.
77. Cooper, *Everyday Utopias*, 7.
78. Levitas, *Utopia as Method*, xiii; see also Hage, "Dwelling."
79. Michel Foucault, "What Is Enlightenment?" in *The Foucault Reader*, ed. Paul Rabinow (New York: Pantheon, 1984); cited in Cooper, *Everyday Utopias*, 34.
80. Cooper, *Everyday Utopias*, 25.
81. Evelyn Schulz, "Beyond Modernism," in *Future Living: Collective Housing in Japan*, ed. Claudia Hildner (Basel: Birkhäuser, 2014).
82. Lawrence Aronson, *City of Love and Revolution: Vancouver in the Sixties* (Vancouver: New Star Books, 2010); Jill Wade, *Houses for All: The Struggle for Social Housing in Vancouver, 1919–50* (Vancouver: UBC Press, 1994); Alfreda Lynne Wilson, "Bringing Home the Bread and Roses: A Case Study of Women and Co-operative Housing in Vancouver, British Columbia" (MA thesis, Simon Fraser University, Vancouver, 1997).
83. Levitas, *Utopia as Method*, 18.
84. Ibid., 198.
85. Sargisson, "Second-Wave Cohousing," 51.
86. Ibid., 50.
87. Sargisson, *Fool's Gold*, 178.
88. Sargisson, "Second-Wave Cohousing," 29.

89. Ibid., 42.
90. Lucy Sargisson, "Strange Places: Estrangement, Utopianism, and Intentional Communities," *Utopian Studies* 18, no. 3 (2007).
91. Karin Bradley and Johan Hedrén, "Utopian Thought in the Making of Green Futures," in *Green Utopianism: Perspectives, Politics and Micro-Practices*, ed. Karin Bradley and Johan Hedrén (New York: Routledge, 2014), 9.
92. Sargisson, "Second-Wave Cohousing," 30.
93. Sargisson, "Second-Wave Cohousing"; Sargisson, *Fool's Gold*; Williams, "Predicting an American Future."
94. Lietaert, "Cohousing's Relevance to Degrowth," 580.
95. Cooper, *Everyday Utopias*, 7.
96. Ibid., 5.
97. Levitas, *Utopia as Method*, 4.
98. Brown, "Introduction," 5.
99. Mathews, "Happiness, Culture, and Context," 304.
100. Fischer, *Good Life*, 216.

APPENDIX
The Film Shorts

URL: https://drive.google.com/drive/folders/1WnPcxyyrL86VI5ifHc_cET12XAWdo4mj?usp=sharing

Life at Quayside Village

Exploring Quayside Village

1. Walk through the Neighbourhood (00:00)
2. Jazzy's Tour (00:51)
3. Jazzy's Newsletter (Quayside Quibbler) (01:14)
4. Donya and Jazzy Discuss Cohousing (01:25)
5. Carol Enjoying Her Balcony (02:00)
6. Working in the Common Kitchen (02:15)

Making Community

7. Community Meeting (03:29)
8. Decision Making (03:49)
9. Common Meals (04:22)
10. Gardening (05:37)
11. Beautification (06:39)
12. Recycling (07:25)
13. Composting (09:05)
14. Don's Original Composition (09:30)
15. Community Yoga (09:59)
16. Annual Awards (10:32)

Connecting with the Wider Community

17. Vera's Midwifery Practice (12:31)
18. The Perfect Storm Singers (12:53)
19. Art in the Garden (13:33)

Celebrations

20. Birthday Celebrations (14:26)
21. Vera's Birthday (15:12)
22. Preparing for the 20th Anniversary Party (16:00)
23. The 20th Anniversary Party (16:10)
24. Company B Jazz Band (17:56)

Life at Kankanmori

Exploring Kankanmori

1. Walk through the Neighbourhood (00:00)
2. Haruko Giving a Tour of Her Family's Apartment (01:06)

Making Community

3. Community Meeting (03:27)
4. Children's Meeting (04:07)
5. Common Meals (04:42)
6. Traditional Okinawan Music (05:43)
7. Community Yoga (05:53)
8. Gardening (06:13)
9. The Flower Garden (07:12)
10. The Vegetable Garden (07:32)
11. Children's Painting Project (08:04)
12. Mochi Making (08:57)

Celebrations and Connections with the City

13. Student Presentation (10:22)
14. Decorating for the Christmas Party (10:38)
15. Celebrating Christmas (11:35)
16. 15th Anniversary Presentation (14:08)
17. 15th Anniversary Party (14:28)

Exchange at Kankanmori

1. Quayside Visitors Tour Kankanmori (00:05)
2. A Tour of Shoko's Apartment (00:45)

Meetings

3. The Visitors Attend a Community Meeting (01:46)
4. The Quayside Visitors Give a Presentation (02:27)
5. Afternoon Tea with the Quayside Visitors (02:49)
6. Children's Afternoon Tea (03:22)

Hanging Out

7. The Quayside Visitors Make a Meal (03:46)
8. Common Meal Accounting (05:33)
9. After Dinner Drinking Party (05:56)
10. Yumiko Dresses Connie in a Kimono (06:04)
11. Making Bread Together (06:49)
12. Having a Traditional Japanese Meal (07:42)
13. Building Outdoor Planter Boxes (08:44)
14. Karaoke Night (10:10)
15. Farewell Meal (10:55)

Exchange at Quayside Village

1. Haruko Explores Quayside Village (00:07)
2. Haruko and Carl See the Recycling Room (02:25)
3. Brian Teaches the Visitors about Composting (02:45)

Meetings

4. Carl and Haruko Attend a Thriving Meeting (05:21)
5. Carl Learns about Meeting Cards (06:17)
6. Kankanmori Visitors Attend a Community Meeting (06:30)
7. Carl and Haruko Give a Presentation (08:03)

Hanging Out

8. Decorating for Christmas (08:28)
9. Juhli and Haruko Make Bread (08:37)
10. Haruko Explains the Gifts from Kankanmori (09:28)
11. Playing Games Together (10:01)
12. The Children Build a Fort (10:26)
13. Anna's Birthday Party (10:31)
14. Anna Rings the Dinner Bell (11:14)
15. Farewell Meal with the Visitors (11:28)

BIBLIOGRAPHY

Abbinnett, Ross. *Politics of Happiness: Connecting the Philosophical Ideas of Hegel, Nietzsche and Derrida to the Political Ideologies of Happiness*. New York: Bloomsbury, 2013.

Abrams, Amanda. "Cohousing's Diversity Problem." *CityLab*, 9 August 2017. Retrieved 21 April 2020 from https://www.citylab.com/equity/2017/08/cohousings-diversity-problem/536337/.

Ahmed, Sara. *The Promise of Happiness*. Durham, NC: Duke University Press, 2010.

Aknin, Lara B., Ashley V. Whillans, Michael I. Norton, and Elizabeth W. Dunn. "Happiness and Prosocial Behaviour: An Evaluation of the Evidence." In *World Happiness Report 2019*, edited by John F. Helliwell, Richard Layard, and Jeffrey D. Sachs, 67–86. 2019. Retrieved April 21 2020 from https://worldhappiness.report/ed/2019/.

Allison, Anne. *Precarious Japan*. Durham, NC: Duke University Press, 2013.

Amin, Ash, and Philip Howell. "Thinking the Commons." In *Releasing the Commons: Rethinking the Futures of the Commons*, edited by Ash Amin and Philip Howell, 1–17. New York: Routledge, 2016.

Antonucci, Toni C., Lisa Berkman, Axel Börsch-Supan, Laura L. Carstensen, Linda P. Fried, Frank F. Furstenberg, Dana Goldman, James S. Jackson, Martin Kohli, S. Jay Olshansky, John Rother, John W. Rowe, and Julie Zissimopoulos. "Society and the Individual at the Dawn of the Twenty-First Century." In *Handbook of the Psychology of Aging*, 2nd ed., edited by K. Warner Schaie and Sherry L. Willis, 41–62. Oxford: Academic Press, 2016.

Argyle, Michael. *The Psychology of Happiness*. London: Methuen, 1987.

Aronson, Lawrence. *City of Love and Revolution: Vancouver in the Sixties*. Vancouver: New Star Books, 2010.

Bearne, Suzanne. "Totally Together: Could Communal Living Suit You?" *The Guardian*, 3 February 2018. Retrieved 27 February 2020 from https://www.theguardian.com/money/2018/feb/03/communal-living-communes-cohousing.

Ben-Shahar, Tal. *Happier: Learn the Secrets to Daily Joy and Lasting Fulfillment*. New York: McGraw Hill, 2007.

Berggren, Heidi M. "Cohousing as Civic Society: Cohousing Involvement and Political Participation in the United States." *Social Science Quarterly* 98, no. 1 (2017): 57–72.

Berkman, Lisa F., and Aditi Krishna. "Social Network Epidemiology." In *Social Epidemiology*, 2nd ed., edited by Lisa F. Berkman, Ichiro Kawachi, and M. Maria Glymour, 234–289. Oxford: Oxford University Press, 2014.

Berkman, Lisa F., and Leonard Syme. "Social Networks, Host Resistance, and Mortality: A Nine-Year Follow-Up Study of Alameda County Residents." *American Journal of Epidemiology* 109, no. 2 (1979): 186–204.

Bin Bishr, Aisha. "Happy Cities Agenda." In *Global Happiness and Wellbeing Policy Report 2019*, edited by Global Council for Happiness and Wellbeing, 113–39. 2019. Retrieved 30 August 2019 from www.happinesscouncil.org.

Bok, Derek. *The Politics of Happiness: What Government Can Learn from the New Research on Well-Being*. Princeton, NJ: Princeton University Press, 2010.

Bourdieu, Pierre, and Löic J. D. Wacquant. *An Invitation to Reflexive Sociology*. Chicago: University of Chicago Press, 1992.

Bradley, Karin, and Johan Hedrén. "Utopian Thought in the Making of Green Futures." In *Green Utopianism: Perspectives, Politics and Micro-practices*, edited by Karin Bradley and Johan Hedrén, 2–20. New York: Routledge, 2014.

Brodie, Janine. "Social Literacy and Social Justice in Times of Crisis." *Trudeau Foundation Papers* 4, no. 1 (2012): 115–46.

Brown, Susan Love. "Introduction." In *Intentional Community: An Anthropological Perspective*, edited by Susan Love Brown, 1–15. Albany: State University of New York Press, 2002.

———. "Community as Cultural Critique." In *Intentional Community: An Anthropological Perspective*, edited by Susan Love Brown, 153–79. Albany: State University of New York Press, 2002.

Brown, Susan Love, ed. *Intentional Community: An Anthropological Perspective*. Albany: State University of New York Press, 2002.

Bruckner, Pascal. *Perpetual Euphoria: On the Duty to Be Happy*. Princeton, NJ: Princeton University Press, 2010.

Canadian Cohousing Network. Website. 2020. Retrieved 4 May 2020 from https://www.cohousing.ca.

Carr, Alan. *Positive Psychology: The Science of Happiness and Human Strengths*. London: Routledge, 2004.

CBC. "Where I Live and Why: Co-housing Development in Edmonton." CBC News, 1 October 2019. Retrieved 27 February 2020 from https://www.cbc.ca/player/play/1628975683653.

———. "A Closer Look at How Cohousing Works." CBC News, 12 November 2019. Retrieved 27 February 2020 from https://www.cbc.ca/player/play/1641455683614.

Chang, Shu-Sen, David Stuckler, Paul Yip, and David Gunnell. "Impact of 2008 Global Economic Crisis on Suicide: Time Trend Study in 54 Countries." *British Medical Journal* 347 (2013): 1–15.

Chao, Tzu-Yuan Stessa, Shao-Kuan Liu, Balint Kalman, Hsin-Chieh Cindy Lu, and Miaoqi Cai. "Delivering Community Well-Being from the Happy City Concept: A Practical Approach to Urban Planning and Design." In *Handbook of Community Well-Being Research*, edited by Rhonda Phillips and Cecilia Wong, 435–52. Dordrecht: Springer, 2017.

Chiodelli, Francesco, and Valeria Baglione. "Living Together Privately: For a Cautious Reading of Cohousing." *Urban Research & Practice* 7, no. 1 (2014): 20–34.

Chodorkoff, Dan. *The Anthropology of Utopia: On Social Ecology and Human Development*. Porsgrunn: New Compass Press, 2014.

Christian, Diana Leafe. *Creating a Life Together: Practical Tools to Grow Ecovillages and Intentional Communities*. Gabriola Islands, BC: New Society Publishers, 2003.

Christopher, John Chambers, and Sarah Hickinbottom. "Positive Psychology, Ethnocentrism, and the Disguised Ideology of Individualism." *Theory & Psychology* 18, no. 5 (2008): 563–89.

Cieslik, Mark. *The Happiness Riddle and the Quest for a Good Life*. London: Palgrave Macmillan, 2017.

Clancy, Patricia M. "The Acquisition of Communicative Style in Japanese." In *Making Sense of Language: Readings in Culture and Communication*, 3rd ed., edited by Susan D. Blum, 106–24. New York: Oxford University Press, 2017.

Clapham, David. "Happiness, Well-Being, and Housing Policy." *Policy and Politics* 38, no. 2 (2010): 253–67.

Clark, Andrew E., Sarah Flèche, Richard Layard, Nattavudh Powdthavee, and George Ward. *The Origins of Happiness: The Science of Well-Being over the Life Course*. Princeton, NJ: Princeton University Press, 2018.

Cloutier, Scott, and Deirdre Pfeiffer. "Happiness: An Alternative Objective for Sustainable Community Development." In *Handbook of Community Well-Being Research*, edited by Rhonda Phillips and Cecilia Wong, 85–96. Dordrecht: Springer, 2017.

Cohousing Association of the United States. Website. 2020. Retrieved 4 May 2020 from https://www.cohousing.org.

"Collective Homes a Solution for Those in Japan Who Don't Want to Live Alone." *Japan Times*, 30 August 2016. Retrieved 27 February 2020 from https://www.japantimes.co.jp/news/2016/08/30/national/social-issues/collective-homes-solution-japan-dont-want-live-alone/#.XvLBpy0ZPq0.

"Conflict and Connection." Special issue. *Communities* 104 (1999).

Cooper, Davina. *Everyday Utopias: The Conceptual Life of Promising Spaces*. Durham, NC: Duke University Press, 2014.

Coulmas, Florian. "The Quest for Happiness in Japan." German Institute for Japanese Studies Working Paper 09/1. Tokyo: German Institute for Japanese Studies, 2008.

Csikszentmihalyi, Mihaly. *Flow: The Psychology of Optimal Experience*. New York: HarperCollins, 1990.

———. *Creativity: Flow and the Psychology of Discovery and Invention*. New York: HarperCollins, 1997.

David, Susan, Ilona Boniwell, and Amanda Conley Ayers, eds. *The Oxford Handbook of Happiness*. Oxford: Oxford University Press, 2013.

Davies, William. *The Happiness Industry: How the Government and Big Business Sold Us Well-Being*. London: Verso, 2015.

"Decision-Making in Community." Special issue. *Communities* 109 (2000).

Delgado, Guillermo. "Collaborative Housing at a Crossroad: Critical Reflections from the International Collaborative Housing Conference." In *Living Together—Cohousing Ideas and Realities around the World: Proceedings from the International Collaborative Housing Conference in Stockholm 5–9 May 2010*, edited by Dick Urban Vestbro, 212–23. Stockholm: Division of Urban and Regional Studies, Royal Institute of Technology, in collaboration with Kollektivhus NU, 2010.

DePaulo, Bella. *How We Live Now: Redefining Home and Family in the 21st Century*. New York: Atria Books, 2015.

Diener, Ed, Richard E. Lucas, Ulrich Schimmack, and John F. Helliwell. *Well-Being for Public Policy*. Oxford: Oxford University Press, 2009.

Diener, Ed, and Robert Biswas-Diener. "Social Well-Being: Research and Policy Recommendations." In *Global Happiness Policy Report 2018*, edited by Global Happiness Council, 129–58. 2018. Retrieved 3 September 2018 from http://www.happinesscouncil.org/report/2018/.
———. "Well-Being Interventions to Improve Societies." In *Global Happiness and Wellbeing Policy Report 2019*, edited by Global Council for Happiness and Wellbeing, 95–112. 2019. Retrieved 21 April 2020 from http://www.happinesscouncil.org.
Diener, Ed, Shigehiro Oishi, and Louis Tay, eds. *Handbook of Well-Being*. Salt Lake City, UT: DEF Publishers, 2018.
Dolan, Paul. *Happiness by Design: Change What You Do, Not How You Think*. New York: Hudson Street Press, 2014.
Dolan, Paul, and Mathew P. White. "How Can Measures of Subjective Well-Being Be Used to Inform Public Policy?" *Perspectives on Psychological Science* 2, no. 1 (2007): 71–85.
Dolan, Paul, Tessa Peasgood, and Mathew White. *Review of Research on the Influences on Personal Well-Being and Application to Policy Making*. London: Defra, 2006.
Durand, Martine. "Countries' Experiences with Well-Being and Happiness Metrics." In *Global Happiness Policy Report 2018*, edited by Global Happiness Council, 201–45. 2018. Retrieved 3 September 2018 from http://www.happinesscouncil.org/report/2018/.
Durand, Martine, and Carrie Exton. "Adopting a Well-Being Approach in Central Government: Policy Mechanisms and Practical Tools." In *Global Happiness and Wellbeing Policy Report 2019*, edited by Global Council for Happiness and Wellbeing, 141–62. 2019. Retrieved 21 April 2020 from http://www.happinesscouncil.org.
Durkheim, Émile. *Suicide: A Study in Sociology*. Translated by John A. Spaulding and George Simpson. New York: The Free Press, 1997 [1897].
Durrett, Charles, and Kathryn McCamant. *Creating Cohousing: Building Sustainable Communities*. Gabriola Islands, BC: New Society Publishers, 2011.
Egerö, Bertil. "Introduction: Cohousing—Issues and Challenges." In *Living Together—Cohousing Ideas and Realities around the World: Proceedings from the International Collaborative Housing Conference in Stockholm 5–9 May 2010*, edited by Dick Urban Vestbro, 11–20. Stockholm: Division of Urban and Regional Studies, Royal Institute of Technology, in collaboration with Kollektivhus NU, 2010.
Ehrenreich, Barbara. *Bright-Sided: How the Relentless Promotion of Positive Thinking Has Undermined America*. New York: Henry Holt, 2009.
Farmer, Crystal. "Barriers to Diversity in Community." *Communities* 178 (2018): 17.
Ferguson, Iain. "Neoliberalism, Happiness and Wellbeing." *International Socialism* 117 (2007): 7–13. Retrieved 19 July 2017 from http://isj.org.uk/neoliberalism-happiness-and-wellbeing/.
Fernández-Ríos, Luís, and J. M. Cornes. "A Critical Review of the History and Current Status of Positive Psychology." *Annuary of Clinical and Health Psychology* 5 (2009): 7–13.
Fischer, Edward F. *The Good Life: Aspiration, Dignity, and the Anthropology of Wellbeing*. Stanford, CA: Stanford University Press, 2014.
Foucault, Michel. "What Is Enlightenment?" In *The Foucault Reader*, edited by Paul Rabinow, 32–50. New York: Pantheon, 1984.
Foundation for Intentional Community. Website. 2019. Retrieved 4 May 2020 from www.ic.org.

Fromm, Dorit. *Collaborative Communities: Cohousing, Central Living, and Other New Forms of Housing with Shared Facilities.* New York: Van Nostrand Reinhold, 1991.
Gable, Shelly L., and Christopher Bromberg. "Healthy Social Bonds: A Necessary Condition for Well-Being." In *Handbook of Well-Being*, edited by Ed Diener, Shigehiro Oishi, and Louis Tay, 1–14. Salt Lake City, UT: DEF Publishers, 2018.
Gable, Shelly L., and Jonathan Haidt. "What (and Why) Is Positive Psychology?" *Review of General Psychology* 9, no. 2 (2005): 103–10.
Garciano, Jerome L. "Affordable Cohousing: Challenges and Opportunities for Supportive Relational Networks in Mixed-Income Housing." *Journal of Affordable Housing & Community Development Law* 20, no. 2 (2011): 169–92.
Geertz, Clifford. "On the Nature of Anthropological Understanding." *American Scientist* 63 (1975): 47–53.
Gibson-Graham, J. K., Jenny Cameron, and Stephen Healy. "Commoning as a Postcapitalist Politics." In *Releasing the Commons: Rethinking the Futures of the Commons*, edited by Ash Amin and Philip Howell, 192–212. New York: Routledge, 2016.
Gilman, Robert. "Keynote Address: The Dynamic Planetary Context for Intentional Communities (Proceedings of the 11th Conference of the International Communal Studies Association)." *Social Sciences Directory* 2, no. 3 (2013): 2–31.
Glass, Anne P., and Rebecca S. Vander Plaats. "A Conceptual Model for Aging Better Together Intentionally." *Journal of Aging Studies* 27, no. 4 (2013): 428–42.
Global Council for Happiness and Wellbeing, eds. *Global Happiness and Wellbeing Policy Report 2019.* 2019. Retrieved 21 April 2020 from http://www.happinesscouncil.org.
Goodman, Roger. "Shifting Landscapes: The Social Context of Youth Problems in an Ageing Nation." In *A Sociology of Japanese Youth: From Returnees to NEETs*, edited by Roger Goodman, Yuki Imoto, and Tuukka Toivonen, 159–73. New York: Routledge, 2012.
Grinde, Bjørn, Ragnhild Bang Nes, Ian F. MacDonald, and David Sloan Wilson. "Quality of Life in Intentional Communities." *Social Indicators Research* 137 (2018): 625–40.
Gunnell, Barbara. "The Happiness Industry." *New Statesman*, 6 September 2004. Retrieved 27 February 2020 from https://www.newstatesman.com/node/160445.
Hage, Ghassan. "Dwelling in the Reality of Utopian Thought." *Traditional Dwellings and Settlements Review* 23, no. 1 (2011): 7–13.
Handel, Ariel. "What's in a Home? Toward a Critical Theory of Housing/Dwelling." *Environment and Planning C: Politics and Space* 37, no. 6 (2019): 1045–62.
Helliwell, John F. "Global Happiness Policy Synthesis 2018." In *Global Happiness Policy Report 2018*, edited by Global Happiness Council, 11–26. 2018. Retrieved 3 September 2018 from http://www.happinesscouncil.org/report/2018/.
Helliwell, John F., Richard Layard, and Jeffrey Sachs, eds. *World Happiness Report 2012*. 2012. Retrieved 21 April 2020 from https://worldhappiness.report/ed/2012/.
Helliwell, John F., and Robert D. Putnam. "The Social Context of Well-Being." *Philosophical Transactions of the Royal Society of London* 359, no. 1449 (2004): 1435–46.
Hewitt, Rachel. "Do 'Animal Fluids Move by Hydraulick Laws'? The Politics of the Hydraulic Theory of Emotion." *Lancet Psychiatry* 5, no. 1 (2018): 25–26.
Hildner, Claudia. *Future Living: Collective Housing in Japan.* Basel: Birkhäuser, 2014.
Hitokoto, Hidehumi, and Yukiko Uchida. "Interdependent Happiness: Theoretical Importance and Measurement Validity." *Journal of Happiness Studies* 16, no. 1 (2015): 211–39.

Hoffman, Michael. "Solitude Appears to Have an Image Problem in Japan." *Japan Times*, 11 August 2018. Retrieved 27 February 2020 from https://www.japantimes.co.jp/news/2018/08/11/national/media-national/solitude-appears-image-problem-japan/#.XvK7ey0ZPq0.

Holmes, Douglas R., and George E. Marcus. "Collaboration Today and the Re-imagination of the Classic Scene of Fieldwork Encounter." *Collaborative Anthropologies* 1 (2008): 81–101.

Holthus, Barbara, and Wolfram Manzenreiter. "Conclusion: Happiness as a Balancing Act between Agency and Social Structure." In *Happiness and the Good Life in Japan*, edited by Wolfram Manzenreiter and Barbara Holthus, 243–55. New York: Routledge, 2017.

Holt-Lunstad, Julianne, Theodore F. Robles, and David A. Sbarra. "Advancing Social Connection as a Public Health Priority in the United States." *American Psychologist* 72, no. 6 (2017): 517–30.

Horiguchi, Sachiko. "Hikikomori: How Private Isolation Caught the Public Eye." In *A Sociology of Japanese Youth: From Returnees to NEETs*, edited by Roger Goodman, Yuki Imoto, and Tuukka Toivonen, 122–38. New York: Routledge, 2012.

Huntermoon, Kara. "Why Diversity Is Good for Intentional Community." *Communities* 178 (2018): 45–46.

Intergovernmental Panel on Climate Change. *Global Warming of 1.5°C: An IPCC Special Report on the Impacts of Global Warming of 1.5°C above Pre-industrial Levels and Related Global Greenhouse Gas Emission Pathways, in the Context of Strengthening the Global Response to the Threat of Climate Change, Sustainable Development, and Efforts to Eradicate Poverty*. Geneva: World Meteorological Organization, 2018.

———. "Land Is a Critical Resource, IPCC Report Says." *Intergovernmental Panel on Climate Change*, 8 August 2019. Retrieved 27 February 2020 from https://www.ipcc.ch/2019/08/08/land-is-a-critical-resource_srccl/.

Izquierdo, Carolina. "Well-Being among the Matsigenka of the Peruvian Amazon: Health, Missions, Oil, and 'Progress.'" In *Pursuits of Happiness: Well-Being in Anthropological Perspective*, edited by Gordon Mathews and Carolina Izquierdo, 67–87. New York: Berghahn Books, 2009.

Jackson, Michael. *Life within Limits: Well-Being in a World of Want*. Durham, NC: Duke University Press, 2011.

Jakobsen, Peter, and Henrik Gutzon Larsen. "An Alternative for Whom? The Evolution and Socio-economy of Danish Cohousing." *Urban Research and Practice* 12, no. 4 (2019): 414–30.

James, Wendy. "Well-Being: In Whose Opinion, and Who Pays?" In *Culture and Well-Being: Anthropological Approaches to Freedom and Political Ethics*, edited by Alberto Corsín Jiménez, 69–79. London: Pluto, 2008.

Jarvis, Helen. "Saving Space, Sharing Time: Integrated Infrastructures of Daily Life in Cohousing." *Environment and Planning A: Economy and Space* 43, no. 3 (2011): 560–77.

Joshanloo, Mohsen, and Dan Weijers. "Aversion to Happiness across Cultures: A Review of Where and Why People Are Averse to Happiness." *Journal of Happiness Studies* 15, no. 3 (2014): 717–35.

Kamau, Lucy Jayne. "Liminality, Communitas, Charisma, and Community." In *Intentional Community: An Anthropological Perspective*, edited by Susan Love Brown, 17–40. Albany: State University of New York Press, 2002.

Kankanmori Collective House Inc. Website. 2020. Retrieved 17 June 2020 from http://www.collectivehouse.co.jp.
Kankanmori Residents. *The Collective House, Kankanmori: This Is the Alternative Way of Living in Modern Japan*. Tokyo: Domesushupan, 2014.
Kavedžija, Iza. "The Good Life in Balance: Insights from Aging Japan." In *Values of Happiness: Toward an Anthropology of Purpose in Life*, edited by Harry Walker and Iza Kavedžija, 83–108. Chicago: HAU Books, 2016.
Kawachi, Ichiro, Bruce P. Kennedy, Kimberly Lochner, and Deborah Prothrow-Stith. "Social Capital, Income Inequality, and Mortality." *American Journal of Public Health* 87, no. 9 (1997): 1491–98.
Kawano, Satsuki, Glenda S. Roberts, and Susan Orpett Long. "Introduction: Differentiation and Uncertainty." In *Capturing Contemporary Japan: Differentiation and Uncertainty*, edited by Satsuki Kawano, Glenda S. Roberts, and Susan Orpett Long, 1–24. Honolulu: University of Hawai'i Press, 2014.
Keay, Douglas. "Interview with Margaret Thatcher, September 23." *Woman's Own*, 23 September 1987.
Keefe, Janice, Melissa Andrew, Pamela Fancey, and Madelyn Hall. *A Profile of Social Isolation in Canada*. Halifax: Nova Scotia Centre on Aging and the Department of Family Studies and Gerontology, Mount Saint Vincent University, 2006.
Keenan, John. "Dubai Wants to Be 'World's Happiest City.' Report Says It Has a Long Way to Go." *The Guardian*, 16 March 2016. Retrieved 20 July 2017 from https://www.theguardian.com/cities/2016/mar/16/world-happiest-city-dubai-happiness-index-report.
Kingfisher, Catherine. *Western Welfare in Decline: Globalization and Women's Poverty*. Philadelphia: University of Pennsylvania Press, 2002.
———. "Happiness: Notes on History, Culture and Governance." *Health, Culture and Society* 5, no. 1 (2013): 67–82.
Kingwell, Mark. *In Pursuit of Happiness: Better Living from Plato to Prozac*. Toronto: Penguin, 1998.
Kitanaka, Junko. *Depression in Japan: Psychiatric Cures for a Society in Distress*. Princeton, NJ: Princeton University Press, 2012.
Klein, Naomi. *No Is Not Enough: Resisting the New Shock Politics and Winning the World We Need*. Toronto: Random House, 2017.
Klein, Stefan. *The Science of Happiness: How Our Brains Make Us Happy—And What We Can Do to Get Happier*. Translated by Stephen Lehmann. Cambridge: Da Capo Press, 2006.
Klinenberg, Eric. *Going Solo: The Extraordinary Rise and Surprising Appeal of Living Alone*. New York: Penguin, 2012.
Lassiter, Luke Eric. *The Chicago Guide to Collaborative Ethnography*. Chicago: University of Chicago Press, 2005.
Leach, Anna. "Happy Together: Lonely Baby Boomers Turn to Co-housing." *The Guardian*, 15 August 2018. Retrieved 27 February 2020 from https://www.theguardian.com/world/2018/aug/15/happy-together-lonely-baby-boomers-turn-to-co-housing.
Leheny, David. "What's Behind What Ails Japan." In *Critical Issues in Contemporary Japan*, edited by Jeff Kingston, 288–99. New York: Routledge, 2014.
Levitas, Ruth. *Utopia as Method: The Imaginary Reconstitution of Society*. New York: Palgrave Macmillan, 2013.

Lietaert, Matthieu. "Cohousing's Relevance to Degrowth Theories." *Journal of Cleaner Production* 18, no. 6 (2010): 576–80.
Linley, P. Alex, Stephen Joseph, Susan Harrington, and Alex M. Wood. "Positive Psychology: Past, Present, and (Possible) Future." *Journal of Positive Psychology* 1, no. 1 (2006): 3–16.
Lockyer, Joshua. "Intentional Communities and Sustainability." *Communal Societies* 30, no. 1 (2010): 17–30.
Lockyer, Joshua, and James R. Veteto, eds. *Environmental Anthropology Engaging Ecotopia: Bioregionalism, Permaculture, and Ecovillages*. New York: Berghahn Books, 2013.
Lubik, Amy, and Tom Kosatsky. "Public Health Should Promote Co-operative Housing and Cohousing." *Canadian Journal of Public Health* 110 (2019): 121–26.
Ludwig, Yana. "Cross-Class Cooperation and Land Access." *Communities* 182 (2019): 25–26.
Lutz, Catherine A. *Unnatural Emotions: Everyday Sentiments on a Micronesian Atoll and Their Challenge to Western Theory*. Chicago: University of Chicago Press, 1988.
MacCulloch, Robert. "How Political Systems and Social Welfare Policies Affect Well-Being." In *Handbook of Well-Being*, edited by Ed Diener, Shigehiro Oishi, and Louis Tay, 1–9. Salt Lake City, UT: DEF Publishers, 2018.
Mageo, Jeannette M. *Theorizing Self in Samoa: Emotions, Genders, and Sexualities*. Ann Arbor: University of Michigan Press, 1998.
Malinowski, Bronislaw. *Myth in Primitive Psychology*. London: Norton, 1926.
Mallett, Shelley. "Understanding Home: A Critical Review of the Literature." *Sociological Review* 52, no. 1 (2004): 62–89.
Manzenreiter, Wolfram, and Barbara Holthus. "Introduction: Happiness in Japan through the Anthropological Lens." In *Happiness and the Good Life in Japan*, edited by Wolfram Manzenreiter and Barbara Holthus, 1–12. New York: Routledge, 2017.
Mathews, Gordon. *What Makes Life Worth Living? How Japanese and Americans Make Sense of Their Worlds*. Berkeley: University of California Press, 1996.
———. "Happiness and the Pursuit of a Life Worth Living: An Anthropological Approach." In *Happiness and Public Policy: Theory, Case Studies and Implications*, edited by Yew-Kwang Ng and Lok Sang Ho, 147–68. New York: Palgrave Macmillan, 2006.
———. "Finding and Keeping a Purpose in Life: Well-Being and *Ikigai* in Japan and Elsewhere." In *Pursuits of Happiness: Well-Being in Anthropological Perspective*, edited by Gordon Mathews and Carolina Izquierdo, 167–85. New York: Berghahn Books, 2009.
———. "Happiness, Culture, and Context." *International Journal of Wellbeing* 2, no. 4 (2012): 299–312.
———. "Happiness in Neoliberal Japan." In *Happiness and the Good Life in Japan*, edited by Wolfram Manzenreiter and Barbara Holthus, 227–42. New York: Routledge, 2017.
———. "Wellbeing." In *The International Encyclopedia of Anthropology*, edited by Hilary Callan, 1–5. 2018. Retrieved 27 February 2020 from https://doi.org/10.1002/9781118924396.wbiea1627.
Mathews, Gordon, and Carolina Izquierdo, eds. *Pursuits of Happiness: Well-Being in Anthropological Perspective*. New York: Berghahn Books, 2009.

Mathews, Gordon, and Carolina Izquierdo. "Anthropology, Happiness, and Well-Being." In *Pursuits of Happiness: Well-Being in Anthropological Perspective*, edited by Gordon Mathews and Carolina Izquierdo, 1–19. New York: Berghahn Books, 2009.

———. "Towards an Anthropology of Well-Being." In *Pursuits of Happiness: Well-Being in Anthropological Perspective*, edited by Gordon Mathews and Carolina Izquierdo, 248–66. New York: Berghahn Books, 2009.

McCamant, Kathryn, and Charles Durrett. *Cohousing: A Contemporary Approach to Housing Ourselves*. Berkeley: Habitat Press/Ten Speed Press, 1988.

McCurry, Justin. "Concern in Japan over High Number of 'Lonely Deaths' While Living with Others." *The Guardian*, 8 December 2020. Retrieved 18 December 2020 from https://www.theguardian.com/world/2020/dec/08/concern-lonely-deaths-japan-dementia.

McDonald, Matthew, and Jean O'Callaghan. "Positive Psychology: A Foucauldian Critique." *Humanistic Psychologist* 36, no. 2 (2008): 127–42.

McLeod-Macy, Jennifer, and Erin Roulston. "3rd Annual Canadian Mental Health Check-Up." *Ipsos Public Perspectives*, April 2017. Retrieved 27 February 2020 from https://www.ipsos.com/sites/default/files/2017-08/IpsosPA_PublicPerspectives_CA_April percent202017 percent20Mental percent20Health.pdf.

McMahon, Darrin M. *Happiness: A History*. New York: Grove Press, 2006.

———. "What Does the Ideal of Happiness Mean?" *Social Research* 77, no. 2 (2010): 469–90.

Meltzer, Graham. "Cohousing: Linking Communitarianism and Sustainability." *Communal Societies* 19 (1999): 85–100.

———. "Cohousing: Verifying the Importance of Community in the Application of Environmentalism." *Journal of Architectural and Planning Research* 17, no. 2 (2000): 110–32.

———. *Sustainable Community: Learning from the Cohousing Model*. Victoria: Trafford, 2005.

———. "'Urban Biotope'—Japanese Style." *Communities* 129 (2005): 57–59.

Montgomery, Charles. *Happy City: Transforming Our Lives through Urban Design*. Toronto: Anchor Canada, 2013.

Moore, Henrietta L. "'Visions of the Good Life': Anthropology and the Study of Utopia." *Cambridge Journal of Anthropology* 14, no. 3 (1990): 13–33.

———. *Still Life: Hopes, Desires and Satisfactions*. Cambridge: Polity Press, 2011.

Moore, Suzanne. "The Self-Care Industry Is Peddling Exhausting, Dangerous Drivel." *The Guardian*, 7 May 2018. Retrieved 27 February 2020 from https://www.theguardian.com/commentisfree/2018/may/07/the-self-care-industry-is-peddling-exhausting-dangerous-drivel.

More, Thomas. *Utopia*. Translated by Paul Turner. New York: Penguin, 1965 [1515].

Morris, Betsy. "Making Cohousing Affordable: Strategies and Successes." *Communities* 158 (2013): 36–75.

Mulgan, Geoff. "Well-Being and Public Policy." In *The Oxford Handbook of Happiness*, edited by Susan David, Ilona Boniwell, and Amanda Conley Ayers, 517–32. Oxford: Oxford University Press, 2013.

Myers, David G. "Human Connections and the Good Life: Balancing Individuality and Community in Public Policy." In *Positive Psychology in Practice*, edited by P. Alex Linley and Stephen Joseph, 641–57. Hoboken, NJ: Wiley, 2004.

Nair, Roshini. "The Architecture of Loneliness: How Vancouver's Highrises Contribute to Isolation." CBC News, 25 November 2018. Retrieved 27 February 2020 from https://www.cbc.ca/news/canada/british-columbia/the-architecture-of-loneliness-how-vancouver-s-highrises-contribute-to-isolation-1.4919548.

Nicol, Lee Ann. *Sustainable Collective Housing: Policy and Practice for Multi-family Dwellings*. New York: Routledge, 2013.

Nightingale, Andrea. "Commoning for Inclusion? Commons, Exclusion, Property and Socio-natural Becomings." *International Journal of the Commons* 13, no. 1 (2019): 16–35.

Norton, Max. "Appendix: Inventory of Policy Ideas from Theme Chapters." In *Global Happiness Policy Report 2018*, edited by Global Happiness Council, 247–60. 2018. Retrieved 24 August 2019 from http://www.happinesscouncil.org/report/2018/.

Ogihara, Yuji, Hiroyo Fujita, Hitoshi Tominaga, Sho Ishigaki, Takuya Kashimoto, Ayano Takahashi, Kyoko Toyohara, and Yukiko Uchida. "Are Common Names Becoming Less Common? The Rise in Uniqueness and Individualism in Japan." *Frontiers in Psychology* 6, no. 1490 (2015): 1–14.

O'Hashi, Alan. "Bridging Social and Cultural Divides in Cohousing." *Communities* 178 (2018): 24.

Oishi, Shigehiro. "Culture and Subjective Well-Being: Conceptual and Measurement Issues." In *Handbook of Well-Being*, edited by Ed Diener, Shigehiro Oishi, and Louis Tay, 1–15. Salt Lake City, UT: DEF Publishers, 2018.

Organisation for Economic Co-operation and Development. *The Well-Being of Nations: The Role of Human and Social Capital*. Paris: OECD Publishing, 2001.

———. *Health at a Glance 2017: OECD Indicators*. Paris: OECD Publishing, 2017.

———. *Accelerating Climate Action: Refocusing Policies through a Well-Being Lens*. Paris: OECD Publishing, 2019.

———. "Climate Change Mitigation through a Well-Being Lens: 'Putting People at the Centre of Climate Action.'" *Organisation for Economic Co-operation and Development*, 2019. Retrieved 21 April 2020 from https://www.oecd.org/environment/cc/flyer-climate-change-mitigation-through-a-well-being-lens.pdf.

———. *How's Life? 2020: Measuring Well-Being*. Paris: OECD Publishing, 2020.

Ostrom, Elinor. *Governing the Commons: The Evolution of Institutions for Collective Action*. Cambridge: Cambridge University Press, 1990.

Oved, Yaacov. "The Globalization of Communes." *Social Sciences Directory* 2, no. 3 (2013): 93–96.

PBS. "Cohousing Communities Help Prevent Social Isolation." *PBS NewsHour*, 12 February 2017. Retrieved 4 May 2020 from https://www.pbs.org/newshour/show/cohousing-communities-help-prevent-social-isolation.

Pekkanen, Robert J., Yutaka Tsujinaka, and Hidehiro Yamamoto. *Neighborhood Associations and Local Governance in Japan*. New York: Routledge, 2014.

Putnam, Robert D. *Bowling Alone: The Collapse and Revival of American Community*. New York: Simon and Schuster, 2000.

Putnam, Robert D., and Lewis M. Feldstein. *Better Together: Restoring the American Community*. New York: Simon & Schuster, 2003.

Rappaport, Joanne. "Beyond Participant Observation: Collaborative Ethnography as Theoretical Innovation." *Collaborative Anthropologies* 1 (2008): 1–31.

Robbins, Joel. "Beyond the Suffering Subject: Toward an Anthropology of the Good." *Journal of the Royal Anthropological Institute* 19, no. 3 (2013): 447–62.

Robertson, Roland. *Globalization: Social Theory and Global Culture*. London: Sage, 1992.
Roth, Chris. "Undressing and Addressing the Elephant in the Room." *Communities* 178 (2018): 8–9.
Ruiu, Maria Laura. "The Social Capital of Cohousing Communities." *Sociology* 50, no. 2 (2016): 400–415.
Sachs, Jeffrey D. "Introduction to the 2019 Global Happiness and Wellbeing Policy Report." In *Global Happiness and Wellbeing Policy Report 2019*, edited by Global Council for Happiness and Wellbeing, 3–7. 2019. Retrieved 21 April 2020 from http://www.happinesscouncil.org.
Samanani, Farhan, and Johannes Lenhard. "House and Home." In *The Cambridge Encyclopedia of Anthropology*, edited by Felix Stein, Sian Lazar, Matei Candea, Hildegard Diemberger, Joel Robbins, Andrew Sanchez, and Rupert Stasch, 1–18. 2019. Retrieved 27 February 2020 from http://doi.org/10.29164/19home.
Sanford, A. Whitney. *Living Sustainably: What Intentional Communities Can Teach Us about Democracy, Simplicity, and Nonviolence*. Lexington: University Press of Kentucky, 2017.
Sargisson, Lucy. "Strange Places: Estrangement, Utopianism, and Intentional Communities." *Utopian Studies* 18, no. 3 (2007): 393–424.
———. "Second-Wave Cohousing: A Modern Utopia?" *Utopian Studies* 23, no. 1 (2012): 28–56.
———. *Fool's Gold? Utopianism in the Twenty-First Century*. New York: Palgrave Macmillan, 2012.
Sargisson, Lucy, and Lyman Tower Sargent. *Living in Utopia: New Zealand's Intentional Communities*. New York: Routledge, 2004.
Schaub, Laird. "The Paralysis of Racism in Social Change Groups." *Communities* 155 (2012): 19–20.
Schehr, Robert C. *Dynamic Utopia: Establishing Intentional Communities as a New Social Movement*. Westport, CT: Bergin and Garvey, 1997.
Schensul, Stephen L., Jean J. Schensul, Merrill Singer, Margaret Weeks, and Marie Brault. "Participatory Methods and Community-Based Collaborations." In *Handbook of Methods in Cultural Anthropology*, 2nd ed., edited by H. Russell Bernard and Clarence C. Gravlee, 185–214. Lanham, MD: Rowman and Littlefield, 2015.
Schulz, Evelyn. "Beyond Modernism." In *Future Living: Collective Housing in Japan*, edited by Claudia Hildner, 11–26. Basel: Birkhäuser, 2014.
Seligman, Martin. *Authentic Happiness: Using the New Positive Psychology to Realize Your Potential for Lasting Fulfillment*. New York: Free Press, 2002.
———. *Learned Optimism: How to Change Your Mind and Your Life*. New York: Vintage, 2006.
———. *Flourish: A Visionary New Understanding of Happiness and Well-Being*. New York: Free Press, 2012.
Seligman, Martin, and Mihaly Csikszentmihalyi. "Positive Psychology: An Introduction." *American Psychologist* 55, no. 1 (2000): 5–14.
Shah, Hetan, and Nic Marks. *A Well-Being Manifesto for a Flourishing Society*. London: New Economics Foundation, 2004.
Shore, Cris, and Susan Wright. "Policy: A New Field of Anthropology." In *Anthropology of Policy: Critical Perspectives on Governance and Power*, edited by Cris Shore and Susan Wright, 3–39. New York: Routledge, 1997.

Solomon, Robert C. *True to Our Feelings: What Our Emotions Are Really Telling Us*. New York: Oxford University Press, 2007.
Spiro, Melford E. *Kibbutz: Venture in Utopia*. Cambridge: Harvard University Press, 1956.
———. "Utopia and Its Discontents: The Kibbutz and Its Historical Vicissitudes." *American Anthropologist* 106, no. 3 (2004): 556–68.
Stiglitz, Joseph E., Amartya Sen, and Jean-Paul Fitoussi. *Report by the Commission on the Measurement of Economic Performance and Social Progress*. Paris: Commission on the Measurement of Economic Performance and Social Progress, 2009.
Sugimoto, Yoshio. *An Introduction to Japanese Society*, 4th ed. Cambridge: Cambridge University Press, 2014.
Tang, Jackie, Nora Galbraith, and Johnny Truong. *Living Alone in Canada*. Ottawa: Statistics Canada, 2019.
Thin, Neil. "Happiness and the Sad Topics of Anthropology." Wellbeing in Developing Countries Working Paper No. 10. Bath: Wellbeing in Developing Countries ESRC Research Group, 2005.
———. *Social Happiness: Theory into Policy and Practice*. Bristol: The Policy Press, 2012.
———. "Qualitative Approaches to Culture and Well-Being." In *Handbook of Well-Being*, edited by Ed Diener, Shigehiro Oishi, and Louis Tay, 1–20. Salt Lake City, UT: DEF Publishers, 2018.
Thompson, Sam. "Introduction to Happiness and Society." In *The Oxford Handbook of Happiness*, edited by Susan David, Ilona Boniwell, and Amanda Conley Ayers, 427–30. Oxford: Oxford University Press, 2013.
Throop, C. Jason. "Ambivalent Happiness and Virtuous Suffering." In *Values of Happiness: Toward an Anthropology of Purpose in Life*, edited by Harry Walker and Iza Kavedžija, 29–57. Chicago: HAU Books, 2016.
Tiefenbach, Tim, and Florian Kohlbacher. "Happiness from the Viewpoint of Economics: Findings from Recent Survey Data in Japan." German Institute for Japanese Studies Working Paper 13/1. Tokyo: German Institute for Japanese Studies, 2013.
———. "Happiness and Life Satisfaction in Japan by Gender and Age." German Institute for Japanese Studies Working Paper 13/2. Tokyo: German Institute for Japanese Studies, 2013.
Tom, Allison. "Inclusivity and Disability." *Communities* 180 (2018): 37–39.
Tummers, Lidewij. "The Re-emergence of Self-Managed Co-housing in Europe: A Critical Review of Co-housing Research." *Urban Studies* 53, no. 10 (2016): 2023–40.
Uchida, Yukiko, and Shinobu Kitayama. "Happiness and Unhappiness in East and West: Themes and Variations." *Emotion* 9, no. 4 (2009): 441–56.
Uchida, Yukiko, and Yuji Ogihara. "Personal or Interpersonal Construal of Happiness: A Cultural Psychological Perspective." *International Journal of Wellbeing* 2, no. 4 (2012): 354–69.
Uchida, Yukiko, Yuji Ogihara, and Shintaro Fukushima. "Cultural Construal of Wellbeing—Theories and Empirical Evidence." In *Global Handbook of Quality of Life*, edited by Wolfgang Glatzer, Laura Camfield, Valerie Møller, and Mariano Rojas, 823–37. New York: Springer, 2015.
UK Cohousing Network. Website. 2020. Retrieved 4 May 2020 from https://cohousing.org.uk.
United Nations. "Happiness Should Have Greater Role in Development Policy—UN Member States." *UN News*, 19 July 2011. Retrieved 1 May 2020 from https://news.un.org/en/story/2011/07/382052.

———. *World Urbanization Prospects: The 2018 Revision*. New York: United Nations Department of Economic and Social Affairs, Population Division, 2018.

———. "Human Development Reports." *United Nations Development Programme*. Retrieved 2 May 2020 from http://hdr.undp.org/.

van Uchelen, Collin. "Individualism, Collectivism, and Community Psychology." In *Handbook of Community Psychology*, edited by Julian Rappaport and Edward Seidman, 65–78. New York: Kluwer Academic/Plenum Publishers, 2000.

Velicu, Irina, and Gustavo García-López. "Thinking the Commons through Ostrom and Butler: Boundedness and Vulnerability." *Theory, Culture & Society* 35, no. 6 (2018): 55–73.

Verde, Tom. "There's Community and Consensus. But It's No Commune." *The Independent*, 10 February 2018. Retrieved 27 February 2020 from https://www.independent.co.uk/news/community-consensus-commune-cohousing-retirement-younger-everybody-loves-raymond-a8199316.html.

Vestbro, Dick Urban. "History of Cohousing—Internationally and in Sweden." In *Living Together—Cohousing Ideas and Realities around the World: Proceedings from the International Collaborative Housing Conference in Stockholm 5–9 May 2010*, edited by Dick Urban Vestbro, 42–55. Stockholm: Division of Urban and Regional Studies, Royal Institute of Technology, in collaboration with Kollektivhus NU, 2010.

Wade, Jill. *Houses for All: The Struggle for Social Housing in Vancouver, 1919–50*. Vancouver: UBC Press, 1994.

Waldinger, Robert. "What Makes a Good Life? Lessons from the Longest Study on Happiness." TED Talk, November 2015. Retrieved 20 July 2017 from https://www.ted.com/talks/robert_waldinger_what_makes_a_good_life_lessons_from_the_longest_study_on_happiness?language=en.

Walker, Harry, and Iza Kavedžija. "Introduction: Values of Happiness." In *Values of Happiness: Toward an Anthropology of Purpose in Life*, edited by Harry Walker and Iza Kavedžija, 1–28. Chicago: HAU Books, 2016.

Webster, Noah J., Kristine J. Ajrouch, and Toni C. Antonucci. "Living Healthier, Living Longer: The Benefits of Residing in Community." *Generations* 37, no. 4 (2014): 28–32.

Williams, Jo. "Predicting an American Future for Cohousing." *Futures* 40, no. 3 (2008): 268–86.

Wilson, Alfreda Lynne. "Bringing Home the Bread and Roses: A Case Study of Women and Co-operative Housing in Vancouver, British Columbia." MA thesis, Simon Fraser University, Vancouver 1997.

Winter, Joanna, and Charles Durrett. "Achieving Affordability with Cohousing." *Communities* 158 (2013): 34–74.

Woodward, Alison. "Communal Housing in Sweden: A Remedy for the Stress of Everyday Life?" In *New Households, New Housing*, edited by Karen A. Franck and Sherry Ahrentzen, 71–94. New York: Van Nostrand Reinhold, 1989.

World Meteorological Organization. "Urgency of Climate Action Highlighted for U.N. Summit Preparatory Meeting." *World Meteorological Organization*, 28 June 2019. Retrieved 27 February 2020 from https://public.wmo.int/en/media/press-release/urgency-of-climate-action-highlighted-un-summit-preparatory-meeting.

Wright, Robert. "The Evolution of Despair." *Time*, 24 June 2001. Retrieved 18 December 2020 from http://content.time.com/time/magazine/article/0,9171,134603,00.html.

Zevnik, Luka. *Critical Perspectives in Happiness Research: The Birth of Modern Happiness*. New York: Springer, 2014.

Zhang, Donia. "Cooperative Housing and Cohousing in Canada: The Pursuit of Happiness in the Common Courtyards." *Journal of Architectural Research and Development* 2, no. 1 (2018): 12–22.

INDEX

A
aging, 18, 46, 49, 51, 59, 61, 66, 71–72, 73–74, 91, 110–11, 116–17, 138, 141, 147, 181, 191–92, 195, 199, 201
Antonucci, Toni C., 185
Aotearoa/New Zealand, 13, 14, 196

B
Baglione, Valeria, 193
Berggren, Heidi M., 195
Berkman, Lisa, 16
Bin Bishr, Aisha, 10, 16
Biswas-Diener, Robert, 4, 9, 10, 198, 199–200
Brodie, Janine, 17
Bromberg, Christopher, 9
Brown, Susan, 11, 208

C
Canada
   Canadian Cohousing Network, 31n81, 52, 79, 192
   cohousing in, 18–19, 24, 52, 145, 146–47, 192, 205–6
   collectivism and individualism in, 1–2, 18–19, 67, 82, 124–25, 164–65, 206
   orientations to happiness and well-being, 18, 82, 212n36
childcare
   and safety, 48, 50, 59, 64, 104–5, 161
   shared, 36, 42–43, 45–46, 47–48, 50–51, 58–59, 62, 64–66, 67–68, 71–72, 73–74, 83–84, 86, 88, 101, 102, 104–5, 109–11, 114, 119, 122, 123, 126, 129–31, 133, 135, 137–38, 141, 147, 149, 150, 151, 156–57, 160–62, 163, 180, 183–84n6, 204, 210
   shortages, 45, 50–51, 59, 67, 138
Chiodelli, Francesco, 193
Clancy, Patricia, 134
Clapham, David, 16–17
Clark, Andrew, 196
cohousing
   age and generation in, 18, 191–92, 199, 201
   and the built environment, 14, 15, 68–69, 153, 181, 187–88, 192, 193–94, 196, 199, 203, 204–5, 200, 202, 206, 209
   and civic engagement, 16, 101, 188–91, 192, 195, 198–99, 201, 206–8
   common meals in, 68, 153, 195, 204
   common property in, 4, 15, 16, 68, 181, 187–88, 192, 193–94, 196, 202, 204, 206, 207, 209
   common space in, 15, 68, 181, 187–88, 192, 200, 202, 204, 206, 209
   community in, 10–12, 14, 15–17, 19, 23, 67–69, 79, 141–43, 145–46, 153, 181–83, 185–96, 198–203, 204–10
   and cultural context, 18–19, 67, 146–47, 153, 181–82, 190–91, 192, 187, 201–3, 204–7
   diversity in, 67–68, 153, 185, 187–88, 189–90, 191–93, 199, 200, 201, 207–8
   economy of, 4, 15, 16, 181, 188, 189, 190, 192–93, 194, 199, 200, 202, 204, 206, 207
   and environmental sustainability, 4–5, 10, 15–16, 17, 18, 19, 22, 23–24, 101, 181, 185, 187, 193–94, 196, 199–200, 202–3, 206, 207–9
   governance and decision-making in, 16, 18, 68, 79, 99, 153, 187–88, 190, 194, 195–96, 202, 204

and government policy, 5, 13, 23, 46, 51, 60–61, 70n21, 73, 85, 101–2, 106n18, 181, 187, 190, 196, 198–201, 203, 207–8 (*see also* government; policy)
happiness and well-being in, 3–4, 10–11, 15–17, 19, 22, 23, 35, 68, 71–72, 105, 141–43, 145, 147, 168, 181, 182–83, 185–91, 194–96, 198–203, 204–5, 206–10
history of, 13–14, 181, 205–6
and home, 16–17, 199, 206
and independence/interdependence, 3, 4, 15, 16, 18, 19, 67–68, 141–43, 187–89, 195, 201–3, 206, 208–9
and individualism/collectivism, 15, 67–68, 141–43, 185, 187–88, 189, 194, 195, 201–3, 206, 208–9
and integration with/separation from society, 14–15, 16, 18, 101, 187, 188–91, 193, 195, 201, 203–5, 206–8
as intentional community, 3, 11–13, 189, 194, 208
loneliness, as a response to, 3–4, 10–11, 16, 23–24, 45, 51–52, 67–68, 71, 185–87, 196, 202–3, 208–9
in the media, 5, 13, 101, 138, 189, 193, 207
and neighborhood integration, 15, 16, 187, 188–91, 193–94, 201, 206–8
organizational structures of, 14, 15, 68–69, 79, 99, 145–46, 153, 181–83, 187–91, 193–96, 200–203, 204–10
private space in, 3, 15, 187–88, 200, 204, 206–7, 209
and public health, 4, 16, 199–200
residents of, 19, 67–69, 145–46, 153, 181–83, 185–96, 199–203, 204–10
social capital in, 189–91
and social connection, 3–4, 10–11, 14–16, 23, 67–68, 79, 141–43, 145–46, 153, 181–83, 185–96, 198–203, 204–10
as social critique, 14–15, 18, 185, 203–5, 206–8
as a social experiment, 105, 145, 194, 209
and social sustainability, 3, 5, 15, 17, 18, 22, 23–24, 101, 187, 194, 196, 198–200, 202–3, 206, 207–9
and unofficial policy, 68–69, 195–96 (*see also* policy)
and urbanization, 3–4, 185, 187, 193, 208
as a utopic model, 14, 69, 187, 203–5, 206–8 (*see also* utopia)
See also intentional community; Kankanmori; Quayside Village; urban cohousing
Cohousing Association of the United States, 31n81, 79, 192
collective housing. *See* cohousing
commons/commoning, 12, 205
community
in cohousing, 10–12, 14, 15–17, 19, 23, 67–69, 79, 141–43, 145–46, 153, 181–83, 185–96, 198–203, 204–10
and happiness and well-being, 3–4, 6–7, 10–12, 15–16, 23, 68, 137, 141–43, 147, 168, 181, 182–83, 185–91, 194–96, 198–203, 204, 208–10
Cooper, Davina, 205, 208
Coulmas, Florian, 18
Csikszentmihalyi, Mihaly, 6
cultural psychology
collective/structural well-being, 7, 8–9
interdependent happiness, 7
See also well-being

D

Delgado, Guillermo, 203
Denmark, 13
influence on development of Quayside Village, 145
Diener, Ed, 4, 8–9, 10, 198, 199–200
diversity
and happiness and well-being, 47–48, 50–51, 67–68, 71–73, 77, 78–79, 81–83, 96, 101, 109–11, 142–43, 185, 187–88, 189–93, 193, 199, 201
at Kankanmori, 35, 38, 43, 45, 47–48, 50–51, 67–68, 109–11, 141, 142–43, 147, 153, 187–88, 191–93, 201, 207–8
at Quayside Village, 35, 53–54, 65–66, 67–68, 71–74, 77, 78–79, 81–83, 96, 101, 110–11, 153, 187–88, 191–93, 201, 207–8
Durand, Martine, 200–201

Durkheim, Emile, 4
Durrett, Charles, 13, 32n86, 145, 193

E
Egerö, Bertil, 14
environmental sustainability
  and environmental crisis, 4–5, 23–24, 185, 194, 200, 208–9
  and happiness and well-being, 15–16, 22, 187, 193–94, 197, 198–99, 202–3, 208–9
  See also under cohousing; Kankanmori; Quayside Village
exchanges between Kankanmori and Quayside Village
  and collaboration, 20–22, 146–52, 167–68, 181–83, 183–84n6, 187, 195
  and differences between the communities, 23, 65, 116, 135, 145, 146–47, 151–68, 170–72, 181–83, 184n17, 195
  as experiential, 20, 146–47, 151–52, 167–68, 181–83, 183–84n6
  impacts on Kankanmori, 23, 146–47, 151–52, 167–68, 169, 173–77, 179–83, 195
  impacts on Quayside Village, 23, 146–47, 151–52, 162–63, 167–74, 176, 177–79, 181–83, 195
  and reflexivity, 20, 146–47, 151–52, 162–63, 167–68, 173, 177, 179, 181–83
  and similarities between the communities, 23, 65, 135, 146–47, 151–55, 160, 167–68, 181–83, 195
  See also Kankanmori; methodology; Quayside Village
Exton, Carrie, 200–201

F
Feldstein, Lewis, 190
film shorts, 21–22, 146, 151
Fischer, Edward
  well-being "tool kit," 10, 23, 209
Foucault, Michel, 205
Foundation for Intentional Community, 12, 31n78, 31n81, 79, 192–93
Fukushima, Shintaro, 7, 9

G
Gable, Shelly, 9
Gilman, Robert, 12–13
Global Happiness Policy Report, 4, 10, 199–200, 201, 203. *See also* government; policy; well-being
Global Happiness and Well-Being Policy Report, 3, 196–97, 199–200, 201, 203. *See also* government; policy; well-being
good life. *See* well-being
government
  and cohousing development, 5, 13, 23, 46, 51, 60–61, 70n21, 73, 85, 101–2, 106n18, 181, 187, 190, 196, 198–201, 203, 207–8
  and happiness and well-being, 2, 8, 9, 11, 196–201, 203, 212n36 (*see also* policy)
Grinde, Bjørn, 15–16
Gross National Happiness Index, 2

H
happiness. *See* well-being
happiness economics, 2, 8, 194, 196–97, 200–201
Helliwell, John, 197, 200–201
Hitokoto, Hidehumi, 7
Holthus, Barbara, 134, 142
home
  as dwelling, 17, 199
  and happiness and well-being, 16–17, 199–200
  and housing policy, 16–17, 60–61, 69–70n16, 70n21, 85, 106n18, 198–200
  as process, 17, 199
hydraulic theory of emotion, 82, 101, 165

I
individualism
  and approaches to happiness and well-being, 2–3, 5–11, 15, 18, 23, 24, 68, 82, 137, 141–43, 147, 185, 187, 188, 194, 196–98, 201–3, 204, 208–9 (*see also* well-being)
  and capitalism, 2, 12, 194, 196–98, 209
  and consumption, 2, 15, 18, 23–24, 51–52, 194, 200, 207

as culturally and historically specific, 5–8, 18, 36, 41–42, 45, 47, 51–52, 82, 185, 198, 202
and environmental destruction, 23–24, 194, 200 (*see also* environmental sustainability)
and hyperindividualism, 2–3, 9, 10, 15, 18, 23–24, 185, 187, 189
ideology of separation, 3, 5–6, 17
and loneliness, 1–4, 5, 7–8, 17, 23–24, 36, 41–42, 45, 47, 51–52, 68, 185, 187, 202–3
and private property, 3, 17, 200
intentional community
and authoritarianism, 204
as a critique of society, 12, 14–15, 204, 207
and environmental sustainability, 12–13, 15–16, 187, 193–94, 208
as a global social movement, 12–13, 20–21, 101, 145, 192–93, 205, 207, 208
happiness and well-being in, 11–13, 15–16, 194, 208 (*see also* well-being)
history of, 11–13
in the media, 5, 13, 101, 138, 189, 193, 207
networks for the exchange of ideas about, 5, 13, 20–21, 101, 145–46, 181–82, 190, 205, 207
and policy, 5, 13, 23, 194 (*see also* government; policy)
and social sustainability, 12–13, 187, 194, 208
types of, 11–12
utopian socialism, 12, 204 (*see also* utopia)
See also cohousing; Kankanmori; Quayside Village; urban cohousing
Intergovernmental Panel on Climate Change, 4
International Collaborative Housing Conference, 14
International Communal Studies Association, 12–13
isolation. *See* loneliness
Izquierdo, Carolina, 11, 200, 201

J
Jackson, Michael, 201
James, Wendy, 8, 198
Japan
collective housing in, 18–19, 24, 36–37, 45, 46, 47, 51–52, 69n2, 69n15, 133–34, 137–38, 143, 146–47, 175–76, 184n17, 191–92, 204, 205–6
collectivism and individualism in, 1–2, 9, 18–19, 36, 41–42, 45, 47, 51–52, 67, 109, 124–25, 133–34, 137, 141–43, 164, 206
Commission on Measuring Well-Being, 9
jichikai (neighborhood association), 111–12
kodokushi (lonely death), 1
National Survey of Lifestyle Preferences, 1–2
orientations to happiness and well-being, 9, 18, 51–52, 137, 141–43, 196
Jarvis, Helen, 190, 196

K
Kankanmori
and aging, 46, 49, 51, 110–11, 116–17, 138, 141, 181, 191–92, 195, 201
architecture and spatial arrangement, 22, 23, 35, 37–39, 40, 49, 68–69, 108, 109, 110, 111, 117–18, 119, 120, 122–28, 129–34, 135, 136, 137, 138–39, 140, 141, 142, 144n12, 144n25, 151, 152–53, 156, 159, 161–62, 163–64, 165–67, 172, 173, 174–75, 179, 181, 183, 187–88, 192, 193, 200, 202, 206, 209
balance of individual and community in, 38, 46–47, 48–49, 50, 51, 67–68, 108–9, 111, 112–17, 118–19, 122–25, 134–35, 137, 139, 140–43, 143n9, 155–57, 158–60, 162–67, 170–72, 174–75, 176–81, 184n17, 185–86, 187–88, 191, 192, 195, 197, 201–3, 206, 208–9
childcare in, 36, 42–43, 45–46, 47–48, 50–51, 67–68, 109–11, 114, 119, 122, 123, 126, 129–31, 133, 135, 137–38, 141, 147, 150, 151, 156–57, 160–62, 163, 180, 183–84n6, 210 (*see also* childcare)
common meals, 36, 39–41, 42, 48, 49, 50, 65, 68, 108–9, 110, 111, 115,

116, 118, 119–20, 121–22, 123–24, 126–31, 132–33, 134, 135–36, 137, 138, 139, 144n25, 150–51, 152–55, 157–59, 162, 163, 164, 168–70, 172–73, 174, 176–77, 178, 180, 181, 210
 common property, 39, 68, 111, 112, 114, 116, 117–20, 125–28, 129–31, 133–34, 135, 136, 137, 139, 144n12, 144n25, 150, 153–54, 157, 159, 162, 164, 172, 173, 176–77, 181, 188, 192, 193, 202, 206, 207, 209
 common space, 38–39, 40, 65, 68, 107n26, 108, 109, 110, 111, 112, 114, 116, 117–18, 119, 120, 121–28, 129–34, 135–36, 137, 139, 140, 144n12, 144n25, 151, 152–53, 154, 156, 161–62, 163–64, 165–67, 172, 173, 174, 176–77, 179, 181, 187–88, 192, 200, 202, 206, 209, 210
 community engagement, 40, 44–45, 109, 112, 114, 124, 136, 137–39, 140, 182, 185–86, 188–89, 190, 191–92, 195, 201, 206–8
 cultural context of, 18–19, 45, 47, 51–52, 67, 109, 122, 124–25, 133–34, 137–38, 141–43, 146–47, 153, 155, 159, 161, 163–65, 167, 170, 173, 175–76, 180, 181–82, 184n17, 187, 190–92, 201–3, 205–7
 demographics, 22, 40, 43–50, 110–11, 141, 153, 192
 disagreement and conflict, 36, 65, 111, 115–16, 119–20, 125, 134–35, 165, 170–71, 177, 202
 diversity, 38, 43, 45, 47–48, 50–51, 67–68, 109–11, 141, 142–43, 147, 153, 187–88, 191–93, 201, 207–8
 and environmental sustainability, 22, 35, 39, 67, 109, 127–28, 139, 140, 150, 181, 187, 193, 202–3, 206, 207–9
 history and development, 18, 22, 23, 35–40, 41–42, 44–45, 109–11, 144n15, 145–46, 175–76, 181, 183, 183n1, 185, 205–6
 kakari (committee system), 174–75
 loneliness, as a response to, 10–11, 41–42, 45, 47–48, 49, 50, 51–52, 67–68, 109, 142, 185–86, 202–3, 208–9

mori-ken (Kankanmori currency), 118–19, 126–27, 130–31, 153, 172, 173, 181, 183
nijikai (second party), 131
official and unofficial sociality, 23, 135–37, 139, 162–63, 164, 169–70, 172–73, 178–79, 188
reasons for moving in, 22, 35–36, 40–43, 44–52, 67–68, 110–11, 121–22, 138–39, 141, 149–50, 185–87, 188, 192
residents of, 22, 35–36, 39–52, 67–69, 107n26, 108–43, 143n9, 143n10, 144n15, 144n25, 145–83, 183n1, 183–84n6, 184n17, 185–89, 190–92, 193, 195, 197, 200–203, 205–10
social connection and community formation in, 18, 22–23, 35–43, 44–52, 67–69, 107n26, 108–43, 143n9, 144n25, 145–83, 183n1, 183–84n6, 184n17, 185–93, 195, 197, 200–203, 205–10
social events, 36, 40–41, 46–47, 48–49, 50, 51, 110, 120, 121, 126, 131–33, 135–37, 138–39, 151, 152–53, 158–59, 162–63, 164, 169–70, 172–73, 178–79, 180, 182, 186, 188, 189, 202
and social sustainability, 22, 187, 202–3, 206, 207–9
unit rental and ownership, 40–41, 45, 110–11, 118–19, 139–41, 163, 166–67, 188, 192
Kankanmori, organizational structures and governance of, 22–23, 39–40, 45–46, 65, 68–69, 109–11, 117, 121–22, 133–36, 137, 139–41, 146, 147, 153, 158–60, 165, 168, 170–72, 176–77, 179–80, 181, 187–88, 190, 197, 200, 202–3
 committees, 40, 46, 65, 111–18, 119–22, 123, 126–27, 129, 130, 131–33, 135–36, 137, 138, 140, 150, 156, 170–72, 173, 174–75, 176–77, 179–81, 183
 community meetings, 40–41, 110, 112, 119–20, 122, 126, 133, 134, 140, 151, 155–57, 160, 163–64, 174–75, 176, 177–81, 184n17

decision-making, 40, 68, 111, 119–20, 132, 134, 147, 150, 153, 174–75, 188, 202
Kankanmori, philosophy and values of, 22–23, 40, 68–69, 109–11, 117, 121–22, 133–36, 137, 139–41, 146, 153, 158–60, 165, 168, 170–72, 176–77, 179–80, 181, 188, 189, 191–92, 193, 195, 197, 202–3
  everyone is equal, 22–23, 110, 111–22, 132, 134–35, 137, 139, 156, 158, 164, 165, 171, 176, 180, 206
  to have independent and private space as well as communal space, 23, 109, 114, 122–27, 133–35, 137, 141–43
  to share space and time with others, 109, 114, 121–27, 128–37, 138–39, 141–43, 189, 190
  to spend time together in common activities, 109, 121–22, 125–26, 128–37, 138–39, 141–43, 188
Kavedžija, Iza, 137, 141–42, 201–2
Kawano, Satsuki, 36
Klein, Naomi, 18
Klein, Stefan, 9
Kosatsky, Tom, 16, 199
Koyabe, Ikuko, 32n86, 34n123, 35, 122, 185, 192
  and development of collective housing in Japan, 36–38, 40, 41–42, 45, 137, 142, 175–76

L

Layard, Richard, 197
Lenhard, Johannes, 17
Levitas, Ruth, 203–4, 206
Lietaert, Matthieu, 3, 207
Lockyer, Joshua, 194
loneliness
  and the built environment, 1–2, 3–4, 17, 41–42, 49, 56, 142, 185–87, 196
  effects on happiness and well-being, 1–3, 4, 7–8, 10–11, 16, 68, 185–87, 196, 202–3, 208–9
  See also under cohousing; Kankanmori; Quayside Village
Long, Susan Orpett, 36
Lubik, Amy, 16, 199

M

Manzenreiter, Wolfram, 134, 142
Marks, Nic, 198
Mathews, Gordon, 11, 200, 201, 209
McCamant, Kathryn, 13, 32n86, 145
Meltzer, Graham, 15, 22, 134, 185, 194
mental health, 1–2, 5–6, 197, 199–200.
  See also well-being
methodology
  collaboration between communities, 20–22, 146–52, 167–68, 181–83, 183–84n6, 187, 195 (*see also* exchanges between Kankanmori and Quayside Village)
  collaboration with residents, 19–22, 23, 107n25, 146–47, 187
  community comparison, 18–19, 23, 146–47, 187, 195
  film shorts, 21–22, 146, 151
  participant observation, 19, 151–52
  reciprocity, 146
  translation, 18–19, 146–47
Montgomery, Charles, 3, 5–6, 22
Moore, Suzanne, 7
More, Thomas, 11–12, 203

N

neoliberalism
  and individualism, 7–8, 198
Netherlands, the, 13, 196

O

Ogihara, Yuji, 7, 9
O'Hashi, Alan, 192
Organisation for Economic Co-operation and Development
  and approaches to happiness and well-being, 2, 194, 196, 197
  and environmental sustainability, 194, 197
  and policy development, 2, 194, 196, 197
Oved, Yaacov, 12

P

policy
  as charter for social action, 68, 195
  community policy, 10, 60–61, 197–200
  and environmental sustainability, 194, 197, 198–200

government policy, 2, 8, 9, 11, 196–201, 212n36
  and happiness and well-being, 2, 8, 9, 10, 11, 23, 194, 196–201, 203, 208, 212n36
  and housing, 16–17, 60–61, 69–70n16, 70n21, 85, 106n18, 198–200
  and social sustainability, 194, 196–200
  See also government
positive psychology
  individualization, 2, 6, 7, 8–10, 185, 202
  and self-sufficiency, 8
  and work on the self, 6, 8
  See also individualism; well-being
poverty, 7–8, 200
public health
  benefits of cohousing for, 4, 16, 199–200
  crisis of loneliness, 1–2
  determinants of health, 1–2, 4, 16
Putnam, Robert, 2, 190

Q

Quayside Village
  and aging, 59, 61, 66, 71–72, 73–74, 91, 110–11, 191–92, 201
  architecture and spatial arrangement, 22, 23, 35, 52–55, 66–67, 68–69, 71–72, 73, 74–78, 79, 81, 84, 85, 89, 90, 91–95, 96–97, 102, 103–5, 107n25, 122, 126, 128, 151, 152–53, 155, 159, 161–62, 163–64, 165–67, 172, 173, 174–75, 179, 181, 183, 187–88, 192, 193, 202, 206, 209–10
  balance of individual and community in, 53, 54–55, 56, 60, 61–63, 64–65, 66–68, 71–73, 77–84, 85–88, 90, 91, 96–97, 104–5, 116, 122, 151, 155–57, 158–60, 162–67, 170–72, 174–75, 176–81, 187–88, 195, 197, 201–3, 206, 208–9
  childcare in, 58–59, 62, 64–66, 67–68, 71–72, 73–74, 83–84, 86, 88, 101, 102, 104–5, 110–11, 147, 149, 160–62, 183–84n6
  common meals, 53, 55–56, 65, 73, 76, 83–85, 87, 88–90, 92, 93, 100, 102, 105, 129, 148, 150–51, 152–55, 157–59, 161, 163, 169–70, 172–73, 176–77, 178, 181, 186
  common property, 55, 62, 66–67, 68, 74–76, 80–81, 85, 87, 89–90, 91–95, 96–97, 101, 102, 103, 106n18, 107n25, 126, 128, 149, 150, 153–54, 157–58, 161, 168, 172, 173, 176–77, 181, 188, 192, 193, 202, 206, 207, 209
  common space, 53–55, 68, 73, 75–78, 79, 80–81, 85, 86, 87, 88–90, 91–95, 96–97, 101, 102, 103–4, 106n18, 107n26, 122, 126, 128, 148–49, 152–53, 154, 157, 158, 161–63, 165–67, 172, 173, 174, 176–77, 179, 181, 187–88, 192, 202, 206, 209, 210
  cultural context of, 18–19, 67, 73, 74, 82, 146–47, 153, 155, 159, 161, 163–65, 167, 180, 181–82, 187, 190–91, 201–3, 205–7
  demographics, 22, 57–66, 73–74, 153–54, 192
  disagreement and conflict, 60, 61–63, 65, 66–67, 72–73, 77–84, 86–87, 88, 94, 96–101, 105, 106n13, 106n18, 116, 120, 134–35, 170–71, 177, 202
  diversity, 35, 53–54, 65–66, 67–68, 71–74, 77, 78–79, 81–83, 96, 101, 110–11, 153, 187–88, 191–93, 201, 207–8
  and environmental sustainability, 22, 52, 53, 55, 59–60, 67, 71–73, 74–77, 81, 85, 101–2, 110, 127–28, 140, 149, 150, 181, 186, 187, 193, 202–3, 206, 207–9
  history and development, 18, 22, 23, 35–36, 52–55, 58–59, 71–74, 87, 145–46, 181, 183, 185, 205–6
  loneliness, as a response to, 10–11, 56–57, 59, 65, 66, 67–68, 71, 104–5, 185, 202–3, 208–9
  reasons for moving in, 22, 35–36, 52–53, 55–57, 58–68, 86, 105, 148–49, 185, 187, 188, 192, 209
  residents of, 22, 35–36, 55–69, 71–105, 106n19, 107n25, 107n26, 110–11, 116, 120, 126, 127, 129, 133–35, 136, 137, 138, 139, 145–83, 185–89, 190–92, 193, 195, 197, 200–203, 205–10

social connection and community formation in, 18, 22, 35–36, 52–57, 58–69, 71–105, 106n18, 107n26, 110–11, 116, 120, 126, 127, 129, 134–35, 136, 137, 138, 139, 145–83, 183–84n6, 185–93, 195, 197, 200–203, 205–10
social events, 59, 61–63, 64–65, 66–67, 72–73, 77–78, 83–84, 87–90, 92, 94–95, 101–2, 105, 136, 151, 152–53, 158–59, 162–63, 169–70, 172–73, 178–79, 182, 186, 188, 189, 195, 210
and social sustainability, 22, 59, 77, 101, 187, 202–3, 206, 207–9 (*see also* social sustainability)
unit ownership and rental, 52, 54, 55–56, 59–61, 64, 71–72, 73–74, 116, 139, 163, 166–67, 188, 192
Quayside Village, organizational structures and governance of, 22, 65, 66–67, 68–69, 71–74, 84–85, 88, 91, 95, 96, 100, 106n18, 110–11, 146, 147, 153, 158–60, 165, 168, 170–72, 176–77, 179–80, 181, 187–88, 190, 195, 197, 202–3
committees, 72, 74, 76, 77–78, 84, 85–88, 95, 97–99, 106n19, 116, 148, 150, 152–53, 156, 157, 170–72, 173, 174–75, 176–77, 179–81, 183
community meetings, 60, 72, 73–74, 77–84, 85–87, 91–92, 95, 96–100, 101, 104, 106n8, 106n18, 110, 120, 147, 148, 151, 152–53, 155–57, 160–61, 163–64, 174–75, 176, 177–80, 206
decision-making, 53, 60, 61–63, 66–67, 68, 72–73, 77–84, 85, 86, 94–95, 96–99, 101, 106n13, 106n18, 120, 147–48, 150, 152–53, 174–75, 188, 191, 202
Quayside Village, philosophy and values of, 22–23, 68–69, 71–74, 82–83, 84–85, 88, 91, 95, 96, 100, 110–11, 146, 153, 158–60, 165, 168, 170–72, 176–77, 179–80, 181, 188, 189, 191–92, 193, 195, 197, 202–3
camaraderie, 61–63, 66–67, 73, 74, 84–101

communication, 61–63, 66–67, 72–73, 74, 77–84, 95–101
community engagement, 65–66, 73, 77, 87–88, 101–2, 138, 178, 188–89, 190, 191–92, 199, 201, 206–8
each-according-to-their-strengths, each-according-to-their-desires, 22, 85–88, 156, 158, 165, 171, 178, 206
environmental stewardship, 22, 72, 73, 74–77, 110, 193
trust, 72, 74, 77–84, 95–101, 187–88

R
Roberts, Glenda, 36
Ruiu, Maria Laura, 190

S
Sachs, Jeffrey, 194, 196–97
Samanani, Farhan, 17
Sargent, Lyman Tower, 14
Sargisson, Lucy, 11, 14, 16, 66, 189, 204, 206–7
Schehr, Robert, 13
Seligman, Martin, 6, 9
Shah, Hetan, 198
social capital, 189–9
social connection. *See under* cohousing; Kankanmori; Quayside Village; well-being
social sustainability, 1–2, 3, 5, 12–13, 15, 17, 18, 22, 23–24, 59, 77, 101, 187, 194, 196–200, 202–3, 206, 207–9. *See also under* cohousing; Kankanmori; Quayside Village; well-being
Sweden
cohousing in, 13, 14, 199
influence on development of Kankanmori, 36–37, 45, 46, 129, 131, 137, 144n15, 145, 175–76, 183n1

T
Thatcher, Margaret, 5
therapy, 2, 6, 8. *See also* well-being
Thin, Neil, 1, 147
Thompson, Sam, 5

U
Uchida, Yukiko, 7, 9
UK Cohousing Network, 31n81, 192

United Nations, 2, 77, 196, 197, 199
urban cohousing
  characteristics of, 3–5, 10–11, 14–15, 18–19, 22, 101, 181, 187, 189–91, 193–94, 195–96, 203–9
  environmental benefits of, 4–5, 10, 15, 18, 22, 101, 187, 193–94, 203, 207–9
  and integration with/separation from society, 14–15, 18, 101, 189–91, 193–94, 195–96, 203–5, 206–8
  need for, 3–5, 10–11, 18
  See also cohousing; intentional community
urbanization
  difficulties associated with, 3–4, 69–70n16, 185
  global state of, 3, 187, 208
  and urban design, 3–4, 10, 185, 193
utopia
  and authoritarianism, 204
  cohousing as model of, 14, 69, 187, 203–5, 206–8
  as critique of social arrangements, 14, 203–5, 206–8
  and emphasis on the collective, 11–12, 24, 204–5
  as heterotopia, 205
  practical utopia, 204, 207–8
  utopia as method, 204–5, 206–8

V
van Uchelen, Collin, 5–6

W
Waldinger, Robert, 4
Walker, Harry, 201–2
welfare, 8, 198
well-being
  anthropological approaches to, 6–7, 8, 200, 201–3
  and the built environment, 10, 187–88, 198–200, 209
  and cohousing, 3–4, 10–11, 15–17, 19, 22, 23, 35, 68, 71–72, 105, 141–43, 145, 147, 168, 181, 182–83, 185–91, 194–96, 198–203, 204–5, 206–10 (*see also* cohousing)
  as collaborative, 1, 3–4, 6–7, 8–11, 15–16, 23, 24, 68, 137, 141–43, 147, 168, 181, 182–83, 185–91, 194–96, 198–203, 204, 208–10
  and community, 3–4, 6–7, 10–12, 15–16, 23, 68, 137, 141–43, 147, 168, 181, 182–83, 185–91, 194–96, 198–203, 204, 208–10 (*see also* community)
  and culture, 5–8, 10, 11, 18, 51–52, 82, 141–43, 147, 201–3
  and diversity, 47–48, 50–51, 67–68, 71–73, 77, 78–79, 81–83, 96, 101, 109–11, 142–43, 185, 187–88, 189–93, 193, 199, 201
  emphasis on the individual, 2–3, 5–11, 15, 18, 23, 24, 68, 82, 137, 141–43, 147, 185, 187, 188, 194, 196–98, 201–3, 204, 208–9 (*see also* individualism)
  and environmental sustainability, 15–16, 22, 187, 193–94, 197, 198–99, 202–3, 208–9
  happiness economics (*see* happiness economics)
  the happiness imperative, 7
  the "happiness industry," 2, 7
  history of frameworks of, 2, 5–6, 7–10
  and interdependent happiness, 7
  macro-, micro-, and meso-level approaches to, 10–11, 197–200
  and neoliberalism, 7–8, 198
  in popular culture, 2, 9, 18, 68, 185, 196, 204, 208–9
  positive psychology (*see* positive psychology)
  and social connection, 1, 3–4, 6–7, 8–11, 15–16, 23, 24, 68, 137, 141–43, 147, 168, 181, 182–83, 185–91, 194–96, 198–203, 204, 208–10
  and social sustainability, 22, 187, 194, 196–200, 202–3, 208–9
  and urban planning, 3–4, 10, 193, 198–200 (*see also* urbanization)
  and use of terminology, 24
Williams, Jo, 16, 207
Winter, Joanna, 193
World Happiness Report, 197, 199–200, 203. *See also* government; policy; well-being
World Meteorological Association, 4
Wright, Robert, 1, 2

www.ingramcontent.com/pod-product-compliance
Lightning Source LLC
Chambersburg PA
CBHW051535020426
42333CB00016B/1947